I0528449

שופטים

THE
ISRAEL
BIBLE

JUDGES

EDITED BY

Rabbi Tuly Weisz

The Israel Bible: Judges

First Edition, 2021

The Israel Bible was produced by Israel365 in cooperation with Teach for Israel and is used with permission from Teach for Israel. All rights reserved. The English translation was adapted by Israel365 from the JPS Tanakh. Copyright © 1985 by the Jewish Publication Society. All rights reserved.

Cover image used under license from Shutterstock.com

ISBN 978-1-957109-32-9

A CIP catalogue record for this title is available from the British Library

The Israel Bible: Judges is a holy book that contains the name of God and should be treated with respect.

Table of Contents

Introduction

The Hebrew Bible is commonly known as the *Tanakh* which stands for *Torah* (the Five Books of Moses), *Neviim* (the Prophets) and *Ketuvim* (the Writings). The *Tanakh* consists of 24 books that are considered by Jews to be the word of God. While these books have been referred to as the "Old Testament," many Jews reject this label since it implies the replacement of the Hebrew Bible with something newer and prefer the more authentic Jewish name.

The *Tanakh* is not only the most important book known to man, it is God's word that is perfect and absolute. It is therefore a daunting undertaking to publish an edition of the *Tanakh*, and the responsibilities are awesome. There is no room for error or carelessness in dealing with the eternal word of God. Further, upon embarking on such a serious initiative, we ask ourselves if our efforts are gratuitous. Considering the many editions of the Bible in print, is there truly a need for yet another one?

While there are numerous Bibles in circulation today, its most central aspect – the Land of Israel – has often been overlooked. References to Israel appear on nearly every page, and the city of Jerusalem is specifically referred to hundreds of times throughout the Bible. The essential link between Israel and *Torah* is emphasized repeatedly in verses such as, "For instruction (*Torah*) shall come forth from *Tzion*, the word of *Hashem* from *Yerushalayim*" (Micah 4:2).

The miraculous return of the People of Israel to the Land of Israel in our own generation provides the perfect moment for a new volume to fill this void in biblical literature. *The Israel Bible* includes many special features elucidating God's focus on Israel throughout *Tanakh* and there are many additional, multimedia features available on our website **www.theisraelbible.com**.

Ordering and Presentation – In presenting *The Israel Bible*, our goal is to spread awareness of the biblical significance of the Land of Israel as well as the Jewish people's eternal connection to the land, based on the text of the *Tanakh*, the Hebrew Bible. We aim to honor "the God, the People and the Land of Israel" from an Orthodox Jewish perspective. To that end, *The Israel Bible* follows the traditional Jewish ordering of the books and the customary Hebrew division of chapters. Therefore, for example, we count 24 books of *Tanakh* with *Sefer Divrei Hayamim* (Chronicles) appearing last. It is our hope that our rich content will speak to all Jews and non-Jews who appreciate Israel as the God given land of the Jewish people.

English Translation – Throughout history, Jews have studied the Bible in Hebrew, as any form of translation would miss much of the nuance of the original holy tongue in which *Torah* has been transmitted since the days of Moses. However, as many Jews settled in America in the 19th Century, the need for an English translation became necessary. To be sure, there were already English translations prepared over the centuries by Christians, but in the words of the original editors of the Jewish Publication Society (JPS), "The Jew cannot afford to have his Bible translation prepared for him by others. He cannot have it as a gift, even as he cannot borrow his soul from others."

JPS set out in the late 1800s to publish an authoritative English translation "in the spirit of Jewish tradition." It was compiled over decades by some of the leading Jewish scholars of the time. They formed committees and subcommittees to compare existing English versions, considering medieval and modern Jewish commentators. The monumental JPS translation, originally published in 1917, has been updated in recent years, and *The Israel Bible* is proud to utilize the 1984 New Jewish Publication Society (NJPS) version with its modern, clear language, as well as its wide-ranging acceptance as an accurate and high-quality translation. We applied the NJPS translation verbatim, except for a select list of nouns which we replaced with their traditional Hebrew names. This is true even when we found the NJPS translation to be different than the popular translation of a word or phrase and when the NJPS switched the order of the text for the sake of clarity (see, for example, Ezekiel 24:22–24).

Hebrew Transliteration – To give our readers an authentic *Tanakh* experience, every verse that has commentary is transliterated from Hebrew into English. The Hebrew alphabet chart includes our standards for transliteration and pronunciation of Hebrew verses, enabling readers of *The Israel Bible* to decipher key biblical passages in the holy language. Readers can hear the entire Bible read in Hebrew on our website **www.theisraelbible.com**.

There are various standards when it comes to transliterating Hebrew words into English letters. While we have relied primarily on the classical Hebrew transliteration, we have occasionally deviated for the sake of simplicity, clarity and to reflect common usage.

In addition to whole verses, we have also transliterated many proper nouns in the English translation so that our readers can learn the names of key biblical figures and locations in their Hebrew form. As a rule, we chose to transliterate names of people that were central in the establishment and functioning of the nation of Israel, as well as significant places in the Holy Land. Therefore, regarding Adam's sons, for example, only *Shet* (Seth) is transliterated since it was from him that *Noach* (Noah), and ultimately *Avraham* (Abraham), descended. For this reason, there might be verses or sections of *The Israel Bible* that contains multiple names and only some of them are transliterated.

For the same reason, we have transliterated the names of the books of *Tanakh* when referring to them in our introductions and commentary. When referencing a specific chapter or verse, however, we use the English names of the books in our citations for clarity. We also transliterated ideas and concepts that are central to Judaism such as *Shabbat* (Sabbath), the names of the Jewish holidays and the *Beit Hamikdash* (Temple), as well as biblical measurements. Finally, the name of God is transliterated. Out of respect, Orthodox Jews generally refer to the Lord as *Hashem*, which literally means 'the Name.' Referring to God as *Hashem* reminds us that we feel close to Him but also recognize our distance at the same time. To stress this moniker, we transliterated both the Tetragrammaton as well as the name *Elohim* as *Hashem*.

Study Notes – Our unique commentary was compiled by Orthodox Jewish scholars who live in Israel. It is an anthology in the sense that most of the commentary is not original, but draws from traditional teachings of early Jewish Sages and modern rabbinic commentators. We also include quotations from individuals who have played a significant part in the past century of modern Israeli history including Israeli prime ministers, poets and military leaders.

Our commentary can be broken into four categories, three of which are identified by an icon at the beginning of the study note:

 Israel lessons are indicated with an icon bearing the map of Israel and focus on the Land of Israel and the modern State of Israel.

 Jewish lessons are indicated with a *Torah* scroll and teach a concept in Judaism or a classic idea from rabbinic thought.

 Hebrew lessons are represented by an icon bearing the letter *aleph* and focus on the meaning of a Hebrew word or phrase.

All other comments are considered general comments and are not assigned an icon.

Supplemental Material – In addition to our unique translation and original commentary, *The Israel Bible* offers supplementary material to enrich the learning experience of our readers. Before every book of *Tanakh,* we provide an introduction, as well as information, generally in the form of a map, a chart or a list, which is central to the specific book.

Maps – As the purpose of *The Israel Bible* is to highlight the biblical significance of the Land of Israel, significant time was spent researching and preparing maps to bring the physical contours of the holy land to life with great accuracy. However, since there is a lack of information regarding the precise locations of certain ancient cities, some of the places on our maps are approximate or subject to debate. In these cases, we followed the opinion that we are most comfortable with, but acknowledge that there is room for disagreement. We continue to produce new maps, which are available on our website **www.theisraelbible.com/maps**.

Torah **Readings** – The *Torah* is not just a work that is studied privately, it is also read out loud in synagogue. Every *Shabbat* and holiday a portion of the *Torah* is read, as well as a related section from *Neviim*, the prophets, called the *haftarah*. We included the blessings recited before and after the reading of the *Torah*, a list of the weekly *Torah* portions and their corresponding *haftarot*, and a chart of the *Torah* readings for special days with their corresponding *haftarot*. Readers can always find the current week's *Torah* portion by visiting **www.theisraelbible.com/weekly-torah-portion**. In this volume, we indicate where a new *Torah* portion begins by highlighting the Hebrew verse number with a gray box so readers can follow along with the communal *Torah* readings. Furthermore, we have included prayers for the State of Israel and the soldiers of the Israel Defense Forces (IDF) that are generally recited following the *Torah* reading in synagogue. It is our constant prayer that God watch over the State of Israel and the members of the IDF, who defend Israel every hour of every day.

In 1948, the State of Israel was created providing a modern answer to Isaiah's ancient question, "Is a nation born all at once?" (Isaiah 66:8). *The Israel Bible* was first published in the 70th year of God's miraculous restoration of the People of Israel to the Land of Israel. Jewish wisdom teaches that 70 is a significant number: *Moshe* (Moses) translated the *Torah* into 70 languages for all 70 nations of the world. From our very origins, the Jewish people were meant to be a light unto the 70 nations, spreading God's truth to the masses.

In the seven decades since the modern rebirth of the State of Israel, God's plan has been unfolding with unprecedented speed, dramatic highs and heartbreaking lows. Never has Israel been at the forefront of the world's attention as it is in our generation. Efforts to vilify the Jewish State seem to spread every day across the globe. At the same time, so does the growing movement of millions of non-Jewish biblical Zionists who stand with the nation of Israel as an expression of their commitment to God's word. As we seek to understand the clash of these two conflicting worldviews, the need for *The Israel Bible* has never been so important.

Standing on the great shoulders of those who came before us and emanating from the land that has always served as the birthplace for the Bible, we conclude with a heartfelt prayer: May the Almighty bless our efforts in offering this *Tanakh* to influence the hearts, minds and actions of its readers. In this way, it is our hope to spread God's name so that the publication of *The Israel Bible* brings us one step closer to the final redemption of Israel and the entire world.

Rabbi Tuly Weisz
Editor, *The Israel Bible*

Foreword

The mandate to study God's word daily is interestingly not found in the Five Books of Moses (Pentateuch), but rather in the first book of our prophetic writings: "Let not this Book of the Teaching cease from your lips, but recite it day and night, so that you may observe faithfully all that is written in it. Only then will you prosper in your undertakings and only then will you be successful" (Joshua 1:8). Charged with bringing the Israelites into the land covenantally promised to Abraham, Isaac and Jacob, God ensures Joshua of His protection if the nation observes His ways as dictated in the Divine constitution known as the *Torah*.

In Jewish tradition, Joshua (1:8) is directly linked with Deuteronomy (11:14), "You shall gather in your new grain and wine, and oil."[1] Our Sages deduced from this scriptural combination the importance of merging *Torah* study with a profession. Completely dedicating oneself to the study of *Torah* without having the financial means to sustain this lifestyle can lead one to eventually straying from observance of God's will. Poverty and crime can have an intimate relationship.

We must also be careful that our work does not affect our daily study of Scripture. The addiction of becoming a workaholic and not making *Torah* study a priority can also lead one into temptations that can violate our personal relationship with Him as well as our fellow human beings. The goal is to achieve a healthy balance between our study of God's word and our daily work.

The Deuteronomic verse quoted above is part of the second section of the Shema[2] that discusses the concept of reward and punishment. Sanctifying God by fulfilling His commandments results in the Land of Israel practically benefitting from rains that occur in the right season and reaping the abundance from the fields. However, if the nation follows pagan gods and practices, the consequences are devastating – famine and death. The Land of Israel is intrinsically linked with the keeping of the *Torah*. Covenant Land comes with covenant responsibility.

---

1. Talmud Bavli Berachot 35b
2. Consisting of three sections within the Five Books of Moses (Deut. 6:4–8; 11:13–22 and Numbers 15:37–42), the *Shema* is proclamation of accepting God's Kingdom in our lives, loyalty to His commandments and remembering His redemptive act of liberating us from Egypt. Jews recite the *Shema* twice a day as stated in Deut. 6:7.

Born into slavery, Joshua is now leading His people into the Promised Land. More than 500 years separates him from his ancestral forefather Abraham. The historical narratives that took place between Abraham leaving everything behind to follow God in Genesis 12 and the death of Moses in the last chapter of Deuteronomy are filled with intrigue, suspense, joy, sorrow and hope. What began as a family is now a nation actualizing its mission to be a kingdom of priests to the world. However, for the Israelites to succeed in the Land of Israel, they must see the *Torah* as the only compass to direct their lives.

The biblical episodes after our first entry into the land are well known. Our ancestors' triumphs and sins are all on public record. We learned the harsh reality of Leviticus (18:28) "So let not the land spew you out for defiling it as it spewed out the nation that came before you." Twice, we lost the privilege to be stewards of the Land of Israel and to fulfill our nation state mandate to be a light to the world. However, when the annals of history were ready to archive the Jewish people after the Holocaust, God kept His covenantal promise and gathered us from the four corners of the globe to come home. The year 1948 was a game changer. Biblical prophecies were and are being realized. We are now living in the birth pangs of the messianic era.

In our morning prayers, we recite a series of blessings over the *Torah* that include petitioning God to have a sweet tooth for His word, to study it without any ulterior motive and to have Him to teach it to us. They are some congregations that invoke the following liturgical prayer after the completion of these blessings: *May the Torah be my faith and El Shaddai my help. Blessed be the name of His glorious kingdom forever and all time.*

According to Jewish tradition, the neglect of not blessing the *Torah* before engaging in its study was one of the reasons for the destruction of the Temple.[3] This is deduced from the redundancy of words in Jeremiah (9:12) that talks about Israel not following God: " ... Because they forsook the teaching I had set before them. They did not obey Me and they did not follow it [did not make a blessing before studying it]." Our inability to properly cherish God's greatest gift to the world, the *Torah,* led to our eventual exile from our land.

On Israel's Independence Day, Jews around the world recite Psalms 113–118 to express our gratitude to God for His Divine hand in helping establish the State of Israel. We have learned from our past and realize the privilege to see firsthand the land, people and *Torah* operating all together in our generation.

---

3. Babylonian Talmud Nedarim 81a

When Rabbi Tuly Weisz approached me about his intent to publish *The Israel Bible* that would highlight commentary about the special relationship between the land and people, I saw this project as another way to publicly demonstrate our appreciation to God for having the State of Israel. In addition, it is another educational tool to ensure biblical literacy. If we are to truly enjoy the Land of Israel, it is incumbent upon us to continually study the *Torah*. Isaiah once prophesied that the Jewish people would return to Zion with songs, "crowned with everlasting joy" (35:10). *The Israel Bible* provides us the lyrical content to express our joy in living in the land that God calls holy.

Rabbi Shlomo Riskin
Chief Rabbi of Efrat
Founder of the Center for Jewish-Christian
Understanding & Cooperation (CJCUC)

Introduction to Sefer Shoftim
The Book of Judges

Introduction and Commentary by Rabbi Shmuel Jablon

The rabbis of the Talmud (*Bava Batra* 15b) teach that *Sefer Shoftim* (Judges), the second book of the Prophets, was written by the prophet *Shmuel*. This book tells the story of 390 difficult years of Israelite history, ending with the statement, "In those days there was no king in *Yisrael*; everyone did as he pleased" (Judges 21:24–25). This verse, which appears several times in the book of *Shoftim*, sums up this challenging era. During this period, the Children of Israel often turned away from *Hashem's Torah*, and fell prey to the cardinal sins of idolatry, murder and sexual immorality. In return, God often allowed Israel's enemies to oppress them. In *Sefer Shoftim*, we read of the Israelites suffering at the hands of Moabites, Canaanites, Midianites, Ammonites and Philistines. All too often throughout this period, though they were living in their own land, the Children of Israel were not actually a free people.

However, not everything described in this book is tragic. After each descent into sin and subjugation, we learn about the judges who fostered spiritual reawakening and led the Israelites to military victories and salvation. In the era prior to Israel's kings, the judges provided leadership to all who were willing to follow.

These judges, drawn from various tribes of Israel, included some of the most heroic figures in Jewish history. For example, we learn about *Otniel*, who was both a *Torah* scholar and a warrior, about *Devora*, the prophetess and judge who sang to *Hashem* after Israel's miraculous victory, and about *Shimshon*, the symbol of great physical strength and willingness to sacrifice everything for the People of Israel. Throughout this book, we see that the judges served as both worldly and spiritual leaders. When the Israelites followed their guidance, they prospered.

Thus, *Sefer Shoftim* depicts a repeating cycle, in which sins, punishment and suffering are followed by repentance, military victory and spiritual growth.

The lesson that success in the Land of Israel depends on following the God of Israel emerges as a consistent theme.

The books of the Prophets were written to teach lessons that would be needed to guide future generations. In his commentary to *Sefer Shoftim* (upon which much of the following commentary is based), Israeli scholar Rabbi Shlomo Aviner writes, "In the future there would be difficult and complicated situations faced by the People of Israel. Due to the prophecy of the *Shoftim*, the nation would be able to learn and strengthen itself."

Rabbi Aviner teaches that as our generation faces complicated challenges, we must look to *Sefer Shoftim* for inspiration and for lessons about how to muster the spiritual and physical strength necessary to cope with these challenges.

Chart of the Judges of Israel

The following is a chart of the Judges of Israel, the tribes they were from, and the amount of time they served, based on *Sefer Shoftim*.

Name	Tribe	Approximate Years	Relevant Verses
Otniel son of *Kenaz*	Yehuda	40	Judges 3:8–11
Ehud son of *Gera*	Binyamin	80	Judges 3:15–30
Shamgar son of *Anat*	Not recorded	1	Judges 3:31
Devora wife of *Lapidot*	Efraim	40	Judges 4–5
Gidon son of *Yoash*	Menashe	40	Judges 6–6
Avimelech son of *Gidon*	Menashe	3	Judges 9:1–56
Tola son of *Puah*	Yissachar	23	Judges 10:1–2
Yair the Giladite	Menashe	22	Judges 10:3–5
Yiftach the Giladite	Menashe	6	Judges 11:1–12:7
Ivtzan of *Beit Lechem*	Yehuda	7	Judges 12:8–10
Eilon the Zebulunite	Zevulun	10	Judges 12:11–12
Avdon son of *Hillel*	Efraim	8	Judges 12:13–15
Shimshon son of *Manoach*	Dan	20	Judges 13–16
Eli the Kohen	Levi	40	I Samuel 1–4
Shmuel the Navi	Levi	11	I Samuel 1–17

Judges

1 ¹ After the death of *Yehoshua*, the Israelites inquired of *Hashem*, "Which of us shall be the first to go up against the Canaanites and attack them?"

א וַיְהִי אַחֲרֵי מוֹת יְהוֹשֻׁעַ וַיִּשְׁאֲלוּ בְּנֵי יִשְׂרָאֵל בַּיהֹוָה לֵאמֹר מִי יַעֲלֶה־לָּנוּ אֶל־הַכְּנַעֲנִי בַּתְּחִלָּה לְהִלָּחֶם בּוֹ:

² *Hashem* replied, "Let [the tribe of] *Yehuda* go up. I now deliver the land into their hands."

ב וַיֹּאמֶר יְהֹוָה יְהוּדָה יַעֲלֶה הִנֵּה נָתַתִּי אֶת־הָאָרֶץ בְּיָדוֹ:

³ *Yehuda* then said to their brother-tribe *Shimon*, "Come up with us to our allotted territory and let us attack the Canaanites, and then we will go with you to your allotted territory." So *Shimon* joined them.

ג וַיֹּאמֶר יְהוּדָה לְשִׁמְעוֹן אָחִיו עֲלֵה אִתִּי בְגוֹרָלִי וְנִלָּחֲמָה בַּכְּנַעֲנִי וְהָלַכְתִּי גַם־אֲנִי אִתְּךָ בְּגוֹרָלֶךָ וַיֵּלֶךְ אִתּוֹ שִׁמְעוֹן:

⁴ When *Yehuda* advanced, *Hashem* delivered the Canaanites and the Perizzites into their hands, and they defeated ten thousand of them at Bezek.

ד וַיַּעַל יְהוּדָה וַיִּתֵּן יְהֹוָה אֶת־הַכְּנַעֲנִי וְהַפְּרִזִּי בְּיָדָם וַיַּכּוּם בְּבֶזֶק עֲשֶׂרֶת אֲלָפִים אִישׁ:

⁵ At Bezek, they encountered Adoni-bezek, engaged him in battle, and defeated the Canaanites and the Perizzites.

ה וַיִּמְצְאוּ אֶת־אֲדֹנִי בֶזֶק בְּבֶזֶק וַיִּלָּחֲמוּ בּוֹ וַיַּכּוּ אֶת־הַכְּנַעֲנִי וְאֶת־הַפְּרִזִּי:

⁶ Adoni-bezek fled, but they pursued him and captured him; and they cut off his thumbs and his big toes.

ו וַיָּנָס אֲדֹנִי בֶזֶק וַיִּרְדְּפוּ אַחֲרָיו וַיֹּאחֲזוּ אֹתוֹ וַיְקַצְּצוּ אֶת־בְּהֹנוֹת יָדָיו וְרַגְלָיו:

⁷ And Adoni-bezek said, "Seventy kings, with thumbs and big toes cut off, used to pick up scraps under my table; as I have done, so *Hashem* has requited me." They brought him to *Yerushalayim* and he died there.

ז וַיֹּאמֶר אֲדֹנִי־בֶזֶק שִׁבְעִים מְלָכִים בְּהֹנוֹת יְדֵיהֶם וְרַגְלֵיהֶם מְקֻצָּצִים הָיוּ מְלַקְּטִים תַּחַת שֻׁלְחָנִי כַּאֲשֶׁר עָשִׂיתִי כֵּן שִׁלַּם־לִי אֱלֹהִים וַיְבִיאֻהוּ יְרוּשָׁלַםִ וַיָּמָת שָׁם:

⁸ The Judites attacked *Yerushalayim* and captured it; they put it to the sword and set the city on fire.

ח וַיִּלָּחֲמוּ בְנֵי־יְהוּדָה בִּירוּשָׁלַםִ וַיִּלְכְּדוּ אוֹתָהּ וַיַּכּוּהָ לְפִי־חָרֶב וְאֶת־הָעִיר שִׁלְּחוּ בָאֵשׁ:

⁹ After that the Judites went down to attack the Canaanites who inhabited the hill country, the *Negev*, and the Shephelah.

ט וְאַחַר יָרְדוּ בְּנֵי יְהוּדָה לְהִלָּחֵם בַּכְּנַעֲנִי יוֹשֵׁב הָהָר וְהַנֶּגֶב וְהַשְּׁפֵלָה:

¹⁰ The Judites marched against the Canaanites who dwelt in *Chevron*, and they defeated Sheshai, Ahiman, and Talmai. (The name of *Chevron* was formerly *Kiryat Arba*.)

י וַיֵּלֶךְ יְהוּדָה אֶל־הַכְּנַעֲנִי הַיּוֹשֵׁב בְּחֶבְרוֹן וְשֵׁם־חֶבְרוֹן לְפָנִים קִרְיַת אַרְבַּע וַיַּכּוּ אֶת־שֵׁשַׁי וְאֶת־אֲחִימַן וְאֶת־תַּלְמָי:

¹¹ From there they marched against the inhabitants of Debir (the name of Debir was formerly *Kiryat Sefer*).

יא וַיֵּלֶךְ מִשָּׁם אֶל־יוֹשְׁבֵי דְּבִיר וְשֵׁם־דְּבִיר לְפָנִים קִרְיַת־סֵפֶר:

¹² And *Kalev* announced, "I will give my daughter Achsah in marriage to the man who attacks and captures *Kiryat Sefer*."

יב וַיֹּאמֶר כָּלֵב אֲשֶׁר־יַכֶּה אֶת־קִרְיַת־סֵפֶר וּלְכָדָהּ וְנָתַתִּי לוֹ אֶת־עַכְסָה בִתִּי לְאִשָּׁה:

13 His younger kinsman, *Otniel* the Kenizzite, captured it; and *Kalev* gave him his daughter Achsah in marriage.

יג וַיִּלְכְּדָהּ עָתְנִיאֵל בֶּן־קְנַז אֲחִי כָלֵב הַקָּטֹן מִמֶּנּוּ וַיִּתֶּן־לוֹ אֶת־עַכְסָה בִתּוֹ לְאִשָּֽׁה׃

va-yil-k'-DAH ot-nee-AYL ben k'-NAZ a-KHEE kha-LAYV ha-ka-TON mi-ME-nu va-yi-ten LO et akh-SAH vi-TO l'-i-SHAH

14 When she came [to him], she induced him to ask her father for some property. She dismounted from her donkey, and *Kalev* asked her, "What is the matter?"

יד וַיְהִי בְּבוֹאָהּ וַתְּסִיתֵהוּ לִשְׁאֹל מֵאֵת־אָבִיהָ הַשָּׂדֶה וַתִּצְנַח מֵעַל הַחֲמוֹר וַיֹּאמֶר־לָהּ כָּלֵב מַה־לָּֽךְ׃

15 She replied, "Give me a present, for you have given me away as *Negev*-land; give me springs of water." And *Kalev* gave her Upper and Lower Gulloth.

טו וַתֹּאמֶר לוֹ הָבָה־לִּי בְרָכָה כִּי אֶרֶץ הַנֶּגֶב נְתַתָּנִי וְנָתַתָּה לִי גֻּלֹּת מָיִם וַיִּתֶּן־לָהּ כָּלֵב אֵת גֻּלֹּת עִלִּית וְאֵת גֻּלֹּת תַּחְתִּֽית׃

16 The descendants of the Kenite, the father-in-law of *Moshe*, went up with the Judites from the City of Palms to the wilderness of *Yehuda*; and they went and settled among the people in the *Negev* of Arad.

טז וּבְנֵי קֵינִי חֹתֵן מֹשֶׁה עָלוּ מֵעִיר הַתְּמָרִים אֶת־בְּנֵי יְהוּדָה מִדְבַּר יְהוּדָה אֲשֶׁר בְּנֶגֶב עֲרָד וַיֵּלֶךְ וַיֵּשֶׁב אֶת־הָעָֽם׃

17 And *Yehuda* with its brother-tribe *Shimon* went on and defeated the Canaanites who dwelt in Zephath. They proscribed it, and so the town was named Hormah.

יז וַיֵּלֶךְ יְהוּדָה אֶת־שִׁמְעוֹן אָחִיו וַיַּכּוּ אֶת־הַכְּנַעֲנִי יוֹשֵׁב צְפַת וַיַּחֲרִימוּ אוֹתָהּ וַיִּקְרָא אֶת־שֵׁם־הָעִיר חָרְמָֽה׃

18 And *Yehuda* captured *Azza* and its territory, *Ashkelon* and its territory, and Ekron and its territory.

יח וַיִּלְכֹּד יְהוּדָה אֶת־עַזָּה וְאֶת־גְּבוּלָהּ וְאֶת־אַשְׁקְלוֹן וְאֶת־גְּבוּלָהּ וְאֶת־עֶקְרוֹן וְאֶת־גְּבוּלָֽהּ׃

19 *Hashem* was with *Yehuda*, so that they took possession of the hill country; but they were not able to dispossess the inhabitants of the plain, for they had iron chariots.

יט וַיְהִי יְהוָה אֶת־יְהוּדָה וַיֹּרֶשׁ אֶת־הָהָר כִּי לֹא לְהוֹרִישׁ אֶת־יֹשְׁבֵי הָעֵמֶק כִּי־רֶכֶב בַּרְזֶל לָהֶֽם׃

20 They gave *Chevron* to *Kalev*, as *Moshe* had promised; and he drove the three Anakites out of there.

כ וַיִּתְּנוּ לְכָלֵב אֶת־חֶבְרוֹן כַּאֲשֶׁר דִּבֶּר מֹשֶׁה וַיּוֹרֶשׁ מִשָּׁם אֶת־שְׁלֹשָׁה בְּנֵי הָעֲנָֽק׃

21 The Benjaminites did not dispossess the Jebusite inhabitants of *Yerushalayim*; so the Jebusites have dwelt with the Benjaminites in *Yerushalayim* to this day.

כא וְאֶת־הַיְבוּסִי יֹשֵׁב יְרוּשָׁלִַם לֹא הוֹרִישׁוּ בְּנֵי בִנְיָמִן וַיֵּשֶׁב הַיְבוּסִי אֶת־בְּנֵי בִנְיָמִן בִּירוּשָׁלִַם עַד הַיּוֹם הַזֶּֽה׃

1:13 His younger kinsman, *Otniel* the Kenizzite, captured it This verse, describing the conquest of *Kiryat Sefer*, demonstrates *Otniel* the Kenizzite's power as a military leader. However, *Otniel* is more than just a strategic tactician. The classic commentator *Rashi* (Joshua 15:15) notes that *Kiryat Sefer*, which means 'the city of the book,' gets its name from an incident that occurred after *Moshe's* death. Due to the people's profound sadness, many biblical laws were forgotten. However, *Otniel*, with his great intellectual prowess, relearns and restores these commandments. Hence, we see that *Otniel* is not only a great warrior; he is also a great *Torah* scholar. Similarly, today's Israeli army has many soldier-scholars who combine "the book and the sword" in their service of God and the Jewish people.

Israeli soldier with his prayer shawl and phylacteries

Judges

22 The House of *Yosef*, for their part, advanced against *Beit El*, and *Hashem* was with them.

כב וַיַּעֲלוּ בֵית־יוֹסֵף גַּם־הֵם בֵּית־אֵל וַיהוָֹה עִמָּם:

23 While the House of *Yosef* were scouting at *Beit El* (the name of the town was formerly Luz),

כג וַיָּתִירוּ בֵית־יוֹסֵף בְּבֵית־אֵל וְשֵׁם־הָעִיר לְפָנִים לוּז:

24 their patrols saw a man leaving the town. They said to him, "Just show us how to get into the town, and we will treat you kindly."

כד וַיִּרְאוּ הַשֹּׁמְרִים אִישׁ יוֹצֵא מִן־הָעִיר וַיֹּאמְרוּ לוֹ הַרְאֵנוּ נָא אֶת־מְבוֹא הָעִיר וְעָשִׂינוּ עִמְּךָ חָסֶד:

25 He showed them how to get into the town; they put the town to the sword, but they let the man and all his relatives go free.

כה וַיַּרְאֵם אֶת־מְבוֹא הָעִיר וַיַּכּוּ אֶת־הָעִיר לְפִי־חָרֶב וְאֶת־הָאִישׁ וְאֶת־כָּל־מִשְׁפַּחְתּוֹ שִׁלֵּחוּ:

26 The man went to the Hittite country. He founded a city and named it Luz, and that has been its name to this day.

כו וַיֵּלֶךְ הָאִישׁ אֶרֶץ הַחִתִּים וַיִּבֶן עִיר וַיִּקְרָא שְׁמָהּ לוּז הוּא שְׁמָהּ עַד הַיּוֹם הַזֶּה:

27 *Menashe* did not dispossess [the inhabitants of] *Beit-Shean* and its dependencies, or [of] Taanach and its dependencies, or the inhabitants of Dor and its dependencies, or the inhabitants of Ibleam and its dependencies, or the inhabitants of Megiddo and its dependencies. The Canaanites persisted in dwelling in this region.

כז וְלֹא־הוֹרִישׁ מְנַשֶּׁה אֶת־בֵּית־שְׁאָן וְאֶת־בְּנוֹתֶיהָ וְאֶת־תַּעְנַךְ וְאֶת־בְּנֹתֶיהָ וְאֶת־יֹשֵׁב [יֹשְׁבֵי] דוֹר וְאֶת־בְּנוֹתֶיהָ וְאֶת־יוֹשְׁבֵי יִבְלְעָם וְאֶת־בְּנֹתֶיהָ וְאֶת־יוֹשְׁבֵי מְגִדּוֹ וְאֶת־בְּנוֹתֶיהָ וַיּוֹאֶל הַכְּנַעֲנִי לָשֶׁבֶת בָּאָרֶץ הַזֹּאת:

28 And when *Yisrael* gained the upper hand, they subjected the Canaanites to forced labor; but they did not dispossess them.

כח וַיְהִי כִּי־חָזַק יִשְׂרָאֵל וַיָּשֶׂם אֶת־הַכְּנַעֲנִי לָמַס וְהוֹרֵישׁ לֹא הוֹרִישׁוֹ:

29 Nor did *Efraim* dispossess the Canaanites who inhabited Gezer; so the Canaanites dwelt in their midst at Gezer.

כט וְאֶפְרַיִם לֹא הוֹרִישׁ אֶת־הַכְּנַעֲנִי הַיּוֹשֵׁב בְּגָזֶר וַיֵּשֶׁב הַכְּנַעֲנִי בְּקִרְבּוֹ בְּגָזֶר:

30 *Zevulun* did not dispossess the inhabitants of Kitron or the inhabitants of Nahalol; so the Canaanites dwelt in their midst, but they were subjected to forced labor.

ל זְבוּלֻן לֹא הוֹרִישׁ אֶת־יוֹשְׁבֵי קִטְרוֹן וְאֶת־יוֹשְׁבֵי נַהֲלֹל וַיֵּשֶׁב הַכְּנַעֲנִי בְּקִרְבּוֹ וַיִּהְיוּ לָמַס:

31 *Asher* did not dispossess the inhabitants of Acco or the inhabitants of Sidon, Ahlab, Achzib, Helbah, Aphik, and Rehob.

לא אָשֵׁר לֹא הוֹרִישׁ אֶת־יֹשְׁבֵי עַכּוֹ וְאֶת־יוֹשְׁבֵי צִידוֹן וְאֶת־אַחְלָב וְאֶת־אַכְזִיב וְאֶת־חֶלְבָּה וְאֶת־אֲפִיק וְאֶת־רְחֹב:

32 So the Asherites dwelt in the midst of the Canaanites, the inhabitants of the land, for they did not dispossess them.

לב וַיֵּשֶׁב הָאָשֵׁרִי בְּקֶרֶב הַכְּנַעֲנִי יֹשְׁבֵי הָאָרֶץ כִּי לֹא הוֹרִישׁוֹ:

33 *Naftali* did not dispossess the inhabitants of *Beit Shemesh* or the inhabitants of Beth-anath. But they settled in the midst of the Canaanite inhabitants of the land, and the inhabitants of *Beit Shemesh* and Beth-anath had to perform forced labor for them.

לג נַפְתָּלִי לֹא־הוֹרִישׁ אֶת־יֹשְׁבֵי בֵית־שֶׁמֶשׁ וְאֶת־יֹשְׁבֵי בֵית־עֲנָת וַיֵּשֶׁב בְּקֶרֶב הַכְּנַעֲנִי יֹשְׁבֵי הָאָרֶץ וְיֹשְׁבֵי בֵית־שֶׁמֶשׁ וּבֵית עֲנָת הָיוּ לָהֶם לָמַס:

³⁴ The Amorites pressed the Danites into the hill country; they would not let them come down to the plain.

לד וַיִּלְחֲצוּ הָאֱמֹרִי אֶת־בְּנֵי־דָן הָהָרָה כִּי־ לֹא נְתָנוֹ לָרֶדֶת לָעֵמֶק:

³⁵ The Amorites also persisted in dwelling in Har-heres, in Aijalon, and in Shaalbim. But the hand of the House of *Yosef* bore heavily on them and they had to perform forced labor.

לה וַיּוֹאֶל הָאֱמֹרִי לָשֶׁבֶת בְּהַר־חֶרֶס בְּאַיָּלוֹן וּבְשַׁעַלְבִים וַתִּכְבַּד יַד בֵּית־יוֹסֵף וַיִּהְיוּ לָמַס:

³⁶ The territory of the Amorites extended from the Ascent of Akrabbim – from Sela – onward.

לו וּגְבוּל הָאֱמֹרִי מִמַּעֲלֵה עַקְרַבִּים מֵהַסֶּלַע וָמָעְלָה:

2 ¹ An angel of *Hashem* came up from *Gilgal* to Bochim and said, "I brought you up from Egypt and I took you into the land which I had promised on oath to your fathers. And I said, 'I will never break My covenant with you.

ב א וַיַּעַל מַלְאַךְ־יְהֹוָה מִן־הַגִּלְגָּל אֶל־ הַבֹּכִים וַיֹּאמֶר אַעֲלֶה אֶתְכֶם מִמִּצְרַיִם וָאָבִיא אֶתְכֶם אֶל־הָאָרֶץ אֲשֶׁר נִשְׁבַּעְתִּי לַאֲבֹתֵיכֶם וָאֹמַר לֹא־אָפֵר בְּרִיתִי אִתְּכֶם לְעוֹלָם:

va-YA-al mal-akh a-do-NAI min ha-gil-GAL el ha-bo-KHEEM va-YO-mer a-a-LEH et-KHEM mi-mitz-RA-yim va-a-VEE et-KHEM el ha-A-retz a-SHER nish-BA-tee la-a-VO-tay-KHEM va-o-MAR lo a-FAYR b'-ree-TEE i-t'-KHEM l'-o-LAM

² And you, for your part, must make no covenant with the inhabitants of this land; you must tear down their altars.' But you have not obeyed Me – look what you have done!

ב וְאַתֶּם לֹא־תִכְרְתוּ בְרִית לְיוֹשְׁבֵי הָאָרֶץ הַזֹּאת מִזְבְּחוֹתֵיהֶם תִּתֹּצוּן וְלֹא־ שְׁמַעְתֶּם בְּקֹלִי מַה־זֹּאת עֲשִׂיתֶם:

³ Therefore, I have resolved not to drive them out before you; they shall become your oppressors, and their gods shall be a snare to you."

ג וְגַם אָמַרְתִּי לֹא־אֲגָרֵשׁ אוֹתָם מִפְּנֵיכֶם וְהָיוּ לָכֶם לְצִדִּים וֵאלֹהֵיהֶם יִהְיוּ לָכֶם לְמוֹקֵשׁ:

⁴ As the angel of *Hashem* spoke these words to all the Israelites, the people broke into weeping.

ד וַיְהִי כְּדַבֵּר מַלְאַךְ יְהֹוָה אֶת־הַדְּבָרִים הָאֵלֶּה אֶל־כָּל־בְּנֵי יִשְׂרָאֵל וַיִּשְׂאוּ הָעָם אֶת־קוֹלָם וַיִּבְכּוּ:

⁵ So they named that place Bochim, and they offered sacrifices there to *Hashem*.

ה וַיִּקְרְאוּ שֵׁם־הַמָּקוֹם הַהוּא בֹּכִים וַיִּזְבְּחוּ־שָׁם לַיהֹוָה:

⁶ When *Yehoshua* dismissed the people, the Israelites went to their allotted territories and took possession of the land.

ו וַיְשַׁלַּח יְהוֹשֻׁעַ אֶת־הָעָם וַיֵּלְכוּ בְנֵי־ יִשְׂרָאֵל אִישׁ לְנַחֲלָתוֹ לָרֶשֶׁת אֶת־ הָאָרֶץ:

2:1 An angel of *Hashem* came up from *Gilgal* to Bochim The angel, who is actually a human prophet according to *Metzudat David*, reiterates God's promise that He will never erase the covenant made with the Patriarchs, according to which the Land of Israel belongs to the Children of Israel. Rabbi Tzvi Yehuda Kook, who was dean of the Mercaz Harav Yeshiva and a prominent leader of Religious Zionism, teaches that whenever the Bible describes a covenant between *Hashem* and the People of Israel, it is not a mutual agreement. Rather, it is a promise that God makes, which the Jewish people must embrace. As this covenant is completely divine, it can never be changed or broken. The establishment of the State of Israel after thousands of years of exile is clearly a fulfillment of this divine covenant.

Rabbi Tzvi Yehuda Kook (1891–1982)

7 The people served *Hashem* during the lifetime of *Yehoshua* and the lifetime of the older people who lived on after *Yehoshua* and who had witnessed all the marvelous deeds that *Hashem* had wrought for *Yisrael*.

ז וַיַּעַבְד֤וּ הָעָם֙ אֶת־יְהֹוָ֔ה כֹּ֖ל יְמֵ֣י יְהוֹשֻׁ֑עַ וְכֹ֣ל ׀ יְמֵ֣י הַזְּקֵנִ֗ים אֲשֶׁ֨ר הֶאֱרִ֤יכוּ יָמִים֙ אַחֲרֵ֣י יְהוֹשֻׁ֔עַ אֲשֶׁ֣ר רָא֗וּ אֵ֣ת כׇּל־מַעֲשֵׂ֤ה יְהֹוָה֙ הַגָּד֔וֹל אֲשֶׁ֥ר עָשָׂ֖ה לְיִשְׂרָאֵֽל׃

8 *Yehoshua* son of *Nun*, the servant of *Hashem*, died at the age of one hundred and ten years,

ח וַיָּ֛מׇת יְהוֹשֻׁ֥עַ בִּן־נ֖וּן עֶ֣בֶד יְהֹוָ֑ה בֶּן־מֵאָ֥ה וְעֶ֖שֶׂר שָׁנִֽים׃

9 and was buried on his own property, at Timnath-heres in the hill country of *Efraim*, north of Mount Gaash.

ט וַיִּקְבְּר֤וּ אוֹתוֹ֙ בִּגְב֣וּל נַחֲלָת֔וֹ בְּתִמְנַת־חֶ֖רֶס בְּהַ֣ר אֶפְרָ֑יִם מִצְּפ֖וֹן לְהַר־גָּֽעַשׁ׃

10 And all that generation were likewise gathered to their fathers. Another generation arose after them, which had not experienced [the deliverance of] *Hashem* or the deeds that He had wrought for *Yisrael*.

י וְגַם֙ כׇּל־הַדּ֣וֹר הַה֔וּא נֶאֶסְפ֖וּ אֶל־אֲבוֹתָ֑יו וַיָּ֩קׇם֩ דּ֨וֹר אַחֵ֜ר אַחֲרֵיהֶ֗ם אֲשֶׁ֤ר לֹא־יָֽדְעוּ֙ אֶת־יְהֹוָ֔ה וְגַם֙ אֶת־הַֽמַּעֲשֶׂ֔ה אֲשֶׁ֥ר עָשָׂ֖ה לְיִשְׂרָאֵֽל׃

11 And the Israelites did what was offensive to *Hashem*. They worshiped the Baalim

יא וַיַּעֲשׂ֧וּ בְנֵֽי־יִשְׂרָאֵ֛ל אֶת־הָרַ֖ע בְּעֵינֵ֣י יְהֹוָ֑ה וַיַּעַבְד֖וּ אֶת־הַבְּעָלִֽים׃

12 and forsook *Hashem*, the God of their fathers, who had brought them out of the land of Egypt. They followed other gods, from among the gods of the peoples around them, and bowed down to them; they provoked *Hashem*.

יב וַיַּעַזְב֞וּ אֶת־יְהֹוָ֣ה ׀ אֱלֹהֵ֣י אֲבוֹתָ֗ם הַמּוֹצִ֣יא אוֹתָם֮ מֵאֶ֣רֶץ מִצְרַ֒יִם֒ וַיֵּלְכ֞וּ אַחֲרֵ֣י ׀ אֱלֹהִ֣ים אֲחֵרִ֗ים מֵאֱלֹהֵ֤י הָֽעַמִּים֙ אֲשֶׁר֙ סְבִיב֣וֹתֵיהֶ֔ם וַיִּֽשְׁתַּחֲו֖וּ לָהֶ֑ם וַיַּכְעִ֖סוּ אֶת־יְהֹוָֽה׃

13 They forsook *Hashem* and worshiped Baal and the Ashtaroth.

יג וַיַּעַזְב֖וּ אֶת־יְהֹוָ֑ה וַיַּעַבְד֥וּ לַבַּ֖עַל וְלָעַשְׁתָּרֽוֹת׃

14 Then *Hashem* was incensed at *Yisrael*, and He handed them over to foes who plundered them. He surrendered them to their enemies on all sides, and they could no longer hold their own against their enemies.

יד וַיִּֽחַר־אַ֤ף יְהֹוָה֙ בְּיִשְׂרָאֵ֔ל וַֽיִּתְּנֵם֙ בְּיַד־שֹׁסִ֔ים וַיָּשֹׁ֖סּוּ אוֹתָ֑ם וַֽיִּמְכְּרֵ֞ם בְּיַ֤ד אֽוֹיְבֵיהֶם֙ מִסָּבִ֔יב וְלֹא־יָ֣כְל֣וּ ע֔וֹד לַעֲמֹ֖ד לִפְנֵ֥י אוֹיְבֵיהֶֽם׃

15 In all their campaigns, the hand of *Hashem* was against them to their undoing, as *Hashem* had declared and as *Hashem* had sworn to them; and they were in great distress.

טו בְּכֹ֣ל ׀ אֲשֶׁ֣ר יָצְא֗וּ יַד־יְהֹוָה֙ הָיְתָה־בָּ֣ם לְרָעָ֔ה כַּֽאֲשֶׁר֙ דִּבֶּ֣ר יְהֹוָ֔ה וְכַאֲשֶׁ֛ר נִשְׁבַּ֥ע יְהֹוָ֖ה לָהֶ֑ם וַיֵּ֥צֶר לָהֶ֖ם מְאֹֽד׃

16 Then *Hashem* raised up chieftains who delivered them from those who plundered them.

טז וַיָּ֥קֶם יְהֹוָ֖ה שֹׁפְטִ֑ים וַיּ֣וֹשִׁיע֔וּם מִיַּ֖ד שֹׁסֵיהֶֽם׃

17 But they did not heed their chieftains either; they went astray after other gods and bowed down to them. They were quick to turn aside from the way their fathers had followed in obedience to the commandments of *Hashem*; they did not do right.

יז וְגַ֤ם אֶל־שֹֽׁפְטֵיהֶם֙ לֹ֣א שָׁמֵ֔עוּ כִּ֣י זָנ֗וּ אַֽחֲרֵי֙ אֱלֹהִ֣ים אֲחֵרִ֔ים וַיִּֽשְׁתַּחֲו֖וּ לָהֶ֑ם סָ֣רוּ מַהֵ֗ר מִן־הַדֶּ֜רֶךְ אֲשֶׁ֨ר הָלְכ֤וּ אֲבוֹתָם֙ לִשְׁמֹ֣עַ מִצְוֺת־יְהֹוָ֔ה לֹא־עָ֖שׂוּ כֵֽן׃

18 When *Hashem* raised up chieftains for them, *Hashem* would be with the chieftain and would save them from their enemies during the chieftain's lifetime; for *Hashem* would be moved to pity by their moanings because of those who oppressed and crushed them.

יח וְכִי־הֵקִים יְהֹוָה לָהֶם שֹׁפְטִים וְהָיָה יְהֹוָה עִם־הַשֹּׁפֵט וְהוֹשִׁיעָם מִיַּד אֹיְבֵיהֶם כֹּל יְמֵי הַשּׁוֹפֵט כִּי־יִנָּחֵם יְהֹוָה מִנַּאֲקָתָם מִפְּנֵי לֹחֲצֵיהֶם וְדֹחֲקֵיהֶם:

19 But when the chieftain died, they would again act basely, even more than the preceding generation – following other gods, worshiping them, and bowing down to them; they omitted none of their practices and stubborn ways.

יט וְהָיָה בְּמוֹת הַשּׁוֹפֵט יָשֻׁבוּ וְהִשְׁחִיתוּ מֵאֲבוֹתָם לָלֶכֶת אַחֲרֵי אֱלֹהִים אֲחֵרִים לְעָבְדָם וּלְהִשְׁתַּחֲוֹת לָהֶם לֹא הִפִּילוּ מִמַּעַלְלֵיהֶם וּמִדַּרְכָּם הַקָּשָׁה:

20 Then *Hashem* became incensed against *Yisrael*, and He said, "Since that nation has transgressed the covenant that I enjoined upon their fathers and has not obeyed Me,

כ וַיִּחַר־אַף יְהֹוָה בְּיִשְׂרָאֵל וַיֹּאמֶר יַעַן אֲשֶׁר עָבְרוּ הַגּוֹי הַזֶּה אֶת־בְּרִיתִי אֲשֶׁר צִוִּיתִי אֶת־אֲבוֹתָם וְלֹא שָׁמְעוּ לְקוֹלִי:

21 I for My part will no longer drive out before them any of the nations that *Yehoshua* left when he died."

כא גַּם־אֲנִי לֹא אוֹסִיף לְהוֹרִישׁ אִישׁ מִפְּנֵיהֶם מִן־הַגּוֹיִם אֲשֶׁר־עָזַב יְהוֹשֻׁעַ וַיָּמֹת:

22 For it was in order to test *Yisrael* by them – [to see] whether or not they would faithfully walk in the ways of *Hashem*, as their fathers had done –

כב לְמַעַן נַסּוֹת בָּם אֶת־יִשְׂרָאֵל הֲשֹׁמְרִים הֵם אֶת־דֶּרֶךְ יְהֹוָה לָלֶכֶת בָּם כַּאֲשֶׁר שָׁמְרוּ אֲבוֹתָם אִם־לֹא:

23 that *Hashem* had left those nations, instead of driving them out at once, and had not delivered them into the hands of *Yehoshua*.

כג וַיַּנַּח יְהֹוָה אֶת־הַגּוֹיִם הָאֵלֶּה לְבִלְתִּי הוֹרִישָׁם מַהֵר וְלֹא נְתָנָם בְּיַד־יְהוֹשֻׁעַ:

3 1 These are the nations that *Hashem* left so that He might test by them all the Israelites who had not known any of the wars of Canaan,

ג א וְאֵלֶּה הַגּוֹיִם אֲשֶׁר הִנִּיחַ יְהֹוָה לְנַסּוֹת בָּם אֶת־יִשְׂרָאֵל אֵת כָּל־אֲשֶׁר לֹא־יָדְעוּ אֵת כָּל־מִלְחֲמוֹת כְּנָעַן:

2 so that succeeding generations of Israelites might be made to experience war – but only those who had not known the former wars:

ב רַק לְמַעַן דַּעַת דֹּרוֹת בְּנֵי־יִשְׂרָאֵל לְלַמְּדָם מִלְחָמָה רַק אֲשֶׁר־לְפָנִים לֹא יְדָעוּם:

3 the five principalities of the Philistines and all the Canaanites, Sidonians, and Hivites who inhabited the hill country of the Lebanon from Mount Baal-hermon to Lebo-hamath.

ג חֲמֵשֶׁת סַרְנֵי פְלִשְׁתִּים וְכָל־הַכְּנַעֲנִי וְהַצִּידֹנִי וְהַחִוִּי יֹשֵׁב הַר הַלְּבָנוֹן מֵהַר בַּעַל חֶרְמוֹן עַד לְבוֹא חֲמָת:

4 These served as a means of testing *Yisrael*, to learn whether they would obey the commandments which *Hashem* had enjoined upon their fathers through *Moshe*.

ד וַיִּהְיוּ לְנַסּוֹת בָּם אֶת־יִשְׂרָאֵל לָדַעַת הֲיִשְׁמְעוּ אֶת־מִצְוֹת יְהֹוָה אֲשֶׁר־צִוָּה אֶת־אֲבוֹתָם בְּיַד־מֹשֶׁה:

5 The Israelites settled among the Canaanites, Hittites, Amorites, Perizzites, Hivites, and Jebusites;

ה וּבְנֵי יִשְׂרָאֵל יָשְׁבוּ בְּקֶרֶב הַכְּנַעֲנִי הַחִתִּי וְהָאֱמֹרִי וְהַפְּרִזִּי וְהַחִוִּי וְהַיְבוּסִי:

6 they took their daughters to wife and gave their own daughters to their sons, and they worshiped their gods.

ו וַיִּקְחוּ אֶת־בְּנוֹתֵיהֶם לָהֶם לְנָשִׁים וְאֶת־בְּנוֹתֵיהֶם נָתְנוּ לִבְנֵיהֶם וַיַּעַבְדוּ אֶת־אֱלֹהֵיהֶם:

7 The Israelites did what was offensive to *Hashem*; they ignored *Hashem* their God and worshiped the Baalim and the Asheroth.

ז וַיַּעֲשׂוּ בְנֵי־יִשְׂרָאֵל אֶת־הָרַע בְּעֵינֵי יְהֹוָה וַיִּשְׁכְּחוּ אֶת־יְהֹוָה אֱלֹהֵיהֶם וַיַּעַבְדוּ אֶת־הַבְּעָלִים וְאֶת־הָאֲשֵׁרוֹת:

8 *Hashem* became incensed at *Yisrael* and surrendered them to King Cushan-rishathaim of Aram-Naharaim; and the Israelites were subject to Cushan-rishathaim for eight years.

ח וַיִּחַר־אַף יְהֹוָה בְּיִשְׂרָאֵל וַיִּמְכְּרֵם בְּיַד כּוּשַׁן רִשְׁעָתַיִם מֶלֶךְ אֲרַם נַהֲרָיִם וַיַּעַבְדוּ בְנֵי־יִשְׂרָאֵל אֶת־כּוּשַׁן רִשְׁעָתַיִם שְׁמֹנֶה שָׁנִים:

9 The Israelites cried out to *Hashem*, and *Hashem* raised a champion for the Israelites to deliver them: *Otniel* the Kenizzite, a younger kinsman of *Kalev*.

ט וַיִּזְעֲקוּ בְנֵי־יִשְׂרָאֵל אֶל־יְהֹוָה וַיָּקֶם יְהֹוָה מוֹשִׁיעַ לִבְנֵי יִשְׂרָאֵל וַיּוֹשִׁיעֵם אֵת עָתְנִיאֵל בֶּן־קְנַז אֲחִי כָלֵב הַקָּטֹן מִמֶּנּוּ:

10 The spirit of *Hashem* descended upon him and he became *Yisrael*'s chieftain. He went out to war, and *Hashem* delivered King Cushan-rishathaim of Aram into his hands. He prevailed over Cushan-rishathaim,

י וַתְּהִי עָלָיו רוּחַ־יְהֹוָה וַיִּשְׁפֹּט אֶת־יִשְׂרָאֵל וַיֵּצֵא לַמִּלְחָמָה וַיִּתֵּן יְהֹוָה בְּיָדוֹ אֶת־כּוּשַׁן רִשְׁעָתַיִם מֶלֶךְ אֲרָם וַתָּעָז יָדוֹ עַל כּוּשַׁן רִשְׁעָתָיִם:

11 and the land had peace for forty years. When *Otniel* the Kenizzite died,

יא וַתִּשְׁקֹט הָאָרֶץ אַרְבָּעִים שָׁנָה וַיָּמָת עָתְנִיאֵל בֶּן־קְנַז:

12 the Israelites again did what was offensive to *Hashem*. And because they did what was offensive to *Hashem*, *Hashem* let King Eglon of Moab prevail over *Yisrael*.

יב וַיֹּסִפוּ בְּנֵי יִשְׂרָאֵל לַעֲשׂוֹת הָרַע בְּעֵינֵי יְהֹוָה וַיְחַזֵּק יְהֹוָה אֶת־עֶגְלוֹן מֶלֶךְ־מוֹאָב עַל־יִשְׂרָאֵל עַל כִּי־עָשׂוּ אֶת־הָרַע בְּעֵינֵי יְהֹוָה:

13 [Eglon] brought the Ammonites and the Amalekites together under his command, and went and defeated *Yisrael* and occupied the City of Palms.

יג וַיֶּאֱסֹף אֵלָיו אֶת־בְּנֵי עַמּוֹן וַעֲמָלֵק וַיֵּלֶךְ וַיַּךְ אֶת־יִשְׂרָאֵל וַיִּירְשׁוּ אֶת־עִיר הַתְּמָרִים:

14 The Israelites were subject to King Eglon of Moab for eighteen years.

יד וַיַּעַבְדוּ בְנֵי־יִשְׂרָאֵל אֶת־עֶגְלוֹן מֶלֶךְ־מוֹאָב שְׁמוֹנֶה עֶשְׂרֵה שָׁנָה:

15 Then the Israelites cried out to *Hashem*, and *Hashem* raised up a champion for them: the Benjaminite *Ehud* son of Gera, a left-handed man. It happened that the Israelites sent tribute to King Eglon of Moab through him.

טו וַיִּזְעֲקוּ בְנֵי־יִשְׂרָאֵל אֶל־יְהֹוָה וַיָּקֶם יְהֹוָה לָהֶם מוֹשִׁיעַ אֶת־אֵהוּד בֶּן־גֵּרָא בֶּן־הַיְמִינִי אִישׁ אִטֵּר יַד־יְמִינוֹ וַיִּשְׁלְחוּ בְנֵי־יִשְׂרָאֵל בְּיָדוֹ מִנְחָה לְעֶגְלוֹן מֶלֶךְ מוֹאָב:

16 So *Ehud* made for himself a two-edged dagger, a *gomed* in length, which he girded on his right side under his cloak.

טז וַיַּעַשׂ לוֹ אֵהוּד חֶרֶב וְלָהּ שְׁנֵי פֵיוֹת גֹּמֶד אָרְכָּהּ וַיַּחְגֹּר אוֹתָהּ מִתַּחַת לְמַדָּיו עַל יֶרֶךְ יְמִינוֹ:

17 He presented the tribute to King Eglon of Moab. Now Eglon was a very stout man.

יז וַיַּקְרֵב אֶת־הַמִּנְחָה לְעֶגְלוֹן מֶלֶךְ מוֹאָב וְעֶגְלוֹן אִישׁ בָּרִיא מְאֹד:

18 When [*Ehud*] had finished presenting the tribute, he dismissed the people who had conveyed the tribute.

יח וַיְהִי כַּאֲשֶׁר כִּלָּה לְהַקְרִיב אֶת־הַמִּנְחָה וַיְשַׁלַּח אֶת־הָעָם נֹשְׂאֵי הַמִּנְחָה:

19 But he himself returned from Pesilim, near *Gilgal*, and said, "Your Majesty, I have a secret message for you." [*Eglon*] thereupon commanded, "Silence!" So all those in attendance left his presence;

יט וְהוּא שָׁב מִן־הַפְּסִילִים אֲשֶׁר אֶת־הַגִּלְגָּל וַיֹּאמֶר דְּבַר־סֵתֶר לִי אֵלֶיךָ הַמֶּלֶךְ וַיֹּאמֶר הָס וַיֵּצְאוּ מֵעָלָיו כָּל־הָעֹמְדִים עָלָיו:

20 and when *Ehud* approached him, he was sitting alone in his cool upper chamber. *Ehud* said, "I have a message for you from *Hashem*"; whereupon he rose from his seat.

כ וְאֵהוּד בָּא אֵלָיו וְהוּא־יֹשֵׁב בַּעֲלִיַּת הַמְּקֵרָה אֲשֶׁר־לוֹ לְבַדּוֹ וַיֹּאמֶר אֵהוּד דְּבַר־אֱלֹהִים לִי אֵלֶיךָ וַיָּקָם מֵעַל הַכִּסֵּא:

*v'-ay-HUD BA ay-LAV v'-hu yo-SHAYV ba-a-li-YAT ha-m'-kay-RAH
a-sher LO l'-va-DO va-YO-mer ay-HUD d'-var e-lo-HEEM
LEE ay-LE-kha va-YA-kom may-AL ha-ki-SAY*

21 Reaching with his left hand, *Ehud* drew the dagger from his right side and drove it into [*Eglon's*] belly.

כא וַיִּשְׁלַח אֵהוּד אֶת־יַד שְׂמֹאלוֹ וַיִּקַּח אֶת־הַחֶרֶב מֵעַל יֶרֶךְ יְמִינוֹ וַיִּתְקָעֶהָ בְּבִטְנוֹ:

22 The fat closed over the blade and the hilt went in after the blade – for he did not pull the dagger out of his belly – and the filth came out.

כב וַיָּבֹא גַם־הַנִּצָּב אַחַר הַלַּהַב וַיִּסְגֹּר הַחֵלֶב בְּעַד הַלַּהַב כִּי לֹא שָׁלַף הַחֶרֶב מִבִּטְנוֹ וַיֵּצֵא הַפַּרְשְׁדֹנָה:

23 Stepping out into the vestibule, *Ehud* shut the doors of the upper chamber on him and locked them.

כג וַיֵּצֵא אֵהוּד הַמִּסְדְּרוֹנָה וַיִּסְגֹּר דַּלְתוֹת הָעֲלִיָּה בַּעֲדוֹ וְנָעָל:

24 After he left, the courtiers returned. When they saw that the doors of the upper chamber were locked, they thought, "He must be relieving himself in the cool chamber."

כד וְהוּא יָצָא וַעֲבָדָיו בָּאוּ וַיִּרְאוּ וְהִנֵּה דַּלְתוֹת הָעֲלִיָּה נְעֻלוֹת וַיֹּאמְרוּ אַךְ מֵסִיךְ הוּא אֶת־רַגְלָיו בַּחֲדַר הַמְּקֵרָה:

25 They waited a long time; and when he did not open the doors of the chamber, they took the key and opened them – and there their master was lying dead on the floor!

כה וַיָּחִילוּ עַד־בּוֹשׁ וְהִנֵּה אֵינֶנּוּ פֹתֵחַ דַּלְתוֹת הָעֲלִיָּה וַיִּקְחוּ אֶת־הַמַּפְתֵּחַ וַיִּפְתָּחוּ וְהִנֵּה אֲדֹנֵיהֶם נֹפֵל אַרְצָה מֵת:

26 But *Ehud* had made good his escape while they delayed; he had passed Pesilim and escaped to Seirah.

כו וְאֵהוּד נִמְלַט עַד הִתְמַהְמְהָם וְהוּא עָבַר אֶת־הַפְּסִילִים וַיִּמָּלֵט הַשְּׂעִירָתָה:

3:20 And when *Ehud* approached him *Ehud* tells the Moabite king Eglon that he has a message for him from God. Eglon stands up, and *Ehud* stabs him, thereby killing the oppressor of the Israelites. Although he delivered no verbal message, *Ehud* told the truth: *Hashem* had instructed him to kill Eglon. At its core, God's message is that ultimately, even if it takes time, He will always save the People of Israel

Girl waving the Israeli flag

from their oppressors. This true message that *Ehud* delivered to Eglon remains equally true in our time. Often the enemies of the Jewish people appear strong, and even claim many innocent victims. But God continues to send the message that ultimately, those who oppress His people will always be destroyed. Over time, the Jews' persecutors all fade away, while the Nation of Israel lives forever.

27 When he got there, he had the *shofar* sounded through the hill country of *Efraim*, and all the Israelites descended with him from the hill country; and he took the lead.

כז וַיְהִי בְּבוֹאוֹ וַיִּתְקַע בַּשּׁוֹפָר בְּהַר אֶפְרָיִם וַיֵּרְדוּ עִמּוֹ בְנֵי־יִשְׂרָאֵל מִן־הָהָר וְהוּא לִפְנֵיהֶם:

28 "Follow me closely," he said, "for *Hashem* has delivered your enemies, the Moabites, into your hands." They followed him down and seized the fords of the *Yarden* against the Moabites; they let no one cross.

כח וַיֹּאמֶר אֲלֵהֶם רִדְפוּ אַחֲרַי כִּי־נָתַן יְהֹוָה אֶת־אֹיְבֵיכֶם אֶת־מוֹאָב בְּיֶדְכֶם וַיֵּרְדוּ אַחֲרָיו וַיִּלְכְּדוּ אֶת־מַעְבְּרוֹת הַיַּרְדֵּן לְמוֹאָב וְלֹא־נָתְנוּ אִישׁ לַעֲבֹר:

29 On that occasion they slew about 10,000 Moabites; they were all robust and brave men, yet not one of them escaped.

כט וַיַּכּוּ אֶת־מוֹאָב בָּעֵת הַהִיא כַּעֲשֶׂרֶת אֲלָפִים אִישׁ כָּל־שָׁמֵן וְכָל־אִישׁ חָיִל וְלֹא נִמְלַט אִישׁ:

30 On that day, Moab submitted to *Yisrael*; and the land was tranquil for eighty years.

ל וַתִּכָּנַע מוֹאָב בַּיּוֹם הַהוּא תַּחַת יַד יִשְׂרָאֵל וַתִּשְׁקֹט הָאָרֶץ שְׁמוֹנִים שָׁנָה:

31 After him came *Shamgar* son of Anath, who slew six hundred Philistines with an ox-goad. He too was a champion of *Yisrael*.

לא וְאַחֲרָיו הָיָה שַׁמְגַּר בֶּן־עֲנָת וַיַּךְ אֶת־פְּלִשְׁתִּים שֵׁשׁ־מֵאוֹת אִישׁ בְּמַלְמַד הַבָּקָר וַיֹּשַׁע גַּם־הוּא אֶת־יִשְׂרָאֵל:

4 1 The Israelites again did what was offensive to *Hashem* – *Ehud* now being dead.

ד א וַיֹּסִפוּ בְּנֵי יִשְׂרָאֵל לַעֲשׂוֹת הָרַע בְּעֵינֵי יְהֹוָה וְאֵהוּד מֵת:

2 And *Hashem* surrendered them to King Jabin of Canaan, who reigned in Hazor. His army commander was Sisera, whose base was Harosheth-goiim.

ב וַיִּמְכְּרֵם יְהֹוָה בְּיַד יָבִין מֶלֶךְ־כְּנַעַן אֲשֶׁר מָלַךְ בְּחָצוֹר וְשַׂר־צְבָאוֹ סִיסְרָא וְהוּא יוֹשֵׁב בַּחֲרֹשֶׁת הַגּוֹיִם:

3 The Israelites cried out to *Hashem*; for he had nine hundred iron chariots, and he had oppressed *Yisrael* ruthlessly for twenty years.

ג וַיִּצְעֲקוּ בְנֵי־יִשְׂרָאֵל אֶל־יְהֹוָה כִּי תְּשַׁע מֵאוֹת רֶכֶב־בַּרְזֶל לוֹ וְהוּא לָחַץ אֶת־בְּנֵי יִשְׂרָאֵל בְּחָזְקָה עֶשְׂרִים שָׁנָה:

4 *Devora*, wife of Lappidoth, was a *Neviah*; she led *Yisrael* at that time.

ד וּדְבוֹרָה אִשָּׁה נְבִיאָה אֵשֶׁת לַפִּידוֹת הִיא שֹׁפְטָה אֶת־יִשְׂרָאֵל בָּעֵת הַהִיא:

ud-vo-RAH i-SHAH n'-vee-AH AY-shet la-pee-DOT HEE
sho-f'-TAH et yis-ra-AYL ba-AYT ha-HEE

4:4 Now *Devora*, a prophetess Throughout Jewish history, many women have followed the example of *Devora*, described in this verse as both a prophetess and a judge, by taking positions of leadership on behalf of their people. One example dates to the early Renaissance period, when another Jewish woman emerged as a great leader of her people. At the time, the Jews of Spain faced the horrific persecutions of the Inquisition. But despite the strict prohibitions against practicing Judaism, many of the forced converts known as *Anussim* or "Crypto-Jews" continued to observe their religion in secret. Dona Gracia (1510–1569) discovered her Jewish identity only after she was married, but from that moment on, she was determined to bring respite to her people. As one of the wealthiest women in Europe, she was able to create an escape network for many of the *Anussim*, and eventually used her position of power to negotiate with Sultan Suleiman the Magnificent for a long term lease on the Tiberias region of the Land of Israel, of which she became the ruling authority. She began to rebuild the Galilee's abandoned towns for other *Anussim* to settle in, and aimed to turn Tiberias into a

Tiberias, Israel

Dona Gracia (1510–1569)

5 She used to sit under the Palm of *Devora*, between *Rama* and *Beit El* in the hill country of *Efraim*, and the Israelites would come to her for decisions.

ה וְהִיא יוֹשֶׁבֶת תַּחַת־תֹּמֶר דְּבוֹרָה בֵּין הָרָמָה וּבֵין בֵּית־אֵל בְּהַר אֶפְרָיִם וַיַּעֲלוּ אֵלֶיהָ בְּנֵי יִשְׂרָאֵל לַמִּשְׁפָּט:

6 She summoned *Barak* son of Abinoam, of Kedesh in *Naftali*, and said to him, "*Hashem*, the God of *Yisrael*, has commanded: Go, march up to Mount *Tavor*, and take with you ten thousand men of *Naftali* and Zevulun.

ו וַתִּשְׁלַח וַתִּקְרָא לְבָרָק בֶּן־אֲבִינֹעַם מִקֶּדֶשׁ נַפְתָּלִי וַתֹּאמֶר אֵלָיו הֲלֹא צִוָּה יְהוָה אֱלֹהֵי־יִשְׂרָאֵל לֵךְ וּמָשַׁכְתָּ בְּהַר תָּבוֹר וְלָקַחְתָּ עִמְּךָ עֲשֶׂרֶת אֲלָפִים אִישׁ מִבְּנֵי נַפְתָּלִי וּמִבְּנֵי זְבֻלוּן:

va-tish-LAKH va-tik-RA l'-va-RAK ben a-vee-NO-am mi-KE-desh naf-ta-LEE va-TO-mer ay-LAV ha-lo tzi-VAH a-do-NAI e-lo-hay yis-ra-AYL LAYKH u-ma-shakh-TA b'-HAR ta-VOR v'-la-kakh-TA i-m'-KHA a-SE-ret a-la-FEEM EESH mi-b'-NAY naf-ta-LEE u-mi-b'-NAY z'-vu-LUN

7 And I will draw Sisera, Jabin's army commander, with his chariots and his troops, toward you up to the Wadi Kishon; and I will deliver him into your hands."

ז וּמָשַׁכְתִּי אֵלֶיךָ אֶל־נַחַל קִישׁוֹן אֶת־סִיסְרָא שַׂר־צְבָא יָבִין וְאֶת־רִכְבּוֹ וְאֶת־הֲמוֹנוֹ וּנְתַתִּיהוּ בְּיָדֶךָ:

8 But *Barak* said to her, "If you will go with me, I will go; if not, I will not go."

ח וַיֹּאמֶר אֵלֶיהָ בָּרָק אִם־תֵּלְכִי עִמִּי וְהָלָכְתִּי וְאִם־לֹא תֵלְכִי עִמִּי לֹא אֵלֵךְ:

9 "Very well, I will go with you," she answered. "However, there will be no glory for you in the course you are taking, for then *Hashem* will deliver Sisera into the hands of a woman." So *Devora* went with *Barak* to Kedesh.

ט וַתֹּאמֶר הָלֹךְ אֵלֵךְ עִמָּךְ אֶפֶס כִּי לֹא תִהְיֶה תִּפְאַרְתְּךָ עַל־הַדֶּרֶךְ אֲשֶׁר אַתָּה הוֹלֵךְ כִּי בְיַד־אִשָּׁה יִמְכֹּר יְהוָה אֶת־סִיסְרָא וַתָּקָם דְּבוֹרָה וַתֵּלֶךְ עִם־בָּרָק קֶדְשָׁה:

10 *Barak* then mustered *Zevulun* and *Naftali* at Kedesh; ten thousand men marched up after him; and *Devora* also went up with him.

י וַיַּזְעֵק בָּרָק אֶת־זְבוּלֻן וְאֶת־נַפְתָּלִי קֶדְשָׁה וַיַּעַל בְּרַגְלָיו עֲשֶׂרֶת אַלְפֵי אִישׁ וַתַּעַל עִמּוֹ דְּבוֹרָה:

11 Now *Chever* the Kenite had separated from the other Kenites, descendants of Hobab, father-in-law of *Moshe*, and had pitched his tent at Elon-bezaanannim, which is near Kedesh.

יא וְחֶבֶר הַקֵּינִי נִפְרָד מִקַּיִן מִבְּנֵי חֹבָב חֹתֵן מֹשֶׁה וַיֵּט אָהֳלוֹ עַד־אֵלוֹן בצענים [בְּצַעֲנַנִּים] אֲשֶׁר אֶת־קֶדֶשׁ:

12 Sisera was informed that *Barak* son of Abinoam had gone up to Mount *Tavor*.

יב וַיַּגִּדוּ לְסִיסְרָא כִּי עָלָה בָּרָק בֶּן־אֲבִינֹעַם הַר־תָּבוֹר:

---

major center of Jewish settlement, trade and learning. Today, visitors to the contemporary city of *Teveria* (Tiberias) can visit the Dona Gracia museum to learn about this fascinating woman who pursued one of the earliest attempts to create a Zionist movement.

4:6 Go, march up to Mount *Tavor*, and take with you ten thousand men The prophetess and judge *Devora* instructs *Barak* in God's name that he is to "march up to Mount *Tavor*" and take ten thousand soldiers with him, to prepare to fight the enemy Sisera. *Metzudat David* points out that taking the soldiers does not mean he was to simply draft them into service. Rather, it means to "draw at their hearts," so that they would overcome their natural fear of Sisera and fight courageously. Rabbi Shlomo Aviner notes that this teaches us an important lesson, which remains relevant to this day: the importance of paying attention to the emotional state of the soldiers of Israel. He writes, "The secret weapon of the Israeli Defense Forces is their morale, strength and courage."

Mount *Tavor* in northern Israel

13 So Sisera ordered all his chariots – nine hundred iron chariots – and all the troops he had to move from Harosheth-goiim to the Wadi Kishon.

יג וַיַּזְעֵק סִיסְרָא אֶת־כָּל־רִכְבּוֹ תְּשַׁע מֵאוֹת רֶכֶב בַּרְזֶל וְאֶת־כָּל־הָעָם אֲשֶׁר אִתּוֹ מֵחֲרֹשֶׁת הַגּוֹיִם אֶל־נַחַל קִישׁוֹן:

14 Then *Devora* said to *Barak*, "Up! This is the day on which *Hashem* will deliver Sisera into your hands: *Hashem* is marching before you." *Barak* charged down Mount *Tavor*, followed by the ten thousand men,

יד וַתֹּאמֶר דְּבֹרָה אֶל־בָּרָק קוּם כִּי זֶה הַיּוֹם אֲשֶׁר נָתַן יְהֹוָה אֶת־סִיסְרָא בְּיָדֶךָ הֲלֹא יְהֹוָה יָצָא לְפָנֶיךָ וַיֵּרֶד בָּרָק מֵהַר תָּבוֹר וַעֲשֶׂרֶת אֲלָפִים אִישׁ אַחֲרָיו:

15 and *Hashem* threw Sisera and all his chariots and army into a panic before the onslaught of *Barak*. Sisera leaped from his chariot and fled on foot

טו וַיָּהָם יְהֹוָה אֶת־סִיסְרָא וְאֶת־כָּל־הָרֶכֶב וְאֶת־כָּל־הַמַּחֲנֶה לְפִי־חֶרֶב לִפְנֵי בָרָק וַיֵּרֶד סִיסְרָא מֵעַל הַמֶּרְכָּבָה וַיָּנָס בְּרַגְלָיו:

16 as *Barak* pursued the chariots and the soldiers as far as Harosheth-goiim. All of Sisera's soldiers fell by the sword; not a man was left.

טז וּבָרָק רָדַף אַחֲרֵי הָרֶכֶב וְאַחֲרֵי הַמַּחֲנֶה עַד חֲרֹשֶׁת הַגּוֹיִם וַיִּפֹּל כָּל־מַחֲנֵה סִיסְרָא לְפִי־חֶרֶב לֹא נִשְׁאַר עַד־אֶחָד:

17 Sisera, meanwhile, had fled on foot to the tent of *Yael*, wife of *Chever* the Kenite; for there was friendship between King Jabin of Hazor and the family of *Chever* the Kenite.

יז וְסִיסְרָא נָס בְּרַגְלָיו אֶל־אֹהֶל יָעֵל אֵשֶׁת חֶבֶר הַקֵּינִי כִּי שָׁלוֹם בֵּין יָבִין מֶלֶךְ־חָצוֹר וּבֵין בֵּית חֶבֶר הַקֵּינִי:

18 *Yael* came out to greet Sisera and said to him, "Come in, my lord, come in here, do not be afraid." So he entered her tent, and she covered him with a blanket.

יח וַתֵּצֵא יָעֵל לִקְרַאת סִיסְרָא וַתֹּאמֶר אֵלָיו סוּרָה אֲדֹנִי סוּרָה אֵלַי אַל־תִּירָא וַיָּסַר אֵלֶיהָ הָאֹהֱלָה וַתְּכַסֵּהוּ בַּשְּׂמִיכָה:

19 He said to her, "Please let me have some water; I am thirsty." She opened a skin of milk and gave him some to drink; and she covered him again.

יט וַיֹּאמֶר אֵלֶיהָ הַשְׁקִינִי־נָא מְעַט־מַיִם כִּי צָמֵאתִי וַתִּפְתַּח אֶת־נֹאוד הֶחָלָב וַתַּשְׁקֵהוּ וַתְּכַסֵּהוּ:

20 He said to her, "Stand at the entrance of the tent. If anybody comes and asks you if there is anybody here, say 'No.'"

כ וַיֹּאמֶר אֵלֶיהָ עֲמֹד פֶּתַח הָאֹהֶל וְהָיָה אִם־אִישׁ יָבוֹא וּשְׁאֵלֵךְ וְאָמַר הֲיֵשׁ־פֹּה אִישׁ וְאָמַרְתְּ אָיִן:

21 Then *Yael* wife of *Chever* took a tent pin and grasped the mallet. When he was fast asleep from exhaustion, she approached him stealthily and drove the pin through his temple till it went down to the ground. Thus he died.

כא וַתִּקַּח יָעֵל אֵשֶׁת־חֶבֶר אֶת־יְתַד הָאֹהֶל וַתָּשֶׂם אֶת־הַמַּקֶּבֶת בְּיָדָהּ וַתָּבוֹא אֵלָיו בַּלָּאט וַתִּתְקַע אֶת־הַיָּתֵד בְּרַקָּתוֹ וַתִּצְנַח בָּאָרֶץ וְהוּא־נִרְדָּם וַיָּעַף וַיָּמֹת:

va-ti-KAKH ya-AYL AY-shet KHE-ver et y'-TAD ha-O-hel va-TA-sem et ha-ma-KE-vet b'-ya-DAH va-ta-VO ay-LAV ba-LAT va-tit-KA et ha-ya-TAYD b'-ra-ka-TO va-titz-NAKH ba-A-retz v'-HU nir-DAM va-YA-af va-ya-MOT

Orna Barbavai
(b. 1962)

4:21 Then *Yael* **wife of** *Chever* **took a tent pin and grasped the mallet** *Yael* is not the only great woman to act as a warrior on behalf of the Nation of Israel. Today, women form an important part of the Israel Defense Forces, serving at its highest levels. In 2011, Orna Barbavai made history, overcoming her under- privileged upbringing to become the first woman in IDF history to reach the rank of *Aluf* (אלוף), 'Major General'. "I am proud to be the first woman to become a major general, and to be part of an organization in which equal- ity is a central principle," Barbivai said. The mother of three retired from the IDF in 2014, but serves as an inspiration

22 Now *Barak* appeared in pursuit of Sisera. *Yael* went out to greet him and said, "Come, I will show you the man you are looking for." He went inside with her, and there Sisera was lying dead, with the pin in his temple.

כג וְהִנֵּה בָרָק רֹדֵף אֶת־סִיסְרָא וַתֵּצֵא יָעֵל לִקְרָאתוֹ וַתֹּאמֶר לוֹ לֵךְ וְאַרְאֶךָּ אֶת־הָאִישׁ אֲשֶׁר־אַתָּה מְבַקֵּשׁ וַיָּבֹא אֵלֶיהָ וְהִנֵּה סִיסְרָא נֹפֵל מֵת וְהַיָּתֵד בְּרַקָּתוֹ:

23 On that day *Hashem* subdued King Jabin of Canaan before the Israelites.

כג וַיַּכְנַע אֱלֹהִים בַּיּוֹם הַהוּא אֵת יָבִין מֶלֶךְ־כְּנָעַן לִפְנֵי בְּנֵי יִשְׂרָאֵל:

24 The hand of the Israelites bore harder and harder on King Jabin of Canaan, until they destroyed King Jabin of Canaan.

כד וַתֵּלֶךְ יַד בְּנֵי־יִשְׂרָאֵל הָלוֹךְ וְקָשָׁה עַל יָבִין מֶלֶךְ־כְּנָעַן עַד אֲשֶׁר הִכְרִיתוּ אֵת יָבִין מֶלֶךְ־כְּנָעַן:

5 1 On that day *Devora* and *Barak* son of Abinoam sang:

ה א וַתָּשַׁר דְּבוֹרָה וּבָרָק בֶּן־אֲבִינֹעַם בַּיּוֹם הַהוּא לֵאמֹר:

2 When locks go untrimmed in *Yisrael*, When people dedicate themselves – Bless *Hashem*!

ב בִּפְרֹעַ פְּרָעוֹת בְּיִשְׂרָאֵל בְּהִתְנַדֵּב עָם בָּרְכוּ יְהֹוָה:

3 Hear, O kings! Give ear, O potentates! I will sing, will sing to *Hashem*, Will hymn *Hashem*, the God of *Yisrael*.

ג שִׁמְעוּ מְלָכִים הַאֲזִינוּ רֹזְנִים אָנֹכִי לַיהֹוָה אָנֹכִי אָשִׁירָה אֲזַמֵּר לַיהֹוָה אֱלֹהֵי יִשְׂרָאֵל:

4 *Hashem*, when You came forth from Seir, Advanced from the country of Edom, The earth trembled; The heavens dripped, Yea, the clouds dripped water,

ד יְהֹוָה בְּצֵאתְךָ מִשֵּׂעִיר בְּצַעְדְּךָ מִשְּׂדֵה אֱדוֹם אֶרֶץ רָעָשָׁה גַּם־שָׁמַיִם נָטָפוּ גַּם־עָבִים נָטְפוּ מָיִם:

5 The mountains quaked – Before *Hashem*, Him of Sinai, Before *Hashem*, God of *Yisrael*.

ה הָרִים נָזְלוּ מִפְּנֵי יְהֹוָה זֶה סִינַי מִפְּנֵי יְהֹוָה אֱלֹהֵי יִשְׂרָאֵל:

6 In the days of *Shamgar* son of Anath, In the days of *Yael*, caravans ceased, And wayfarers went By roundabout paths.

ו בִּימֵי שַׁמְגַּר בֶּן־עֲנָת בִּימֵי יָעֵל חָדְלוּ אֳרָחוֹת וְהֹלְכֵי נְתִיבוֹת יֵלְכוּ אֳרָחוֹת עֲקַלְקַלּוֹת:

7 Deliverance ceased, Ceased in *Yisrael*, Till you arose, O *Devora*, Arose, O mother, in *Yisrael*!

ז חָדְלוּ פְרָזוֹן בְּיִשְׂרָאֵל חָדֵלּוּ עַד שַׁקַּמְתִּי דְּבוֹרָה שַׁקַּמְתִּי אֵם בְּיִשְׂרָאֵל:

kha-d'-LU f'-ra-ZON b'-yis-ra-AYL kha-DAY-lu AD sha-KAM-tee
d'-vo-RAH sha-KAM-tee AYM b'-yis-ra-AYL

8 When they chose new gods, Was there a fighter then in the gates? No shield or spear was seen Among forty thousand in *Yisrael*!

ח יִבְחַר אֱלֹהִים חֲדָשִׁים אָז לָחֶם שְׁעָרִים מָגֵן אִם־יֵרָאֶה וָרֹמַח בְּאַרְבָּעִים אֶלֶף בְּיִשְׂרָאֵל:

---

to countless Israeli young women who enlist in the IDF each year and who know they can reach the highest levels not only in the IDF but throughout Israeli society.

5:7 Deliverance ceased, ceased in *Yisrael*, till you arose, O *Devora* Though one way of translating *f'razon* (פרזון) is 'deliverance,' *Rashi* explains it as "open towns without walls." According to this understanding, *Devora* is saying that prior to her leadership, the Children of Israel had ceased living in small, scattered, non-walled communities, due to fear of attack. However,

the Canaanites continued living in such places, as they were not afraid of the Israelites. The miraculous military victory against Sisera would change this reality. It is interesting to note that in Israel today Jews have also not been afraid to establish small communities in all parts of the land. Miracles of biblical proportions continue in our era as communities of all sizes grow and thrive throughout the Land of Israel.

Small Israeli settlement in the Judean desert

פרזון

Judges

9 My heart is with *Yisrael*'s leaders, With the dedicated of the people – Bless *Hashem*!

ט לִבִּי לְחוֹקְקֵי יִשְׂרָאֵל הַמִּתְנַדְּבִים בָּעָם בָּרְכוּ יְהוָה:

10 You riders on tawny she-asses, You who sit on saddle rugs, And you wayfarers, declare it!

י רֹכְבֵי אֲתֹנוֹת צְחֹרוֹת יֹשְׁבֵי עַל־מִדִּין וְהֹלְכֵי עַל־דֶּרֶךְ שִׂיחוּ:

11 Louder than the sound of archers, There among the watering places Let them chant the gracious acts of *Hashem*, His gracious deliverance of *Yisrael*. Then did the people of *Hashem* March down to the gates!

יא מִקּוֹל מְחַצְצִים בֵּין מַשְׁאַבִּים שָׁם יְתַנּוּ צִדְקוֹת יְהוָה צִדְקֹת פִּרְזֹנוֹ בְּיִשְׂרָאֵל אָז יָרְדוּ לַשְּׁעָרִים עַם־יְהוָה:

12 Awake, awake, O *Devora*! Awake, awake, strike up the chant! Arise, O *Barak*; Take your captives, O son of Abinoam!

יב עוּרִי עוּרִי דְּבוֹרָה עוּרִי עוּרִי דַּבְּרִי־שִׁיר קוּם בָּרָק וּשֲׁבֵה שֶׁבְיְךָ בֶּן־אֲבִינֹעַם:

13 Then was the remnant made victor over the mighty, *Hashem*'s people won my victory over the warriors.

יג אָז יְרַד שָׂרִיד לְאַדִּירִים עָם יְהוָה יְרַד־לִי בַּגִּבּוֹרִים:

14 From *Efraim* came they whose roots are in Amalek; After you, your kin *Binyamin*; From Machir came down leaders, From *Zevulun* such as hold the marshal's staff.

יד מִנִּי אֶפְרַיִם שָׁרְשָׁם בַּעֲמָלֵק אַחֲרֶיךָ בִנְיָמִין בַּעֲמָמֶיךָ מִנִּי מָכִיר יָרְדוּ מְחֹקְקִים וּמִזְּבוּלֻן מֹשְׁכִים בְּשֵׁבֶט סֹפֵר:

15 And *Yissachar*'s chiefs were with *Devora*; As *Barak*, so was *Yissachar* – Rushing after him into the valley. Among the clans of *Reuven* Were great decisions of heart.

טו וְשָׂרַי בְּיִשָּׂשכָר עִם־דְּבֹרָה וְיִשָּׂשכָר כֵּן בָּרָק בָּעֵמֶק שֻׁלַּח בְּרַגְלָיו בִּפְלַגּוֹת רְאוּבֵן גְּדֹלִים חִקְקֵי־לֵב:

16 Why then did you stay among the sheepfolds And listen as they pipe for the flocks? Among the clans of *Reuven* Were great searchings of heart!

טז לָמָּה יָשַׁבְתָּ בֵּין הַמִּשְׁפְּתַיִם לִשְׁמֹעַ שְׁרִקוֹת עֲדָרִים לִפְלַגּוֹת רְאוּבֵן גְּדוֹלִים חִקְרֵי־לֵב:

17 *Gilad* tarried beyond the *Yarden*; And *Dan* – why did he linger by the ships? *Asher* remained at the seacoast And tarried at his landings.

יז גִּלְעָד בְּעֵבֶר הַיַּרְדֵּן שָׁכֵן וְדָן לָמָּה יָגוּר אֳנִיּוֹת אָשֵׁר יָשַׁב לְחוֹף יַמִּים וְעַל מִפְרָצָיו יִשְׁכּוֹן:

18 *Zevulun* is a people that mocked at death, *Naftali* – on the open heights.

יח זְבֻלוּן עַם חֵרֵף נַפְשׁוֹ לָמוּת וְנַפְתָּלִי עַל מְרוֹמֵי שָׂדֶה:

19 Then the kings came, they fought: The kings of Canaan fought At Taanach, by Megiddo's waters – They got no spoil of silver.

יט בָּאוּ מְלָכִים נִלְחָמוּ אָז נִלְחֲמוּ מַלְכֵי כְנַעַן בְּתַעְנַךְ עַל־מֵי מְגִדּוֹ בֶּצַע כֶּסֶף לֹא לָקָחוּ:

20 The stars fought from heaven, From their courses they fought against Sisera.

כ מִן־שָׁמַיִם נִלְחָמוּ הַכּוֹכָבִים מִמְּסִלּוֹתָם נִלְחֲמוּ עִם־סִיסְרָא:

21 The torrent Kishon swept them away, The raging torrent, the torrent Kishon. March on, my soul, with courage!

כא נַחַל קִישׁוֹן גְּרָפָם נַחַל קְדוּמִים נַחַל קִישׁוֹן תִּדְרְכִי נַפְשִׁי עֹז:

NA-khal kee-SHON g'-ra-FAM NA-khal k'-du-MEEM
NA-khal kee-SHON tid-r'-KHEE naf-SHEE OZ

Moshe Dayan
(1915–1981)

5:21 The torrent Kishon swept them away
According to this verse, the Kishon river swept away Sisera's army after it was defeated by the Israelites. Moshe Dayan, an important IDF general, loved the Land of Israel not only as his homeland, but also because it is the land of the Bible. In his book,

22 Then the horses' hoofs pounded As headlong galloped the steeds.

אָז הָלְמוּ עִקְּבֵי־סוּס מִדַּהֲרוֹת דַּהֲרוֹת אַבִּירָיו: כב

23 "Curse Meroz!" said the angel of *Hashem*. "Bitterly curse its inhabitants, Because they came not to the aid of *Hashem*, To the aid of *Hashem* among the warriors."

אוֹרוּ מֵרוֹז אָמַר מַלְאַךְ יְהוָה אֹרוּ אָרוֹר יֹשְׁבֶיהָ כִּי לֹא־בָאוּ לְעֶזְרַת יְהוָה לְעֶזְרַת יְהוָה בַּגִּבּוֹרִים: כג

24 Most blessed of women be *Yael*, Wife of *Chever* the Kenite, Most blessed of women in tents.

תְּבֹרַךְ מִנָּשִׁים יָעֵל אֵשֶׁת חֶבֶר הַקֵּינִי מִנָּשִׁים בָּאֹהֶל תְּבֹרָךְ: כד

25 He asked for water, she offered milk; In a princely bowl she brought him curds.

מַיִם שָׁאַל חָלָב נָתָנָה בְּסֵפֶל אַדִּירִים הִקְרִיבָה חֶמְאָה: כה

26 Her [left] hand reached for the tent pin, Her right for the workmen's hammer. She struck Sisera, crushed his head, Smashed and pierced his temple.

יָדָהּ לַיָּתֵד תִּשְׁלַחְנָה וִימִינָהּ לְהַלְמוּת עֲמֵלִים וְהָלְמָה סִיסְרָא מָחֲקָה רֹאשׁוֹ וּמָחֲצָה וְחָלְפָה רַקָּתוֹ: כו

27 At her feet he sank, lay outstretched, At her feet he sank, lay still; Where he sank, there he lay – destroyed.

בֵּין רַגְלֶיהָ כָּרַע נָפַל שָׁכָב בֵּין רַגְלֶיהָ כָּרַע נָפָל בַּאֲשֶׁר כָּרַע שָׁם נָפַל שָׁדוּד: כז

28 Through the window peered Sisera's mother, Behind the lattice she whined: "Why is his chariot so long in coming? Why so late the clatter of his wheels?"

בְּעַד הַחַלּוֹן נִשְׁקְפָה וַתְּיַבֵּב אֵם סִיסְרָא בְּעַד הָאֶשְׁנָב מַדּוּעַ בֹּשֵׁשׁ רִכְבּוֹ לָבוֹא מַדּוּעַ אֶחֱרוּ פַּעֲמֵי מַרְכְּבוֹתָיו: כח

29 The wisest of her ladies give answer; She, too, replies to herself:

חַכְמוֹת שָׂרוֹתֶיהָ תַּעֲנֶינָּה אַף־הִיא תָּשִׁיב אֲמָרֶיהָ לָהּ: כט

30 "They must be dividing the spoil they have found: A damsel or two for each man, Spoil of dyed cloths for Sisera, Spoil of embroidered cloths, A couple of embroidered cloths round every neck as spoil."

הֲלֹא יִמְצְאוּ יְחַלְּקוּ שָׁלָל רַחַם רַחֲמָתַיִם לְרֹאשׁ גֶּבֶר שְׁלַל צְבָעִים לְסִיסְרָא שְׁלַל צְבָעִים רִקְמָה צֶבַע רִקְמָתַיִם לְצַוְּארֵי שָׁלָל: ל

31 So may all Your enemies perish, *Hashem*! But may His friends be as the sun rising in might! And the land was tranquil forty years.

כֵּן יֹאבְדוּ כָל־אוֹיְבֶיךָ יְהוָה וְאֹהֲבָיו כְּצֵאת הַשֶּׁמֶשׁ בִּגְבֻרָתוֹ וַתִּשְׁקֹט הָאָרֶץ אַרְבָּעִים שָׁנָה: לא

"Living with the Bible," Dayan wrote about the Kishon: "To one who was born in Israel, love of the homeland was not an abstraction. The Rose of Sharon and Mount *Carmel* were very real to me, as were the sweet-scented blossom and the hills whose paths I climbed. Yet this was not enough. I was not content only with the Israel I could see and touch. I also longed for the Israel of antiquity, the Israel of the 'timeless verses' and the 'biblical names', and I wanted to give tangibility to that too. I wished to see not only the river Kishon marking off the fields of Nahalal from those of neighboring Kfar Ye-hoshua; I wished also to visual-ize the biblical Kishon sweeping away the Canaanite chariot forces of Sisera."

The Kishon River with Haifa in the background

6 ¹ Then the Israelites did what was offensive to *Hashem*, and *Hashem* delivered them into the hands of the Midianites for seven years.

א וַיַּעֲשׂוּ בְנֵי־יִשְׂרָאֵל הָרַע בְּעֵינֵי יְהֹוָה וַיִּתְּנֵם יְהֹוָה בְּיַד־מִדְיָן שֶׁבַע שָׁנִים:

² The hand of the Midianites prevailed over *Yisrael*; and because of Midian, the Israelites provided themselves with refuges in the caves and strongholds of the mountains.

ב וַתָּעׇז יַד־מִדְיָן עַל־יִשְׂרָאֵל מִפְּנֵי מִדְיָן עָשׂוּ לָהֶם בְּנֵי יִשְׂרָאֵל אֶת־הַמִּנְהָרוֹת אֲשֶׁר בֶּהָרִים וְאֶת־הַמְּעָרוֹת וְאֶת־הַמְּצָדוֹת:

³ After the Israelites had done their sowing, Midian, Amalek, and the Kedemites would come up and raid them;

ג וְהָיָה אִם־זָרַע יִשְׂרָאֵל וְעָלָה מִדְיָן וַעֲמָלֵק וּבְנֵי־קֶדֶם וְעָלוּ עָלָיו:

⁴ they would attack them, destroy the produce of the land all the way to *Azza*, and leave no means of sustenance in *Yisrael*, not a sheep or an ox or an ass.

ד וַיַּחֲנוּ עֲלֵיהֶם וַיַּשְׁחִיתוּ אֶת־יְבוּל הָאָרֶץ עַד־בּוֹאֲךָ עַזָּה וְלֹא־יַשְׁאִירוּ מִחְיָה בְּיִשְׂרָאֵל וְשֶׂה וָשׁוֹר וַחֲמוֹר:

⁵ For they would come up with their livestock and their tents, swarming as thick as locusts; they and their camels were innumerable. Thus they would invade the land and ravage it.

ה כִּי הֵם וּמִקְנֵיהֶם יַעֲלוּ וְאׇהֳלֵיהֶם יבאו [וּבָאוּ] כְדֵי־אַרְבֶּה לָרֹב וְלָהֶם וְלִגְמַלֵּיהֶם אֵין מִסְפָּר וַיָּבֹאוּ בָאָרֶץ לְשַׁחֲתָהּ:

⁶ *Yisrael* was reduced to utter misery by the Midianites, and the Israelites cried out to *Hashem*.

ו וַיִּדַּל יִשְׂרָאֵל מְאֹד מִפְּנֵי מִדְיָן וַיִּזְעֲקוּ בְנֵי־יִשְׂרָאֵל אֶל־יְהֹוָה:

⁷ When the Israelites cried to *Hashem* on account of Midian,

ז וַיְהִי כִּי־זָעֲקוּ בְנֵי־יִשְׂרָאֵל אֶל־יְהֹוָה עַל אֹדוֹת מִדְיָן:

⁸ *Hashem* sent a *Navi* to the Israelites who said to them, "Thus said *Hashem*, the God of *Yisrael*: I brought you up out of Egypt and freed you from the house of bondage.

ח וַיִּשְׁלַח יְהֹוָה אִישׁ נָבִיא אֶל־בְּנֵי יִשְׂרָאֵל וַיֹּאמֶר לָהֶם כֹּה־אָמַר יְהֹוָה אֱלֹהֵי יִשְׂרָאֵל אָנֹכִי הֶעֱלֵיתִי אֶתְכֶם מִמִּצְרַיִם וָאֹצִיא אֶתְכֶם מִבֵּית עֲבָדִים:

⁹ I rescued you from the Egyptians and from all your oppressors; I drove them out before you, and gave you their land.

ט וָאַצִּל אֶתְכֶם מִיַּד מִצְרַיִם וּמִיַּד כׇּל־לֹחֲצֵיכֶם וָאֲגָרֵשׁ אוֹתָם מִפְּנֵיכֶם וָאֶתְּנָה לָכֶם אֶת־אַרְצָם:

va-a-TZIL et-KHEM mi-YAD mitz-RA-yim u-mi-YAD kol lo-kha-tzay-KHEM va-a-ga-RAYSH o-TAM mi-p'-nay-KHEM va-e-t'-NAH la-KHEM et ar-TZAM

¹⁰ And I said to you, 'I *Hashem* am your God. You must not worship the gods of the Amorites in whose land you dwell.' But you did not obey Me."

י וָאֹמְרָה לָכֶם אֲנִי יְהֹוָה אֱלֹהֵיכֶם לֹא תִירְאוּ אֶת־אֱלֹהֵי הָאֱמֹרִי אֲשֶׁר אַתֶּם יוֹשְׁבִים בְּאַרְצָם וְלֹא שְׁמַעְתֶּם בְּקוֹלִי:

Rabbi Abraham
Isaac Kook
(1865–1935)

Model of the second Temple in Jerusalem

6:9 I rescued you from the Egyptians When the Children of Israel cry out to *Hashem* due to the Midianite persecution, God sends a prophet to remind them that He is the one who brought them out from Egyptian oppression into *Eretz Yisrael*. Rabbi Abraham Isaac Kook, the first *Ashkenazi* chief rabbi of Palestine under the British Mandate and founder of the Mercaz Harav Yeshiva in the early twentieth century, teaches that the exodus was not simply a historical event. It was the beginning of a redemptive process which continues throughout Jewish history. Thus, all future redemptions, including *Gidon's* defeat of Midian and including the State of Israel's defeat of its enemies in our generation, are all part of the ongoing redemption that will culminate with the coming of *Mashiach* and the rebuilding of the *Beit Hamikdash* in *Yerushalayim*.

11 An angel of *Hashem* came and sat under the terebinth at Ophrah, which belonged to *Yoash* the Abiezrite. His son *Gidon* was then beating out wheat inside a winepress in order to keep it safe from the Midianites.

יא וַיָּבֹא מַלְאַךְ יְהֹוָה וַיֵּשֶׁב תַּחַת הָאֵלָה אֲשֶׁר בְּעָפְרָה אֲשֶׁר לְיוֹאָשׁ אֲבִי הָעֶזְרִי וְגִדְעוֹן בְּנוֹ חֹבֵט חִטִּים בַּגַּת לְהָנִיס מִפְּנֵי מִדְיָן:

12 The angel of *Hashem* appeared to him and said to him, "*Hashem* is with you, valiant warrior!"

יב וַיֵּרָא אֵלָיו מַלְאַךְ יְהֹוָה וַיֹּאמֶר אֵלָיו יְהֹוָה עִמְּךָ גִּבּוֹר הֶחָיִל:

13 *Gidon* said to him, "Please, my lord, if *Hashem* is with us, why has all this befallen us? Where are all His wondrous deeds about which our fathers told us, saying, 'Truly *Hashem* brought us up from Egypt'? Now *Hashem* has abandoned us and delivered us into the hands of Midian!"

יג וַיֹּאמֶר אֵלָיו גִּדְעוֹן בִּי אֲדֹנִי וְיֵשׁ יְהֹוָה עִמָּנוּ וְלָמָּה מְצָאַתְנוּ כָּל־זֹאת וְאַיֵּה כָל־נִפְלְאֹתָיו אֲשֶׁר סִפְּרוּ־לָנוּ אֲבוֹתֵינוּ לֵאמֹר הֲלֹא מִמִּצְרַיִם הֶעֱלָנוּ יְהֹוָה וְעַתָּה נְטָשָׁנוּ יְהֹוָה וַיִּתְּנֵנוּ בְּכַף־מִדְיָן:

14 *Hashem* turned to him and said, "Go in this strength of yours and deliver *Yisrael* from the Midianites. I herewith make you My messenger."

יד וַיִּפֶן אֵלָיו יְהֹוָה וַיֹּאמֶר לֵךְ בְּכֹחֲךָ זֶה וְהוֹשַׁעְתָּ אֶת־יִשְׂרָאֵל מִכַּף מִדְיָן הֲלֹא שְׁלַחְתִּיךָ:

15 He said to Him, "Please, my lord, how can I deliver *Yisrael*? Why, my clan is the humblest in *Menashe*, and I am the youngest in my father's household."

טו וַיֹּאמֶר אֵלָיו בִּי אֲדֹנָי בַּמָּה אוֹשִׁיעַ אֶת־יִשְׂרָאֵל הִנֵּה אַלְפִּי הַדַּל בִּמְנַשֶּׁה וְאָנֹכִי הַצָּעִיר בְּבֵית אָבִי:

16 *Hashem* replied, "I will be with you, and you shall defeat Midian to a man."

טז וַיֹּאמֶר אֵלָיו יְהֹוָה כִּי אֶהְיֶה עִמָּךְ וְהִכִּיתָ אֶת־מִדְיָן כְּאִישׁ אֶחָד:

17 And he said to Him, "If I have gained Your favor, give me a sign that it is You who are speaking to me:

יז וַיֹּאמֶר אֵלָיו אִם־נָא מָצָאתִי חֵן בְּעֵינֶיךָ וְעָשִׂיתָ לִּי אוֹת שָׁאַתָּה מְדַבֵּר עִמִּי:

18 do not leave this place until I come back to You and bring out my offering and place it before You." And He answered, "I will stay until you return."

יח אַל־נָא תָמֻשׁ מִזֶּה עַד־בֹּאִי אֵלֶיךָ וְהֹצֵאתִי אֶת־מִנְחָתִי וְהִנַּחְתִּי לְפָנֶיךָ וַיֹּאמַר אָנֹכִי אֵשֵׁב עַד שׁוּבֶךָ:

19 So *Gidon* went in and prepared a kid, and [baked] unleavened bread from an ephah of flour. He put the meat in a basket and poured the broth into a pot, and he brought them out to Him under the terebinth. As he presented them,

יט וְגִדְעוֹן בָּא וַיַּעַשׂ גְּדִי־עִזִּים וְאֵיפַת־קֶמַח מַצּוֹת הַבָּשָׂר שָׂם בַּסַּל וְהַמָּרַק שָׂם בַּפָּרוּר וַיּוֹצֵא אֵלָיו אֶל־תַּחַת הָאֵלָה וַיִּגַּשׁ:

20 the angel of *Hashem* said to him, "Take the meat and the unleavened bread, put them on yonder rock, and spill out the broth." He did so.

כ וַיֹּאמֶר אֵלָיו מַלְאַךְ הָאֱלֹהִים קַח אֶת־הַבָּשָׂר וְאֶת־הַמַּצּוֹת וְהַנַּח אֶל־הַסֶּלַע הַלָּז וְאֶת־הַמָּרַק שְׁפוֹךְ וַיַּעַשׂ כֵּן:

21 The angel of *Hashem* held out the staff that he carried, and touched the meat and the unleavened bread with its tip. A fire sprang up from the rock and consumed the meat and the unleavened bread. And the angel of *Hashem* vanished from his sight.

כא וַיִּשְׁלַח מַלְאַךְ יְהֹוָה אֶת־קְצֵה הַמִּשְׁעֶנֶת אֲשֶׁר בְּיָדוֹ וַיִּגַּע בַּבָּשָׂר וּבַמַּצּוֹת וַתַּעַל הָאֵשׁ מִן־הַצּוּר וַתֹּאכַל אֶת־הַבָּשָׂר וְאֶת־הַמַּצּוֹת וּמַלְאַךְ יְהֹוָה הָלַךְ מֵעֵינָיו:

22 Then *Gidon* realized that it was an angel of *Hashem*; and *Gidon* said, "Alas, O *Hashem*! For I have seen an angel of *Hashem* face to face."

כב וַיַּרְא גִּדְעוֹן כִּי־מַלְאַךְ יְהֹוָה הוּא וַיֹּאמֶר גִּדְעוֹן אֲהָהּ אֲדֹנָי יֱהֹוִה כִּי־עַל־כֵּן רָאִיתִי מַלְאַךְ יְהֹוָה פָּנִים אֶל־פָּנִים:

23 But *Hashem* said to him, "All is well; have no fear, you shall not die."

כג וַיֹּאמֶר לוֹ יְהֹוָה שָׁלוֹם לְךָ אַל־תִּירָא לֹא תָּמוּת:

24 So *Gidon* built there a *Mizbayach* to *Hashem* and called it Adonaishalom. To this day it stands in Ophrah of the Abiezrites.

כד וַיִּבֶן שָׁם גִּדְעוֹן מִזְבֵּחַ לַיהֹוָה וַיִּקְרָא־לוֹ יְהֹוָה שָׁלוֹם עַד הַיּוֹם הַזֶּה עוֹדֶנּוּ בְּעׇפְרַת אֲבִי הָעֶזְרִי:

25 That night *Hashem* said to him: "Take the young bull belonging to your father and another bull seven years old; pull down the altar of Baal which belongs to your father, and cut down the sacred post which is beside it.

כה וַיְהִי בַּלַּיְלָה הַהוּא וַיֹּאמֶר לוֹ יְהֹוָה קַח אֶת־פַּר־הַשּׁוֹר אֲשֶׁר לְאָבִיךָ וּפַר הַשֵּׁנִי שֶׁבַע שָׁנִים וְהָרַסְתָּ אֶת־מִזְבַּח הַבַּעַל אֲשֶׁר לְאָבִיךָ וְאֶת־הָאֲשֵׁרָה אֲשֶׁר־עָלָיו תִּכְרֹת:

26 Then build a *Mizbayach* to *Hashem* your God, on the level ground on top of this stronghold. Take the other bull and offer it as a burnt offering, using the wood of the sacred post that you have cut down."

כו וּבָנִיתָ מִזְבֵּחַ לַיהֹוָה אֱלֹהֶיךָ עַל רֹאשׁ הַמָּעוֹז הַזֶּה בַּמַּעֲרָכָה וְלָקַחְתָּ אֶת־הַפָּר הַשֵּׁנִי וְהַעֲלִיתָ עוֹלָה בַּעֲצֵי הָאֲשֵׁרָה אֲשֶׁר תִּכְרֹת:

27 So *Gidon* took ten of his servants and did as *Hashem* had told him; but as he was afraid to do it by day, on account of his father's household and the townspeople, he did it by night.

כז וַיִּקַּח גִּדְעוֹן עֲשָׂרָה אֲנָשִׁים מֵעֲבָדָיו וַיַּעַשׂ כַּאֲשֶׁר דִּבֶּר אֵלָיו יְהֹוָה וַיְהִי כַּאֲשֶׁר יָרֵא אֶת־בֵּית אָבִיו וְאֶת־אַנְשֵׁי הָעִיר מֵעֲשׂוֹת יוֹמָם וַיַּעַשׂ לָיְלָה:

28 Early the next morning, the townspeople found that the altar of Baal had been torn down and the sacred post beside it had been cut down, and that the second bull had been offered on the newly built *Mizbayach*.

כח וַיַּשְׁכִּימוּ אַנְשֵׁי הָעִיר בַּבֹּקֶר וְהִנֵּה נֻתַּץ מִזְבַּח הַבַּעַל וְהָאֲשֵׁרָה אֲשֶׁר־עָלָיו כֹּרָתָה וְאֵת הַפָּר הַשֵּׁנִי הֹעֲלָה עַל־הַמִּזְבֵּחַ הַבָּנוּי:

29 They said to one another, "Who did this thing?" Upon inquiry and investigation, they were told, "*Gidon* son of *Yoash* did this thing!"

כט וַיֹּאמְרוּ אִישׁ אֶל־רֵעֵהוּ מִי עָשָׂה הַדָּבָר הַזֶּה וַיִּדְרְשׁוּ וַיְבַקְשׁוּ וַיֹּאמְרוּ גִּדְעוֹן בֶּן־יוֹאָשׁ עָשָׂה הַדָּבָר הַזֶּה:

30 The townspeople said to *Yoash*, "Bring out your son, for he must die: he has torn down the altar of Baal and cut down the sacred post beside it!"

ל וַיֹּאמְרוּ אַנְשֵׁי הָעִיר אֶל־יוֹאָשׁ הוֹצֵא אֶת־בִּנְךָ וְיָמֹת כִּי נָתַץ אֶת־מִזְבַּח הַבַּעַל וְכִי כָרַת הָאֲשֵׁרָה אֲשֶׁר־עָלָיו:

31 But *Yoash* said to all who had risen against him, "Do you have to contend for Baal? Do you have to vindicate him? Whoever fights his battles shall be dead by morning! If he is a god, let him fight his own battles, since it is his altar that has been torn down!"

לא וַיֹּאמֶר יוֹאָשׁ לְכֹל אֲשֶׁר־עָמְדוּ עָלָיו הַאַתֶּם תְּרִיבוּן לַבַּעַל אִם־אַתֶּם תּוֹשִׁיעוּן אוֹתוֹ אֲשֶׁר יָרִיב לוֹ יוּמַת עַד־הַבֹּקֶר אִם־אֱלֹהִים הוּא יָרֶב לוֹ כִּי נָתַץ אֶת־מִזְבְּחוֹ:

32 That day they named him *Yerubaal*, meaning "Let Baal contend with him, since he tore down his altar."

לב וַיִּקְרָא־לוֹ בַיּוֹם־הַהוּא יְרֻבַּעַל לֵאמֹר יָרֶב בּוֹ הַבַּעַל כִּי נָתַץ אֶת־מִזְבְּחוֹ:

33 All Midian, Amalek, and the Kedemites joined forces; they crossed over and encamped in the Valley of *Yizrael*.

לג וְכׇל־מִדְיָן וַעֲמָלֵק וּבְנֵי־קֶדֶם נֶאֶסְפוּ יַחְדָּו וַיַּעַבְרוּ וַיַּחֲנוּ בְּעֵמֶק יִזְרְעֶאל:

34 The spirit of *Hashem* enveloped *Gidon*; he sounded the *shofar*, and the Abiezrites rallied behind him.

לד וְרוּחַ יְהֹוָה לָבְשָׁה אֶת־גִּדְעוֹן וַיִּתְקַע בַּשּׁוֹפָר וַיִּזָּעֵק אֲבִיעֶזֶר אַחֲרָיו:

35 And he sent messengers throughout *Menashe*, and they too rallied behind him. He then sent messengers through *Asher, Zevulun,* and *Naftali,* and they came up to meet the Manassites.

לה וּמַלְאָכִים שָׁלַח בְּכָל־מְנַשֶּׁה וַיִּזָּעֵק גַּם־הוּא אַחֲרָיו וּמַלְאָכִים שָׁלַח בְּאָשֵׁר וּבִזְבֻלוּן וּבְנַפְתָּלִי וַיַּעֲלוּ לִקְרָאתָם:

36 And *Gidon* said to *Hashem*, "If You really intend to deliver *Yisrael* through me as You have said –

לו וַיֹּאמֶר גִּדְעוֹן אֶל־הָאֱלֹהִים אִם־יֶשְׁךָ מוֹשִׁיעַ בְּיָדִי אֶת־יִשְׂרָאֵל כַּאֲשֶׁר דִּבַּרְתָּ:

37 here I place a fleece of wool on the threshing floor. If dew falls only on the fleece and all the ground remains dry, I shall know that You will deliver *Yisrael* through me, as You have said."

לז הִנֵּה אָנֹכִי מַצִּיג אֶת־גִּזַּת הַצֶּמֶר בַּגֹּרֶן אִם טַל יִהְיֶה עַל־הַגִּזָּה לְבַדָּהּ וְעַל־כָּל־הָאָרֶץ חֹרֶב וְיָדַעְתִּי כִּי־תוֹשִׁיעַ בְּיָדִי אֶת־יִשְׂרָאֵל כַּאֲשֶׁר דִּבַּרְתָּ:

38 And that is what happened. Early the next day, he squeezed the fleece and wrung out the dew from the fleece, a bowlful of water.

לח וַיְהִי־כֵן וַיַּשְׁכֵּם מִמָּחֳרָת וַיָּזַר אֶת־הַגִּזָּה וַיִּמֶץ טַל מִן־הַגִּזָּה מְלוֹא הַסֵּפֶל מָיִם:

39 Then *Gidon* said to *Hashem*, "Do not be angry with me if I speak just once more. Let me make just one more test with the fleece: let the fleece alone be dry, while there is dew all over the ground."

לט וַיֹּאמֶר גִּדְעוֹן אֶל־הָאֱלֹהִים אַל־יִחַר אַפְּךָ בִּי וַאֲדַבְּרָה אַךְ הַפָּעַם אֲנַסֶּה נָּא רַק־הַפַּעַם בַּגִּזָּה יְהִי־נָא חֹרֶב אֶל־הַגִּזָּה לְבַדָּהּ וְעַל־כָּל־הָאָרֶץ יִהְיֶה־טָּל:

40 *Hashem* did so that night: only the fleece was dry, while there was dew all over the ground.

מ וַיַּעַשׂ אֱלֹהִים כֵּן בַּלַּיְלָה הַהוּא וַיְהִי־חֹרֶב אֶל־הַגִּזָּה לְבַדָּהּ וְעַל־כָּל־הָאָרֶץ הָיָה טָל:

7 1 Early next day, *Yerubaal* – that is, *Gidon* – and all the troops with him encamped above En-harod, while the camp of Midian was in the plain to the north of him, at Gibeath-moreh.

ז א וַיַּשְׁכֵּם יְרֻבַּעַל הוּא גִדְעוֹן וְכָל־הָעָם אֲשֶׁר אִתּוֹ וַיַּחֲנוּ עַל־עֵין חֲרֹד וּמַחֲנֵה מִדְיָן הָיָה־לוֹ מִצָּפוֹן מִגִּבְעַת הַמּוֹרֶה בָּעֵמֶק:

2 *Hashem* said to *Gidon*, "You have too many troops with you for Me to deliver Midian into their hands; *Yisrael* might claim for themselves the glory due to Me, thinking, 'Our own hand has brought us victory.'

ב וַיֹּאמֶר יְהֹוָה אֶל־גִּדְעוֹן רַב הָעָם אֲשֶׁר אִתָּךְ מִתִּתִּי אֶת־מִדְיָן בְּיָדָם פֶּן־יִתְפָּאֵר עָלַי יִשְׂרָאֵל לֵאמֹר יָדִי הוֹשִׁיעָה לִּי:

3 Therefore, announce to the men, 'Let anybody who is timid and fearful turn back, as a bird flies from Mount *Gilad.*'" Thereupon, 22,000 of the troops turned back and 10,000 remained.

ג וְעַתָּה קְרָא נָא בְּאָזְנֵי הָעָם לֵאמֹר מִי־יָרֵא וְחָרֵד יָשֹׁב וְיִצְפֹּר מֵהַר הַגִּלְעָד וַיָּשָׁב מִן־הָעָם עֶשְׂרִים וּשְׁנַיִם אֶלֶף וַעֲשֶׂרֶת אֲלָפִים נִשְׁאָרוּ:

4 "There are still too many troops," *Hashem* said to *Gidon*. "Take them down to the water and I will sift them for you there. Anyone of whom I tell you, 'This one is to go with you,' that one shall go with you; and anyone of whom I tell you, 'This one is not to go with you,' that one shall not go."

ד וַיֹּאמֶר יְהֹוָה אֶל־גִּדְעוֹן עוֹד הָעָם רָב הוֹרֵד אוֹתָם אֶל־הַמַּיִם וְאֶצְרְפֶנּוּ לְךָ שָׁם וְהָיָה אֲשֶׁר אֹמַר אֵלֶיךָ זֶה יֵלֵךְ אִתָּךְ הוּא יֵלֵךְ אִתָּךְ וְכֹל אֲשֶׁר־אֹמַר אֵלֶיךָ זֶה לֹא־יֵלֵךְ עִמָּךְ הוּא לֹא יֵלֵךְ:

5 So he took the troops down to the water. Then *Hashem* said to *Gidon*, "Set apart all those who lap up the water with their tongues like dogs from all those who get down on their knees to drink."

ה וַיּוֹרֶד אֶת־הָעָם אֶל־הַמָּיִם וַיֹּאמֶר יְהֹוָה אֶל־גִּדְעוֹן כֹּל אֲשֶׁר־יָלֹק בִּלְשׁוֹנוֹ מִן־הַמַּיִם כַּאֲשֶׁר יָלֹק הַכֶּלֶב תַּצִּיג אוֹתוֹ לְבָד וְכֹל אֲשֶׁר־יִכְרַע עַל־בִּרְכָּיו לִשְׁתּוֹת:

va-YO-red et ha-AM el ha-MA-yim va-YO-mer a-do-NAI el gid-ON KOL a-sher ya-LOK bil-sho-NO min ha-MA-yim ka-a-SHER ya-LOK ha-KE-lev ta-TZEEG o-TO l'-VAD v'-KHOL a-sher yikh RA al bir-KAV lish-TOT

6 Now those who "lapped" the water into their mouths by hand numbered three hundred; all the rest of the troops got down on their knees to drink.

ו וַיְהִי מִסְפַּר הַמְלַקְקִים בְּיָדָם אֶל־פִּיהֶם שְׁלֹשׁ מֵאוֹת אִישׁ וְכֹל יֶתֶר הָעָם כָּרְעוּ עַל־בִּרְכֵיהֶם לִשְׁתּוֹת מָיִם:

7 Then *Hashem* said to *Gidon*, "I will deliver you and I will put Midian into your hands through the three hundred 'lappers'; let the rest of the troops go home."

ז וַיֹּאמֶר יְהֹוָה אֶל־גִּדְעוֹן בִּשְׁלֹשׁ מֵאוֹת הָאִישׁ הַמְלַקְקִים אוֹשִׁיעַ אֶתְכֶם וְנָתַתִּי אֶת־מִדְיָן בְּיָדֶךָ וְכָל־הָעָם יֵלְכוּ אִישׁ לִמְקֹמוֹ:

8 So [the lappers] took the provisions and *shofarot* that the other men had with them, and he sent the rest of the men of *Yisrael* back to their homes, retaining only the three hundred men. The Midianite camp was below him, in the plain.

ח וַיִּקְחוּ אֶת־צֵדָה הָעָם בְּיָדָם וְאֵת שׁוֹפְרֹתֵיהֶם וְאֵת כָּל־אִישׁ יִשְׂרָאֵל שִׁלַּח אִישׁ לְאֹהָלָיו וּבִשְׁלֹשׁ־מֵאוֹת הָאִישׁ הֶחֱזִיק וּמַחֲנֵה מִדְיָן הָיָה לוֹ מִתַּחַת בָּעֵמֶק:

9 That night *Hashem* said to him, "Come, attack the camp, for I have delivered it into your hands.

ט וַיְהִי בַּלַּיְלָה הַהוּא וַיֹּאמֶר אֵלָיו יְהֹוָה קוּם רֵד בַּמַּחֲנֶה כִּי נְתַתִּיו בְּיָדֶךָ:

10 And if you are afraid to attack, first go down to the camp with your attendant Purah

י וְאִם־יָרֵא אַתָּה לָרֶדֶת רֵד אַתָּה וּפֻרָה נַעַרְךָ אֶל־הַמַּחֲנֶה:

11 and listen to what they say; after that you will have the courage to attack the camp." So he went down with his attendant Purah to the outposts of the warriors who were in the camp.

יא וְשָׁמַעְתָּ מַה־יְדַבֵּרוּ וְאַחַר תֶּחֱזַקְנָה יָדֶיךָ וְיָרַדְתָּ בַּמַּחֲנֶה וַיֵּרֶד הוּא וּפֻרָה נַעֲרוֹ אֶל־קְצֵה הַחֲמֻשִׁים אֲשֶׁר בַּמַּחֲנֶה:

12 Now Midian, Amalek, and all the Kedemites were spread over the plain, as thick as locusts; and their camels were countless, as numerous as the sands on the seashore.

יב וּמִדְיָן וַעֲמָלֵק וְכָל־בְּנֵי־קֶדֶם נֹפְלִים בָּעֵמֶק כָּאַרְבֶּה לָרֹב וְלִגְמַלֵּיהֶם אֵין מִסְפָּר כַּחוֹל שֶׁעַל־שְׂפַת הַיָּם לָרֹב:

13 *Gidon* came there just as one man was narrating a dream to another. "Listen," he was saying, "I had this dream: There was a commotion – a loaf of barley bread was whirling through the Midianite camp. It came to a tent and struck it, and it fell; it turned it upside down, and the tent collapsed."

יג וַיָּבֹא גִדְעוֹן וְהִנֵּה־אִישׁ מְסַפֵּר לְרֵעֵהוּ חֲלוֹם וַיֹּאמֶר הִנֵּה חֲלוֹם חָלַמְתִּי וְהִנֵּה צְלוֹל [צְלִיל] לֶחֶם שְׂעֹרִים מִתְהַפֵּךְ בְּמַחֲנֵה מִדְיָן וַיָּבֹא עַד־הָאֹהֶל וַיַּכֵּהוּ וַיִּפֹּל וַיַּהַפְכֵהוּ לְמַעְלָה וְנָפַל הָאֹהֶל:

Israeli soldier praying
at the Western Wall

7:5 Set apart all those who lap up the water with their tongues For it to be clear to all that the victory of the Israelites would be a miraculous one, *Hashem* orders *Gidon* to reduce the size of his army. He tells *Gidon* to send home all those who kneel down to drink water prior to the battle against Midian. *Rashi* says

that the fact that they kneeled is proof that they had earlier knelt in worship of idols. *Eretz Yisrael* cannot tolerate idolatry (see Deuteronomy 29:24–27). Therefore, those soldiers who have previously engaged in such worship are the ones to be removed from this battle for control of the land.

14 To this the other responded, "That can only mean the sword of the Israelite *Gidon* son of *Yoash*. *Hashem* is delivering Midian and the entire camp into his hands."

יד וַיַּעַן רֵעֵהוּ וַיֹּאמֶר אֵין זֹאת בִּלְתִּי אִם־חֶרֶב גִּדְעוֹן בֶּן־יוֹאָשׁ אִישׁ יִשְׂרָאֵל נָתַן הָאֱלֹהִים בְּיָדוֹ אֶת־מִדְיָן וְאֶת־כָּל־הַמַּחֲנֶה:

15 When *Gidon* heard the dream told and interpreted, he bowed low. Returning to the camp of *Yisrael*, he shouted, "Come on! *Hashem* has delivered the Midianite camp into your hands!"

טו וַיְהִי כִשְׁמֹעַ גִּדְעוֹן אֶת־מִסְפַּר הַחֲלוֹם וְאֶת־שִׁבְרוֹ וַיִּשְׁתָּחוּ וַיָּשָׁב אֶל־מַחֲנֵה יִשְׂרָאֵל וַיֹּאמֶר קוּמוּ כִּי־נָתַן יְהֹוָה בְּיֶדְכֶם אֶת־מַחֲנֵה מִדְיָן:

16 He divided the three hundred men into three columns and equipped every man with a *shofar* and an empty jar, with a torch in each jar.

טז וַיַּחַץ אֶת־שְׁלֹשׁ־מֵאוֹת הָאִישׁ שְׁלֹשָׁה רָאשִׁים וַיִּתֵּן שׁוֹפָרוֹת בְּיַד־כֻּלָּם וְכַדִּים רֵקִים וְלַפִּדִים בְּתוֹךְ הַכַּדִּים:

17 "Watch me," he said, "and do the same. When I get to the outposts of the camp, do exactly as I do.

יז וַיֹּאמֶר אֲלֵיהֶם מִמֶּנִּי תִרְאוּ וְכֵן תַּעֲשׂוּ וְהִנֵּה אָנֹכִי בָא בִּקְצֵה הַמַּחֲנֶה וְהָיָה כַאֲשֶׁר־אֶעֱשֶׂה כֵּן תַּעֲשׂוּן:

18 When I and all those with me blow our *shofarot*, you too, all around the camp, will blow your *shofarot* and shout, 'For *Hashem* and for *Gidon*!'"

יח וְתָקַעְתִּי בַּשּׁוֹפָר אָנֹכִי וְכָל־אֲשֶׁר אִתִּי וּתְקַעְתֶּם בַּשּׁוֹפָרוֹת גַּם־אַתֶּם סְבִיבוֹת כָּל־הַמַּחֲנֶה וַאֲמַרְתֶּם לַיהֹוָה וּלְגִדְעוֹן:

19 *Gidon* and the hundred men with him arrived at the outposts of the camp, at the beginning of the middle watch, just after the sentries were posted. They sounded the *shofarot* and smashed the jars that they had with them,

יט וַיָּבֹא גִדְעוֹן וּמֵאָה־אִישׁ אֲשֶׁר־אִתּוֹ בִּקְצֵה הַמַּחֲנֶה רֹאשׁ הָאַשְׁמֹרֶת הַתִּיכוֹנָה אַךְ הָקֵם הֵקִימוּ אֶת־הַשֹּׁמְרִים וַיִּתְקְעוּ בַּשּׁוֹפָרוֹת וְנָפוֹץ הַכַּדִּים אֲשֶׁר בְּיָדָם:

20 and the three columns blew their *shofarot* and broke their jars. Holding the torches in their left hands and the *shofarot* for blowing in their right hands, they shouted, "A sword for *Hashem* and for *Gidon*!"

כ וַיִּתְקְעוּ שְׁלֹשֶׁת הָרָאשִׁים בַּשּׁוֹפָרוֹת וַיִּשְׁבְּרוּ הַכַּדִּים וַיַּחֲזִיקוּ בְיַד־שְׂמֹאולָם בַּלַּפִּדִים וּבְיַד־יְמִינָם הַשּׁוֹפָרוֹת לִתְקוֹעַ וַיִּקְרְאוּ חֶרֶב לַיהֹוָה וּלְגִדְעוֹן:

21 They remained standing where they were, surrounding the camp; but the entire camp ran about yelling, and took to flight.

כא וַיַּעַמְדוּ אִישׁ תַּחְתָּיו סָבִיב לַמַּחֲנֶה וַיָּרָץ כָּל־הַמַּחֲנֶה וַיָּרִיעוּ וַיָּנִיסוּ [וַיָּנֻסוּ:]

22 For when the three hundred *shofarot* were sounded, *Hashem* turned every man's sword against his fellow, throughout the camp, and the entire host fled as far as Beth-shittah and on to Zererah – as far as the outskirts of Abel-meholah near Tabbath.

כב וַיִּתְקְעוּ שְׁלֹשׁ־מֵאוֹת הַשּׁוֹפָרוֹת וַיָּשֶׂם יְהֹוָה אֵת חֶרֶב אִישׁ בְּרֵעֵהוּ וּבְכָל־הַמַּחֲנֶה וַיָּנָס הַמַּחֲנֶה עַד־בֵּית הַשִּׁטָּה צְרֵרָתָה עַד שְׂפַת־אָבֵל מְחוֹלָה עַל־טַבָּת:

23 And now the men of *Yisrael* from *Naftali* and *Asher* and from all of *Menashe* rallied for the pursuit of the Midianites.

כג וַיִּצָּעֵק אִישׁ־יִשְׂרָאֵל מִנַּפְתָּלִי וּמִן־אָשֵׁר וּמִן־כָּל־מְנַשֶּׁה וַיִּרְדְּפוּ אַחֲרֵי מִדְיָן:

24 *Gidon* also sent messengers all through the hill country of *Efraim* with this order: "Go down ahead of the Midianites and seize their access to the water all along the *Yarden* down to Beth-barah." So all the men of *Efraim* rallied and seized the waterside down to Beth-barah by the *Yarden*.

כד וּמַלְאָכִים שָׁלַח גִּדְעוֹן בְּכָל־הַר אֶפְרַיִם לֵאמֹר רְדוּ לִקְרַאת מִדְיָן וְלִכְדוּ לָהֶם אֶת־הַמַּיִם עַד בֵּית בָּרָה וְאֶת־הַיַּרְדֵּן וַיִּצָּעֵק כָּל־אִישׁ אֶפְרַיִם וַיִּלְכְּדוּ אֶת־הַמַּיִם עַד בֵּית בָּרָה וְאֶת־הַיַּרְדֵּן:

Judges

25 They pursued the Midianites and captured Midian's two generals, Oreb and Zeeb. They killed Oreb at the Rock of Oreb and they killed Zeeb at the Winepress of Zeeb; and they brought the heads of Oreb and Zeeb from the other side of the *Yarden* to *Gidon*.

כה וַיִּלְכְּדוּ שְׁנֵי־שָׂרֵי מִדְיָן אֶת־עֹרֵב וְאֶת־זְאֵב וַיַּהַרְגוּ אֶת־עוֹרֵב בְּצוּר־עוֹרֵב וְאֶת־זְאֵב הָרְגוּ בְיֶקֶב־זְאֵב וַיִּרְדְּפוּ אֶל־מִדְיָן וְרֹאשׁ־עֹרֵב וּזְאֵב הֵבִיאוּ אֶל־גִּדְעוֹן מֵעֵבֶר לַיַּרְדֵּן:

8 ¹ And the men of *Efraim* said to him, "Why did you do that to us – not calling us when you went to fight the Midianites?" And they rebuked him severely.

ח א וַיֹּאמְרוּ אֵלָיו אִישׁ אֶפְרַיִם מָה־הַדָּבָר הַזֶּה עָשִׂיתָ לָּנוּ לְבִלְתִּי קְרֹאות לָנוּ כִּי הָלַכְתָּ לְהִלָּחֵם בְּמִדְיָן וַיְרִיבוּן אִתּוֹ בְּחָזְקָה:

² But he answered them, "After all, what have I accomplished compared to you? Why, *Efraim's* gleanings are better than Abiezer's vintage!

ב וַיֹּאמֶר אֲלֵיהֶם מֶה־עָשִׂיתִי עַתָּה כָּכֶם הֲלֹוא טוֹב עֹלְלוֹת אֶפְרַיִם מִבְצִיר אֲבִיעֶזֶר:

va-YO-mer a-lay-HEM meh a-SEE-tee a-TAH ka-KHEM ha-LO TOV o-l'-LOT ef-RA-yim miv-TZEER a-vee-E-zer

³ *Hashem* has delivered the Midianite generals Oreb and Zeeb into your hands, and what was I able to do compared to you?" And when he spoke in this fashion, their anger against him abated.

ג בְּיֶדְכֶם נָתַן אֱלֹהִים אֶת־שָׂרֵי מִדְיָן אֶת־עֹרֵב וְאֶת־זְאֵב וּמַה־יָּכֹלְתִּי עֲשׂוֹת כָּכֶם אָז רָפְתָה רוּחָם מֵעָלָיו בְּדַבְּרוֹ הַדָּבָר הַזֶּה:

⁴ *Gidon* came to the *Yarden* and crossed it. The three hundred men with him were famished, but still in pursuit.

ד וַיָּבֹא גִדְעוֹן הַיַּרְדֵּנָה עֹבֵר הוּא וּשְׁלֹשׁ־מֵאוֹת הָאִישׁ אֲשֶׁר אִתּוֹ עֲיֵפִים וְרֹדְפִים:

⁵ He said to the people of Succoth, "Please give some loaves of bread to the men who are following me, for they are famished, and I am pursuing Zebah and Zalmunna, the kings of Midian."

ה וַיֹּאמֶר לְאַנְשֵׁי סֻכּוֹת תְּנוּ־נָא כִּכְּרוֹת לֶחֶם לָעָם אֲשֶׁר בְּרַגְלָי כִּי־עֲיֵפִים הֵם וְאָנֹכִי רֹדֵף אַחֲרֵי זֶבַח וְצַלְמֻנָּע מַלְכֵי מִדְיָן:

⁶ But the officials of Succoth replied, "Are Zebah and Zalmunna already in your hands, that we should give bread to your troops?"

ו וַיֹּאמֶר שָׂרֵי סֻכּוֹת הֲכַף זֶבַח וְצַלְמֻנָּע עַתָּה בְּיָדֶךָ כִּי־נִתֵּן לִצְבָאֲךָ לָחֶם:

⁷ "I swear," declared *Gidon*, "when *Hashem* delivers Zebah and Zalmunna into my hands, I'll thresh your bodies upon desert thorns and briers!"

ז וַיֹּאמֶר גִּדְעוֹן לָכֵן בְּתֵת יְהֹוָה אֶת־זֶבַח וְאֶת־צַלְמֻנָּע בְּיָדִי וְדַשְׁתִּי אֶת־בְּשַׂרְכֶם אֶת־קוֹצֵי הַמִּדְבָּר וְאֶת־הַבַּרְקֳנִים:

8:2 But he answered them, "After all, what have I accomplished" Though he has done nothing wrong, *Gidon* nevertheless attempts to pacify the men of *Efraim* who are angry with him, because he recognizes the essential need to avoid civil war. Infighting among the People of Israel always brings disastrous results, such as the destruction of the second *Beit Hamikdash*, which, according to the Talmud (*Yoma* 9b), was destroyed because of baseless hatred. On a number of occasions during the twentieth-century struggle for Jewish independence in the Land of Israel, the main Jewish defense group *Haganah* fought against the rival group *Irgun*, which used more extreme measures against the British authorities. Although it may have been against his own narrow interests, the *Irgun's* leader, Menachem Begin, refused to escalate the violence, saying that civil war must be avoided at all costs. Begin later became Israel's sixth Prime Minister.

Prime Minister Menachem Begin (1913–1992)

8   From there he went up to Penuel and made the same request of them; but the people of Penuel gave him the same reply as the people of Succoth.

ח וַיַּעַל מִשָּׁם פְּנוּאֵל וַיְדַבֵּר אֲלֵיהֶם כָּזֹאת וַיַּעֲנוּ אוֹתוֹ אַנְשֵׁי פְנוּאֵל כַּאֲשֶׁר עָנוּ אַנְשֵׁי סֻכּוֹת:

9   So he also threatened the people of Penuel: "When I come back safe, I'll tear down this tower!"

ט וַיֹּאמֶר גַּם־לְאַנְשֵׁי פְנוּאֵל לֵאמֹר בְּשׁוּבִי בְשָׁלוֹם אֶתֹּץ אֶת־הַמִּגְדָּל הַזֶּה:

10   Now Zebah and Zalmunna were at Karkor with their army of about 15,000; these were all that remained of the entire host of the Kedemites, for the slain numbered 120,000 fighting men.

י וְזֶבַח וְצַלְמֻנָּע בַּקַּרְקֹר וּמַחֲנֵיהֶם עִמָּם כַּחֲמֵשֶׁת עָשָׂר אֶלֶף כֹּל הַנּוֹתָרִים מִכֹּל מַחֲנֵה בְנֵי־קֶדֶם וְהַנֹּפְלִים מֵאָה וְעֶשְׂרִים אֶלֶף אִישׁ שֹׁלֵף חָרֶב:

11   *Gidon* marched up the road of the tent dwellers, up to east of Nobah and Jogbehah, and routed the camp, which was off guard.

יא וַיַּעַל גִּדְעוֹן דֶּרֶךְ הַשְּׁכוּנֵי בָאֳהָלִים מִקֶּדֶם לְנֹבַח וְיָגְבְּהָה וַיַּךְ אֶת־הַמַּחֲנֶה וְהַמַּחֲנֶה הָיָה בֶטַח:

12   Zebah and Zalmunna took to flight, with *Gidon* in pursuit. He captured Zebah and Zalmunna, the two kings of Midian, and threw the whole army into panic.

יב וַיָּנוּסוּ זֶבַח וְצַלְמֻנָּע וַיִּרְדֹּף אַחֲרֵיהֶם וַיִּלְכֹּד אֶת־שְׁנֵי מַלְכֵי מִדְיָן אֶת־זֶבַח וְאֶת־צַלְמֻנָּע וְכָל־הַמַּחֲנֶה הֶחֱרִיד:

13   On his way back from the battle at the Ascent of Heres, *Gidon* son of *Yoash*

יג וַיָּשָׁב גִּדְעוֹן בֶּן־יוֹאָשׁ מִן־הַמִּלְחָמָה מִלְמַעֲלֵה הֶחָרֶס:

14   captured a boy from among the people of Succoth and interrogated him. The latter drew up for him a list of the officials and elders of Succoth, seventy-seven in number.

יד וַיִּלְכָּד־נַעַר מֵאַנְשֵׁי סֻכּוֹת וַיִּשְׁאָלֵהוּ וַיִּכְתֹּב אֵלָיו אֶת־שָׂרֵי סֻכּוֹת וְאֶת־זְקֵנֶיהָ שִׁבְעִים וְשִׁבְעָה אִישׁ:

15   Then he came to the people of Succoth and said, "Here are Zebah and Zalmunna, about whom you mocked me, saying, 'Are Zebah and Zalmunna already in your hands, that we should give your famished men bread?'"

טו וַיָּבֹא אֶל־אַנְשֵׁי סֻכּוֹת וַיֹּאמֶר הִנֵּה זֶבַח וְצַלְמֻנָּע אֲשֶׁר חֵרַפְתֶּם אוֹתִי לֵאמֹר הֲכַף זֶבַח וְצַלְמֻנָּע עַתָּה בְּיָדֶךָ כִּי נִתֵּן לַאֲנָשֶׁיךָ הַיְּעֵפִים לָחֶם:

16   And he took the elders of the city and, [bringing] desert thorns and briers, he punished the people of Succoth with them.

טז וַיִּקַּח אֶת־זִקְנֵי הָעִיר וְאֶת־קוֹצֵי הַמִּדְבָּר וְאֶת־הַבַּרְקֳנִים וַיֹּדַע בָּהֶם אֵת אַנְשֵׁי סֻכּוֹת:

17   As for Penuel, he tore down its tower and killed the townspeople.

יז וְאֶת־מִגְדַּל פְּנוּאֵל נָתָץ וַיַּהֲרֹג אֶת־אַנְשֵׁי הָעִיר:

18   Then he asked Zebah and Zalmunna, "Those men you killed at *Tavor*, what were they like?" "They looked just like you," they replied, "like sons of a king."

יח וַיֹּאמֶר אֶל־זֶבַח וְאֶל־צַלְמֻנָּע אֵיפֹה הָאֲנָשִׁים אֲשֶׁר הֲרַגְתֶּם בְּתָבוֹר וַיֹּאמְרוּ כָּמוֹךָ כְמוֹהֶם אֶחָד כְּתֹאַר בְּנֵי הַמֶּלֶךְ:

19   "They were my brothers," he declared, "the sons of my mother. As *Hashem* lives, if you had spared them, I would not kill you."

יט וַיֹּאמַר אַחַי בְּנֵי־אִמִּי הֵם חַי־יְהֹוָה לוּ הַחֲיִתֶם אוֹתָם לֹא הָרַגְתִּי אֶתְכֶם:

20   And he commanded his oldest son Jether, "Go kill them!" But the boy did not draw his sword, for he was timid, being still a boy.

כ וַיֹּאמֶר לְיֶתֶר בְּכוֹרוֹ קוּם הֲרֹג אוֹתָם וְלֹא־שָׁלַף הַנַּעַר חַרְבּוֹ כִּי יָרֵא כִּי עוֹדֶנּוּ נָעַר:

21 Then Zebah and Zalmunna said, "Come, you slay us; for strength comes with manhood." So *Gidon* went over and killed Zebah and Zalmunna, and he took the crescents that were on the necks of their camels.

כא וַיֹּ֩אמֶר֩ זֶ֨בַח וְצַלְמֻנָּ֜ע ק֤וּם אַתָּה֙ וּפְגַע־בָּ֔נוּ כִּ֥י כָאִ֖ישׁ גְּבוּרָת֑וֹ וַיָּ֣קׇם גִּדְע֗וֹן וַֽיַּהֲרֹג֙ אֶת־זֶ֣בַח וְאֶת־צַלְמֻנָּ֔ע וַיִּקַּח֙ אֶת־הַשַּׂ֣הֲרֹנִ֔ים אֲשֶׁ֖ר בְּצַוְּארֵ֥י גְמַלֵּיהֶֽם׃

22 Then the men of *Yisrael* said to *Gidon*, "Rule over us – you, your son, and your grandson as well; for you have saved us from the Midianites."

כב וַיֹּאמְר֤וּ אִישׁ־יִשְׂרָאֵל֙ אֶל־גִּדְע֔וֹן מְשׇׁל־בָּ֙נוּ֙ גַּם־אַתָּ֔ה גַּם־בִּנְךָ֖ גַּ֣ם בֶּן־בְּנֶ֑ךָ כִּ֥י הוֹשַׁעְתָּ֖נוּ מִיַּ֥ד מִדְיָֽן׃

23 But *Gidon* replied, "I will not rule over you myself, nor shall my son rule over you; *Hashem* alone shall rule over you."

כג וַיֹּ֤אמֶר אֲלֵהֶם֙ גִּדְע֔וֹן לֹֽא־אֶמְשֹׁ֤ל אֲנִי֙ בָּכֶ֔ם וְלֹֽא־יִמְשֹׁ֥ל בְּנִ֖י בָּכֶ֑ם יְהֹוָ֖ה יִמְשֹׁ֥ל בָּכֶֽם׃

24 And *Gidon* said to them, "I have a request to make of you: Each of you give me the earring he received as booty." (They had golden earrings, for they were Ishmaelites.)

כד וַיֹּ֨אמֶר אֲלֵהֶ֜ם גִּדְע֗וֹן אֶשְׁאֲלָ֤ה מִכֶּם֙ שְׁאֵלָ֔ה וּתְנוּ־לִ֕י אִ֖ישׁ נֶ֣זֶם שְׁלָל֑וֹ כִּֽי־נִזְמֵ֤י זָהָב֙ לָהֶ֔ם כִּ֥י יִשְׁמְעֵאלִ֖ים הֵֽם׃

25 "Certainly!" they replied. And they spread out a cloth, and everyone threw onto it the earring he had received as booty.

כה וַיֹּאמְר֖וּ נָת֣וֹן נִתֵּ֑ן וַֽיִּפְרְשׂוּ֙ אֶת־הַשִּׂמְלָ֔ה וַיַּשְׁלִ֣יכוּ שָׁ֔מָּה אִ֖ישׁ נֶ֥זֶם שְׁלָלֽוֹ׃

26 The weight of the golden earrings that he had requested came to 1,700 *shekalim* of gold; this was in addition to the crescents and the pendants and the purple robes worn by the kings of Midian and in addition to the collars on the necks of their camels.

כו וַיְהִ֗י מִשְׁקַ֞ל נִזְמֵ֤י הַזָּהָב֙ אֲשֶׁ֣ר שָׁאָ֔ל אֶ֕לֶף וּשְׁבַע־מֵא֖וֹת זָהָ֑ב לְבַ֣ד מִן־הַשַּׂ֠הֲרֹנִ֠ים וְהַנְּטִפ֤וֹת וּבִגְדֵ֣י הָֽאַרְגָּמָ֗ן שֶׁעַל֙ מַלְכֵ֣י מִדְיָ֔ן וּלְבַ֕ד מִן־הָ֣עֲנָק֔וֹת אֲשֶׁ֖ר בְּצַוְּארֵ֥י גְמַלֵּיהֶֽם׃

27 *Gidon* made an ephod of this gold and set it up in his own town of Ophrah. There all *Yisrael* went astray after it, and it became a snare to *Gidon* and his household.

כז וַיַּ֩עַשׂ֩ אוֹת֨וֹ גִדְע֜וֹן לְאֵפ֗וֹד וַיַּצֵּ֙ג אוֹת֤וֹ בְעִירוֹ֙ בְּעׇפְרָ֔ה וַיִּזְנ֧וּ כׇל־יִשְׂרָאֵ֛ל אַחֲרָ֖יו שָׁ֑ם וַיְהִ֛י לְגִדְע֥וֹן וּלְבֵית֖וֹ לְמוֹקֵֽשׁ׃

28 Thus Midian submitted to the Israelites and did not raise its head again; and the land was tranquil for forty years in *Gidon*'s time.

כח וַיִּכָּנַ֣ע מִדְיָ֗ן לִפְנֵי֙ בְּנֵ֣י יִשְׂרָאֵ֔ל וְלֹ֥א יָסְפ֖וּ לָשֵׂ֣את רֹאשָׁ֑ם וַתִּשְׁקֹ֧ט הָאָ֛רֶץ אַרְבָּעִ֥ים שָׁנָ֖ה בִּימֵ֥י גִדְעֽוֹן׃

29 So *Yerubaal* son of *Yoash* retired to his own house.

כט וַיֵּ֛לֶךְ יְרֻבַּ֥עַל בֶּן־יוֹאָ֖שׁ וַיֵּ֥שֶׁב בְּבֵיתֽוֹ׃

30 *Gidon* had seventy sons of his own issue, for he had many wives.

ל וּלְגִדְע֗וֹן הָי֛וּ שִׁבְעִ֥ים בָּנִ֖ים יֹצְאֵ֣י יְרֵכ֑וֹ כִּֽי־נָשִׁ֥ים רַבּ֖וֹת הָ֥יוּ לֽוֹ׃

31 A son was also born to him by his concubine in *Shechem*, and he named him *Avimelech*.

לא וּפִ֨ילַגְשׁ֜וֹ אֲשֶׁ֣ר בִּשְׁכֶ֗ם יָֽלְדָה־לּ֥וֹ גַם־הִ֖יא בֵּ֑ן וַיָּ֥שֶׂם אֶת־שְׁמ֖וֹ אֲבִימֶֽלֶךְ׃

32 *Gidon* son of *Yoash* died at a ripe old age, and was buried in the tomb of his father *Yoash* at Ophrah of the Abiezrites.

לב וַיָּ֛מׇת גִּדְע֥וֹן בֶּן־יוֹאָ֖שׁ בְּשֵׂיבָ֣ה טוֹבָ֑ה וַיִּקָּבֵ֗ר בְּקֶ֙בֶר֙ יוֹאָ֣שׁ אָבִ֔יו בְּעׇפְרָ֖ה אֲבִ֥י הָעֶזְרִֽי׃

33 After *Gidon* died, the Israelites again went astray after the Baalim, and they adopted Baal-berith as a god.

לג וַיְהִ֗י כַּֽאֲשֶׁר֙ מֵ֣ת גִּדְע֔וֹן וַיָּשׁ֙וּבוּ֙ בְּנֵ֣י יִשְׂרָאֵ֔ל וַיִּזְנ֖וּ אַחֲרֵ֣י הַבְּעָלִ֑ים וַיָּשִׂ֧ימוּ לָהֶ֛ם בַּ֥עַל בְּרִ֖ית לֵאלֹהִֽים׃

34 The Israelites gave no thought to *Hashem* their God, who saved them from all the enemies around them.

לד וְלֹא זָכְרוּ בְּנֵי יִשְׂרָאֵל אֶת־יְהֹוָה אֱלֹהֵיהֶם הַמַּצִּיל אוֹתָם מִיַּד כָּל־אֹיְבֵיהֶם מִסָּבִיב:

35 Nor did they show loyalty to the house of *Yerubaal-Gidon* in return for all the good that he had done for *Yisrael*.

לה וְלֹא־עָשׂוּ חֶסֶד עִם־בֵּית יְרֻבַּעַל גִּדְעוֹן כְּכָל־הַטּוֹבָה אֲשֶׁר עָשָׂה עִם־יִשְׂרָאֵל:

9 1 *Avimelech* son of *Yerubaal* went to his mother's brothers in *Shechem* and spoke to them and to the whole clan of his mother's family. He said,

ט א וַיֵּלֶךְ אֲבִימֶלֶךְ בֶּן־יְרֻבַּעַל שְׁכֶמָה אֶל־אֲחֵי אִמּוֹ וַיְדַבֵּר אֲלֵיהֶם וְאֶל־כָּל־מִשְׁפַּחַת בֵּית־אֲבִי אִמּוֹ לֵאמֹר:

va-YAY-lekh a-vee-ME-lekh ben y'-ru-BA-al sh'-KHE-mah el a-KHAY i-MO
vai-da-BAYR a-lay-HEM v'-el kol mish-PA-khat bayt a-VEE i-MO lay-MOR

2 "Put this question to all the citizens of *Shechem*: Which is better for you, to be ruled by seventy men – by all the sons of *Yerubaal* – or to be ruled by one man? And remember, I am your own flesh and blood."

ב דַּבְּרוּ־נָא בְּאָזְנֵי כָל־בַּעֲלֵי שְׁכֶם מַה־טּוֹב לָכֶם הַמְשֹׁל בָּכֶם שִׁבְעִים אִישׁ כֹּל בְּנֵי יְרֻבַּעַל אִם־מְשֹׁל בָּכֶם אִישׁ אֶחָד וּזְכַרְתֶּם כִּי־עַצְמְכֶם וּבְשַׂרְכֶם אָנִי:

3 His mother's brothers said all this in his behalf to all the citizens of *Shechem*, and they were won over to *Avimelech*; for they thought, "He is our kinsman."

ג וַיְדַבְּרוּ אֲחֵי־אִמּוֹ עָלָיו בְּאָזְנֵי כָּל־בַּעֲלֵי שְׁכֶם אֵת כָּל־הַדְּבָרִים הָאֵלֶּה וַיֵּט לִבָּם אַחֲרֵי אֲבִימֶלֶךְ כִּי אָמְרוּ אָחִינוּ הוּא:

4 They gave him seventy *shekalim* from the temple of Baal-berith; and with this *Avimelech* hired some worthless and reckless fellows, and they followed him.

ד וַיִּתְּנוּ־לוֹ שִׁבְעִים כֶּסֶף מִבֵּית בַּעַל בְּרִית וַיִּשְׂכֹּר בָּהֶם אֲבִימֶלֶךְ אֲנָשִׁים רֵיקִים וּפֹחֲזִים וַיֵּלְכוּ אַחֲרָיו:

5 Then he went to his father's house in Ophrah and killed his brothers, the sons of *Yerubaal*, seventy men on one stone. Only *Yotam*, the youngest son of *Yerubaal*, survived, because he went into hiding.

ה וַיָּבֹא בֵית־אָבִיו עָפְרָתָה וַיַּהֲרֹג אֶת־אֶחָיו בְּנֵי־יְרֻבַּעַל שִׁבְעִים אִישׁ עַל־אֶבֶן אֶחָת וַיִּוָּתֵר יוֹתָם בֶּן־יְרֻבַּעַל הַקָּטֹן כִּי נֶחְבָּא:

6 All the citizens of *Shechem* and all Beth-millo convened, and they proclaimed *Avimelech* king at the terebinth of the pillar at *Shechem*.

ו וַיֵּאָסְפוּ כָּל־בַּעֲלֵי שְׁכֶם וְכָל־בֵּית מִלּוֹא וַיֵּלְכוּ וַיַּמְלִיכוּ אֶת־אֲבִימֶלֶךְ לְמֶלֶךְ עִם־אֵלוֹן מֻצָּב אֲשֶׁר בִּשְׁכֶם:

7 When *Yotam* was informed, he went and stood on top of Mount Gerizim and called out to them in a loud voice. "Citizens of *Shechem*!" he cried, "listen to me, that *Hashem* may listen to you.

ז וַיַּגִּדוּ לְיוֹתָם וַיֵּלֶךְ וַיַּעֲמֹד בְּרֹאשׁ הַר־גְּרִזִים וַיִּשָּׂא קוֹלוֹ וַיִּקְרָא וַיֹּאמֶר לָהֶם שִׁמְעוּ אֵלַי בַּעֲלֵי שְׁכֶם וְיִשְׁמַע אֲלֵיכֶם אֱלֹהִים:

9:1 *Avimelech* son of *Yerubaal* went to his mother's brothers in *Shechem* The city of *Shechem* appears many times in the Bible. *Yaakov* purchases part of the city (Genesis 33:18–20) and later gives it as a special gift to his son *Yosef* (ibid. 49:22–26). Later, when the Children of Israel enter the Land of Israel, they bury *Yosef* in *Shechem*. Other important sites in Israel were also acquired via purchase, such as the Temple Mount in *Yerushalayim* (II Samuel 24) and the cave of Machpelah in *Chevron* (Genesis 23). The Rabbis explain that because of the public nature of these sales, the entire world must recognize Jewish ownership over these three cities.

Tomb of Yosef in Shechem

8 "Once the trees went to anoint a king over themselves. They said to the olive tree, 'Reign over us.'

ח הָל֨וֹךְ הָֽלְכ֤וּ הָֽעֵצִים֙ לִמְשֹׁ֤חַ עֲלֵיהֶם֙ מֶ֔לֶךְ וַיֹּאמְר֥וּ לַזַּ֖יִת מלוכה [מׇלְכָ֥ה] עָלֵֽינוּ׃

9 But the olive tree replied, 'Have I, through whom *Hashem* and men are honored, stopped yielding my rich oil, that I should go and wave above the trees?'

ט וַיֹּ֤אמֶר לָהֶם֙ הַזַּ֔יִת הֶחֳדַ֙לְתִּי֙ אֶת־דִּשְׁנִ֔י אֲשֶׁר־בִּ֛י יְכַבְּד֥וּ אֱלֹהִ֖ים וַאֲנָשִׁ֑ים וְהָ֣לַכְתִּ֔י לָנ֖וּעַ עַל־הָעֵצִֽים׃

10 So the trees said to the fig tree, 'You come and reign over us.'

י וַיֹּאמְר֥וּ הָעֵצִ֖ים לַתְּאֵנָ֑ה לְכִי־אַ֖תְּ מׇלְכִ֥י עָלֵֽינוּ׃

11 But the fig tree replied, 'Have I stopped yielding my sweetness, my delicious fruit, that I should go and wave above the trees?'

יא וַתֹּ֤אמֶר לָהֶם֙ הַתְּאֵנָ֔ה הֶחֳדַ֙לְתִּי֙ אֶת־מׇתְקִ֔י וְאֶת־תְּנוּבָתִ֖י הַטּוֹבָ֑ה וְהָ֣לַכְתִּ֔י לָנ֖וּעַ עַל־הָעֵצִֽים׃

12 So the trees said to the vine, 'You come and reign over us.'

יב וַיֹּאמְר֥וּ הָעֵצִ֖ים לַגָּ֑פֶן לְכִי־אַ֖תְּ מלוכי [מׇלְכִ֥י] עָלֵֽינוּ׃

13 But the vine replied, 'Have I stopped yielding my new wine, which gladdens *Hashem* and men, that I should go and wave above the trees?'

יג וַתֹּ֤אמֶר לָהֶם֙ הַגֶּ֔פֶן הֶחֳדַ֙לְתִּי֙ אֶת־תִּ֣ירוֹשִׁ֔י הַֽמְשַׂמֵּ֥חַ אֱלֹהִ֖ים וַאֲנָשִׁ֑ים וְהָ֣לַכְתִּ֔י לָנ֖וּעַ עַל־הָעֵצִֽים׃

14 Then all the trees said to the thornbush, 'You come and reign over us.'

יד וַיֹּאמְר֥וּ כׇל־הָעֵצִ֖ים אֶל־הָאָטָ֑ד לֵ֥ךְ אַתָּ֖ה מְלׇךְ־עָלֵֽינוּ׃

15 And the thornbush said to the trees, 'If you are acting honorably in anointing me king over you, come and take shelter in my shade; but if not, may fire issue from the thornbush and consume the cedars of Lebanon!'

טו וַיֹּ֣אמֶר הָאָטָד֮ אֶל־הָֽעֵצִים֒ אִ֡ם בֶּאֱמֶ֣ת אַתֶּם֩ מֹשְׁחִ֨ים אֹתִ֤י לְמֶ֙לֶךְ֙ עֲלֵיכֶ֔ם בֹּ֖אוּ חֲס֣וּ בְצִלִּ֑י וְאִם־אַ֕יִן תֵּ֤צֵא אֵשׁ֙ מִן־הָ֣אָטָ֔ד וְתֹאכַ֖ל אֶת־אַרְזֵ֥י הַלְּבָנֽוֹן׃

16 "Now then, if you acted honorably and loyally in making *Avimelech* king, if you have done right by *Yerubaal* and his house and have requited him according to his deserts

טז וְעַתָּ֗ה אִם־בֶּאֱמֶ֤ת וּבְתָמִים֙ עֲשִׂיתֶ֔ם וַתַּמְלִ֖יכוּ אֶת־אֲבִימֶ֑לֶךְ וְאִם־טוֹבָ֤ה עֲשִׂיתֶם֙ עִם־יְרֻבַּ֣עַל וְעִם־בֵּית֔וֹ וְאִם־כִּגְמ֥וּל יָדָ֖יו עֲשִׂ֥יתֶם לֽוֹ׃

17 considering that my father fought for you and saved you from the Midianites at the risk of his life,

יז אֲשֶׁר־נִלְחַ֥ם אָבִ֖י עֲלֵיכֶ֑ם וַיַּשְׁלֵ֤ךְ אֶת־נַפְשׁוֹ֙ מִנֶּ֔גֶד וַיַּצֵּ֥ל אֶתְכֶ֖ם מִיַּ֥ד מִדְיָֽן׃

18 and now you have turned on my father's household, killed his sons, seventy men on one stone, and set up *Avimelech*, the son of his handmaid, as king over the citizens of *Shechem* just because he is your kinsman

יח וְאַתֶּ֞ם קַמְתֶּ֨ם עַל־בֵּ֤ית אָבִי֙ הַיּ֔וֹם וַתַּהַרְג֧וּ אֶת־בָּנָ֛יו שִׁבְעִ֥ים אִ֖ישׁ עַל־אֶ֣בֶן אֶחָ֑ת וַתַּמְלִ֜יכוּ אֶת־אֲבִימֶ֤לֶךְ בֶּן־אֲמָתוֹ֙ עַל־בַּעֲלֵ֣י שְׁכֶ֔ם כִּ֥י אֲחִיכֶ֖ם הֽוּא׃

19 if, I say, you have this day acted honorably and loyally toward *Yerubaal* and his house, have joy in *Avimelech* and may he likewise have joy in you.

יט וְאִם־בֶּאֱמֶ֨ת וּבְתָמִ֧ים עֲשִׂיתֶ֛ם עִם־יְרֻבַּ֥עַל וְעִם־בֵּית֖וֹ הַיּ֣וֹם הַזֶּ֑ה שִׂמְחוּ֙ בַּאֲבִימֶ֔לֶךְ וְיִשְׂמַ֥ח גַּם־ה֖וּא בָּכֶֽם׃

20 But if not, may fire issue from *Avimelech* and consume the citizens of *Shechem* and Beth-millo, and may fire issue from the citizens of *Shechem* and Beth-millo and consume *Avimelech*!"

כ וְאִם־אַ֕יִן תֵּ֤צֵא אֵשׁ֙ מֵאֲבִימֶ֔לֶךְ וְתֹאכַ֛ל אֶת־בַּעֲלֵ֥י שְׁכֶ֖ם וְאֶת־בֵּ֣ית מִלּ֑וֹא וְתֵצֵ֨א אֵ֜שׁ מִבַּעֲלֵ֤י שְׁכֶם֙ וּמִבֵּ֣ית מִלּ֔וֹא וְתֹאכַ֖ל אֶת־אֲבִימֶֽלֶךְ׃

21 With that, *Yotam* fled. He ran to Beer and stayed there, because of his brother *Avimelech*.

כא וַיָּנָס יוֹתָם וַיִּבְרַח וַיֵּלֶךְ בְּאֵרָה וַיֵּשֶׁב שָׁם מִפְּנֵי אֲבִימֶלֶךְ אָחִיו:

22 *Avimelech* held sway over *Yisrael* for three years.

כב וַיָּשַׂר אֲבִימֶלֶךְ עַל־יִשְׂרָאֵל שָׁלֹשׁ שָׁנִים:

23 Then *Hashem* sent a spirit of discord between *Avimelech* and the citizens of *Shechem*, and the citizens of *Shechem* broke faith with *Avimelech*

כג וַיִּשְׁלַח אֱלֹהִים רוּחַ רָעָה בֵּין אֲבִימֶלֶךְ וּבֵין בַּעֲלֵי שְׁכֶם וַיִּבְגְּדוּ בַעֲלֵי־שְׁכֶם בַּאֲבִימֶלֶךְ:

24 to the end that the crime committed against the seventy sons of *Yerubaal* might be avenged, and their blood recoil upon their brother *Avimelech*, who had slain them, and upon the citizens of *Shechem*, who had abetted him in the slaying of his brothers.

כד לָבוֹא חֲמַס שִׁבְעִים בְּנֵי־יְרֻבָּעַל וְדָמָם לָשׂוּם עַל־אֲבִימֶלֶךְ אֲחִיהֶם אֲשֶׁר הָרַג אוֹתָם וְעַל בַּעֲלֵי שְׁכֶם אֲשֶׁר־חִזְּקוּ אֶת־יָדָיו לַהֲרֹג אֶת־אֶחָיו:

25 The citizens of *Shechem* planted ambuscades against him on the hilltops; and they robbed whoever passed by them on the road. Word of this reached *Avimelech*.

כה וַיָּשִׂימוּ לוֹ בַעֲלֵי שְׁכֶם מְאָרְבִים עַל רָאשֵׁי הֶהָרִים וַיִּגְזְלוּ אֵת כָּל־אֲשֶׁר־יַעֲבֹר עֲלֵיהֶם בַּדָּרֶךְ וַיֻּגַּד לַאֲבִימֶלֶךְ:

26 Then Gaal son of Ebed and his companions came passing through *Shechem*, and the citizens of *Shechem* gave him their confidence.

כו וַיָּבֹא גַּעַל בֶּן־עֶבֶד וְאֶחָיו וַיַּעַבְרוּ בִּשְׁכֶם וַיִּבְטְחוּ־בוֹ בַּעֲלֵי שְׁכֶם:

27 They went out into the fields, gathered and trod out the vintage of their vineyards, and made a festival. They entered the temple of their god, and as they ate and drank they reviled *Avimelech*.

כז וַיֵּצְאוּ הַשָּׂדֶה וַיִּבְצְרוּ אֶת־כַּרְמֵיהֶם וַיִּדְרְכוּ וַיַּעֲשׂוּ הִלּוּלִים וַיָּבֹאוּ בֵּית אֱלֹהֵיהֶם וַיֹּאכְלוּ וַיִּשְׁתּוּ וַיְקַלְלוּ אֶת־אֲבִימֶלֶךְ:

28 Gaal son of Ebed said, "Who is *Avimelech* and who are [we] Sh'chemites, that we should serve him? This same son of *Yerubaal* and his lieutenant Zebul once served the men of Hamor, the father of *Shechem*; so why should we serve him?

כח וַיֹּאמֶר גַּעַל בֶּן־עֶבֶד מִי־אֲבִימֶלֶךְ וּמִי־שְׁכֶם כִּי נַעַבְדֶנּוּ הֲלֹא בֶן־יְרֻבַּעַל וּזְבֻל פְּקִידוֹ עִבְדוּ אֶת־אַנְשֵׁי חֲמוֹר אֲבִי שְׁכֶם וּמַדּוּעַ נַעַבְדֶנּוּ אֲנָחְנוּ:

29 Oh, if only this people were under my command, I would get rid of *Avimelech*! One would challenge *Avimelech*, 'Fill up your ranks and come out here!'"

כט וּמִי יִתֵּן אֶת־הָעָם הַזֶּה בְּיָדִי וְאָסִירָה אֶת־אֲבִימֶלֶךְ וַיֹּאמֶר לַאֲבִימֶלֶךְ רַבֶּה צְבָאֲךָ וָצֵאָה:

30 When Zebul, the governor of the city, heard the words of Gaal son of Ebed, he was furious.

ל וַיִּשְׁמַע זְבֻל שַׂר־הָעִיר אֶת־דִּבְרֵי גַּעַל בֶּן־עָבֶד וַיִּחַר אַפּוֹ:

31 He sent messages to *Avimelech* at Tormah to say, "Gaal son of Ebed and his companions have come to *Shechem* and they are inciting the city against you.

לא וַיִּשְׁלַח מַלְאָכִים אֶל־אֲבִימֶלֶךְ בְּתָרְמָה לֵאמֹר הִנֵּה גַעַל בֶּן־עֶבֶד וְאֶחָיו בָּאִים שְׁכֶמָה וְהִנָּם צָרִים אֶת־הָעִיר עָלֶיךָ:

32 Therefore, set out at night with the forces you have with you and conceal yourself in the fields.

לב וְעַתָּה קוּם לַיְלָה אַתָּה וְהָעָם אֲשֶׁר־אִתָּךְ וֶאֱרֹב בַּשָּׂדֶה:

33 Early next morning, as the sun rises, advance on the city. He and his men will thereupon come out against you, and you will do to him whatever you find possible."

לג וְהָיָה בַבֹּקֶר כִּזְרֹחַ הַשֶּׁמֶשׁ תַּשְׁכִּים וּפָשַׁטְתָּ עַל־הָעִיר וְהִנֵּה־הוּא וְהָעָם אֲשֶׁר־אִתּוֹ יֹצְאִים אֵלֶיךָ וְעָשִׂיתָ לּוֹ כַּאֲשֶׁר תִּמְצָא יָדֶךָ:

34 *Avimelech* and all the men with him set out at night and disposed themselves against *Shechem* in four hiding places.

לד וַיָּקָם אֲבִימֶלֶךְ וְכָל־הָעָם אֲשֶׁר־עִמּוֹ לַיְלָה וַיֶּאֶרְבוּ עַל־שְׁכֶם אַרְבָּעָה רָאשִׁים:

35 When Gaal son of Ebed came out and stood at the entrance to the city gate, *Avimelech* and the army with him emerged from concealment.

לה וַיֵּצֵא גַּעַל בֶּן־עֶבֶד וַיַּעֲמֹד פֶּתַח שַׁעַר הָעִיר וַיָּקָם אֲבִימֶלֶךְ וְהָעָם אֲשֶׁר־אִתּוֹ מִן־הַמַּאְרָב:

36 Gaal saw the army and said to Zebul, "That's an army marching down from the hilltops!" But Zebul said to him, "The shadows of the hills look to you like men."

לו וַיַּרְא־גַּעַל אֶת־הָעָם וַיֹּאמֶר אֶל־זְבֻל הִנֵּה־עָם יוֹרֵד מֵרָאשֵׁי הֶהָרִים וַיֹּאמֶר אֵלָיו זְבֻל אֵת צֵל הֶהָרִים אַתָּה רֹאֶה כָּאֲנָשִׁים:

37 Gaal spoke up again, "Look, an army is marching down from Tabbur-erez, and another column is coming from the direction of Elon-meonenim."

לז וַיֹּסֶף עוֹד גַּעַל לְדַבֵּר וַיֹּאמֶר הִנֵּה־עָם יוֹרְדִים מֵעִם טַבּוּר הָאָרֶץ וְרֹאשׁ־אֶחָד בָּא מִדֶּרֶךְ אֵלוֹן מְעוֹנְנִים:

38 "Well," replied Zebul, "where is your boast, 'Who is *Avimelech* that we should serve him'? There is the army you sneered at; now go out and fight it!"

לח וַיֹּאמֶר אֵלָיו זְבֻל אַיֵּה אֵפוֹא פִיךָ אֲשֶׁר תֹּאמַר מִי אֲבִימֶלֶךְ כִּי נַעַבְדֶנּוּ הֲלֹא זֶה הָעָם אֲשֶׁר מָאַסְתָּה בּוֹ צֵא־נָא עַתָּה וְהִלָּחֶם בּוֹ:

39 So Gaal went out at the head of the citizens of *Shechem* and gave battle to *Avimelech*.

לט וַיֵּצֵא גַּעַל לִפְנֵי בַּעֲלֵי שְׁכֶם וַיִּלָּחֶם בַּאֲבִימֶלֶךְ:

40 But he had to flee before him, and *Avimelech* pursued him, and many fell slain, all the way to the entrance of the gate.

מ וַיִּרְדְּפֵהוּ אֲבִימֶלֶךְ וַיָּנָס מִפָּנָיו וַיִּפְּלוּ חֲלָלִים רַבִּים עַד־פֶּתַח הַשָּׁעַר:

41 Then *Avimelech* stayed in Arumah, while Zebul expelled Gaal and his companions and kept them out of *Shechem*.

מא וַיֵּשֶׁב אֲבִימֶלֶךְ בָּארוּמָה וַיְגָרֶשׁ זְבֻל אֶת־גַּעַל וְאֶת־אֶחָיו מִשֶּׁבֶת בִּשְׁכֶם:

42 The next day, when people went out into the fields, *Avimelech* was informed.

מב וַיְהִי מִמָּחֳרָת וַיֵּצֵא הָעָם הַשָּׂדֶה וַיַּגִּדוּ לַאֲבִימֶלֶךְ:

43 Taking the army, he divided it into three columns and lay in ambush in the fields; and when he saw the people coming out of the city, he pounced upon them and struck them down.

מג וַיִּקַּח אֶת־הָעָם וַיֶּחֱצֵם לִשְׁלֹשָׁה רָאשִׁים וַיֶּאֱרֹב בַּשָּׂדֶה וַיַּרְא וְהִנֵּה הָעָם יֹצֵא מִן־הָעִיר וַיָּקָם עֲלֵיהֶם וַיַּכֵּם:

44 While *Avimelech* and the column that followed him dashed ahead and took up a position at the entrance of the city gate, the other two columns rushed upon all that were in the open and struck them down.

מד וַאֲבִימֶלֶךְ וְהָרָאשִׁים אֲשֶׁר עִמּוֹ פָּשְׁטוּ וַיַּעַמְדוּ פֶּתַח שַׁעַר הָעִיר וּשְׁנֵי הָרָאשִׁים פָּשְׁטוּ עַל־כָּל־אֲשֶׁר בַּשָּׂדֶה וַיַּכּוּם:

45 *Avimelech* fought against the city all that day. He captured the city and massacred the people in it; he razed the town and sowed it with salt.

מה וַאֲבִימֶלֶךְ נִלְחָם בָּעִיר כֹּל הַיּוֹם הַהוּא וַיִּלְכֹּד אֶת־הָעִיר וְאֶת־הָעָם אֲשֶׁר־בָּהּ הָרָג וַיִּתֹּץ אֶת־הָעִיר וַיִּזְרָעֶהָ מֶלַח:

46 When all the citizens of the Tower of *Shechem* learned of this, they went into the tunnel of the temple of *El-berith*.

מו וַיִּשְׁמְעוּ כָּל־בַּעֲלֵי מִגְדַּל־שְׁכֶם וַיָּבֹאוּ אֶל־צְרִיחַ בֵּית אֵל בְּרִית:

27

47 When *Avimelech* was informed that all the citizens of the Tower of *Shechem* had gathered [there],

מז וַיֻּגַּד לַאֲבִימֶלֶךְ כִּי הִתְקַבְּצוּ כָּל־בַּעֲלֵי מִגְדַּל־שְׁכֶם:

48 *Avimelech* and all the troops he had with him went up on Mount Zalmon. Taking an ax in his hand, *Avimelech* lopped off a tree limb and lifted it onto his shoulder. Then he said to the troops that accompanied him, "What you saw me do – quick, do the same!"

מח וַיַּעַל אֲבִימֶלֶךְ הַר־צַלְמוֹן הוּא וְכָל־הָעָם אֲשֶׁר־אִתּוֹ וַיִּקַּח אֲבִימֶלֶךְ אֶת־הַקַּרְדֻּמּוֹת בְּיָדוֹ וַיִּכְרֹת שׂוֹכַת עֵצִים וַיִּשָּׂאֶהָ וַיָּשֶׂם עַל־שִׁכְמוֹ וַיֹּאמֶר אֶל־הָעָם אֲשֶׁר־עִמּוֹ מָה רְאִיתֶם עָשִׂיתִי מַהֲרוּ עֲשׂוּ כָמוֹנִי:

49 So each of the troops also lopped off a bough; then they marched behind *Avimelech* and laid them against the tunnel, and set fire to the tunnel over their heads. Thus all the people of the Tower of *Shechem* also perished, about a thousand men and women.

מט וַיִּכְרְתוּ גַם־כָּל־הָעָם אִישׁ שׂוֹכֹה וַיֵּלְכוּ אַחֲרֵי אֲבִימֶלֶךְ וַיָּשִׂימוּ עַל־הַצְּרִיחַ וַיַּצִּיתוּ עֲלֵיהֶם אֶת־הַצְּרִיחַ בָּאֵשׁ וַיָּמֻתוּ גַּם כָּל־אַנְשֵׁי מִגְדַּל־שְׁכֶם כְּאֶלֶף אִישׁ וְאִשָּׁה:

50 *Avimelech* proceeded to Thebez; he encamped at Thebez and occupied it.

נ וַיֵּלֶךְ אֲבִימֶלֶךְ אֶל־תֵּבֵץ וַיִּחַן בְּתֵבֵץ וַיִּלְכְּדָהּ:

51 Within the town was a fortified tower; and all the citizens of the town, men and women, took refuge there. They shut themselves in, and went up on the roof of the tower.

נא וּמִגְדַּל־עֹז הָיָה בְתוֹךְ־הָעִיר וַיָּנֻסוּ שָׁמָּה כָּל־הָאֲנָשִׁים וְהַנָּשִׁים וְכֹל בַּעֲלֵי הָעִיר וַיִּסְגְּרוּ בַּעֲדָם וַיַּעֲלוּ עַל־גַּג הַמִּגְדָּל:

52 *Avimelech* pressed forward to the tower and attacked it. He approached the door of the tower to set it on fire.

נב וַיָּבֹא אֲבִימֶלֶךְ עַד־הַמִּגְדָּל וַיִּלָּחֶם בּוֹ וַיִּגַּשׁ עַד־פֶּתַח הַמִּגְדָּל לְשָׂרְפוֹ בָאֵשׁ:

53 But a woman dropped an upper millstone on *Avimelech*'s head and cracked his skull.

נג וַתַּשְׁלֵךְ אִשָּׁה אַחַת פֶּלַח רֶכֶב עַל־רֹאשׁ אֲבִימֶלֶךְ וַתָּרִץ אֶת־גֻּלְגָּלְתּוֹ:

54 He immediately cried out to his attendant, his arms-bearer, "Draw your dagger and finish me off, that they may not say of me, 'A woman killed him!'" So his attendant stabbed him, and he died.

נד וַיִּקְרָא מְהֵרָה אֶל־הַנַּעַר נֹשֵׂא כֵלָיו וַיֹּאמֶר לוֹ שְׁלֹף חַרְבְּךָ וּמוֹתְתֵנִי פֶּן־יֹאמְרוּ לִי אִשָּׁה הֲרָגָתְהוּ וַיִּדְקְרֵהוּ נַעֲרוֹ וַיָּמֹת:

55 When the men of *Yisrael* saw that *Avimelech* was dead, everyone went home.

נה וַיִּרְאוּ אִישׁ־יִשְׂרָאֵל כִּי מֵת אֲבִימֶלֶךְ וַיֵּלְכוּ אִישׁ לִמְקֹמוֹ:

56 Thus *Hashem* repaid *Avimelech* for the evil he had done to his father by slaying his seventy brothers;

נו וַיָּשֶׁב אֱלֹהִים אֵת רָעַת אֲבִימֶלֶךְ אֲשֶׁר עָשָׂה לְאָבִיו לַהֲרֹג אֶת־שִׁבְעִים אֶחָיו:

57 and *Hashem* likewise repaid the men of *Shechem* for all their wickedness. And so the curse of *Yotam* son of *Yerubaal* was fulfilled upon them.

נז וְאֵת כָּל־רָעַת אַנְשֵׁי שְׁכֶם הֵשִׁיב אֱלֹהִים בְּרֹאשָׁם וַתָּבֹא אֲלֵיהֶם קִלֲלַת יוֹתָם בֶּן־יְרֻבָּעַל:

10 1 After *Avimelech*, *Tola* son of Puah son of Dodo, a man of *Yissachar*, arose to deliver *Yisrael*. He lived at Shamir in the hill country of *Efraim*.

י א וַיָּקָם אַחֲרֵי אֲבִימֶלֶךְ לְהוֹשִׁיעַ אֶת־יִשְׂרָאֵל תּוֹלָע בֶּן־פּוּאָה בֶּן־דּוֹדוֹ אִישׁ יִשָּׂשכָר וְהוּא־יֹשֵׁב בְּשָׁמִיר בְּהַר אֶפְרָיִם:

2 He led *Yisrael* for twenty-three years; then he died and was buried at Shamir.

ב וַיִּשְׁפֹּט אֶת־יִשְׂרָאֵל עֶשְׂרִים וְשָׁלֹשׁ שָׁנָה וַיָּמָת וַיִּקָּבֵר בְּשָׁמִיר:

³ After him arose *Yair* the Giladite, and he led *Yisrael* for twenty-two years.

ג וַיָּקָם אַחֲרָיו יָאִיר הַגִּלְעָדִי וַיִּשְׁפֹּט אֶת־יִשְׂרָאֵל עֶשְׂרִים וּשְׁתַּיִם שָׁנָה:

⁴ (He had thirty sons, who rode on thirty burros and owned thirty boroughs in the region of *Gilad*; these are called Havvoth-jair to this day.)

ד וַיְהִי־לוֹ שְׁלֹשִׁים בָּנִים רֹכְבִים עַל־שְׁלֹשִׁים עֲיָרִים וּשְׁלֹשִׁים עֲיָרִים לָהֶם לָהֶם יִקְרְאוּ חַוֹּת יָאִיר עַד הַיּוֹם הַזֶּה אֲשֶׁר בְּאֶרֶץ הַגִּלְעָד:

⁵ Then *Yair* died and was buried at Kamon.

ה וַיָּמָת יָאִיר וַיִּקָּבֵר בְּקָמוֹן:

⁶ The Israelites again did what was offensive to *Hashem*. They served the Baalim and the Ashtaroth, and the gods of Aram, the gods of Sidon, the gods of Moab, the gods of the Ammonites, and the gods of the Philistines; they forsook *Hashem* and did not serve Him.

ו וַיֹּסִפוּ בְּנֵי יִשְׂרָאֵל לַעֲשׂוֹת הָרַע בְּעֵינֵי יְהוָה וַיַּעַבְדוּ אֶת־הַבְּעָלִים וְאֶת־הָעַשְׁתָּרוֹת וְאֶת־אֱלֹהֵי אֲרָם וְאֶת־אֱלֹהֵי צִידוֹן וְאֵת אֱלֹהֵי מוֹאָב וְאֵת אֱלֹהֵי בְנֵי־עַמּוֹן וְאֵת אֱלֹהֵי פְלִשְׁתִּים וַיַּעַזְבוּ אֶת־יְהוָה וְלֹא עֲבָדוּהוּ:

⁷ And *Hashem*, incensed with *Yisrael*, surrendered them to the Philistines and to the Ammonites.

ז וַיִּחַר־אַף יְהוָה בְּיִשְׂרָאֵל וַיִּמְכְּרֵם בְּיַד־פְּלִשְׁתִּים וּבְיַד בְּנֵי עַמּוֹן:

va-yi-khar AF a-do-NAI b'-yis-ra-AYL va-yim-k'-RAYM
b'-yad p'-lish-TEEM u-v'-YAD b'-NAY a-MON

⁸ That year they battered and shattered the Israelites – for eighteen years – all the Israelites beyond the *Yarden*, in [what had been] the land of the Amorites in *Gilad*.

ח וַיִּרְעֲצוּ וַיְרֹצְצוּ אֶת־בְּנֵי יִשְׂרָאֵל בַּשָּׁנָה הַהִיא שְׁמֹנֶה עֶשְׂרֵה שָׁנָה אֶת־כָּל־בְּנֵי יִשְׂרָאֵל אֲשֶׁר בְּעֵבֶר הַיַּרְדֵּן בְּאֶרֶץ הָאֱמֹרִי אֲשֶׁר בַּגִּלְעָד:

⁹ The Ammonites also crossed the *Yarden* to make war on *Yehuda*, *Binyamin*, and the House of *Efraim*. *Yisrael* was in great distress.

ט וַיַּעַבְרוּ בְנֵי־עַמּוֹן אֶת־הַיַּרְדֵּן לְהִלָּחֵם גַּם־בִּיהוּדָה וּבְבִנְיָמִין וּבְבֵית אֶפְרָיִם וַתֵּצֶר לְיִשְׂרָאֵל מְאֹד:

¹⁰ Then the Israelites cried out to *Hashem*, "We stand guilty before You, for we have forsaken our God and served the Baalim."

י וַיִּזְעֲקוּ בְּנֵי יִשְׂרָאֵל אֶל־יְהוָה לֵאמֹר חָטָאנוּ לָךְ וְכִי עָזַבְנוּ אֶת־אֱלֹהֵינוּ וַנַּעֲבֹד אֶת־הַבְּעָלִים:

¹¹ But *Hashem* said to the Israelites, "[I have rescued you] from the Egyptians, from the Amorites, from the Ammonites, and from the Philistines.

יא וַיֹּאמֶר יְהוָה אֶל־בְּנֵי יִשְׂרָאֵל הֲלֹא מִמִּצְרַיִם וּמִן־הָאֱמֹרִי וּמִן־בְּנֵי עַמּוֹן וּמִן־פְּלִשְׁתִּים:

¹² The Sidonians, Amalek, and Maon also oppressed you; and when you cried out to Me, I saved you from them.

יב וְצִידוֹנִים וַעֲמָלֵק וּמָעוֹן לָחֲצוּ אֶתְכֶם וַתִּצְעֲקוּ אֵלַי וָאוֹשִׁיעָה אֶתְכֶם מִיָּדָם:

¹³ Yet you have forsaken Me and have served other gods. No, I will not deliver you again.

יג וְאַתֶּם עֲזַבְתֶּם אוֹתִי וַתַּעַבְדוּ אֱלֹהִים אֲחֵרִים לָכֵן לֹא־אוֹסִיף לְהוֹשִׁיעַ אֶתְכֶם:

בארצי

10:7 Surrendered them to the Philistines The Philistines are one of the Israelites' long-term enemies. It is interesting to note, however, that they are not among the seven Canaanite nations who initially inhabited the land. Rather, they are a foreign nation that invaded *Eretz Yisrael* via sea.

Ashkelon, one of the five biblical Philistine cities

Yet despite being neither natives nor the recipients of God's promise of the land, they often succeed in persecuting the Children of Israel and holding large amounts of territory in its land. However, in every case, *Hashem* eventually saves the People of Israel from their enemy.

14 Go cry to the gods you have chosen; let them deliver you in your time of distress!"

יד לְכוּ וְזַעֲקוּ אֶל־הָאֱלֹהִים אֲשֶׁר בְּחַרְתֶּם בָּם הֵמָּה יוֹשִׁיעוּ לָכֶם בְּעֵת צָרַתְכֶם:

15 But the Israelites implored *Hashem*: "We stand guilty. Do to us as You see fit; only save us this day!"

טו וַיֹּאמְרוּ בְנֵי־יִשְׂרָאֵל אֶל־יהוה חָטָאנוּ עֲשֵׂה־אַתָּה לָנוּ כְּכָל־הַטּוֹב בְּעֵינֶיךָ אַךְ הַצִּילֵנוּ נָא הַיּוֹם הַזֶּה:

16 They removed the alien gods from among them and served *Hashem*; and He could not bear the miseries of *Yisrael*.

טז וַיָּסִירוּ אֶת־אֱלֹהֵי הַנֵּכָר מִקִּרְבָּם וַיַּעַבְדוּ אֶת־יהוה וַתִּקְצַר נַפְשׁוֹ בַּעֲמַל יִשְׂרָאֵל:

17 The Ammonites mustered and they encamped in *Gilad*; and the Israelites massed and they encamped at *Mitzpa*.

יז וַיִּצָּעֲקוּ בְּנֵי עַמּוֹן וַיַּחֲנוּ בַּגִּלְעָד וַיֵּאָסְפוּ בְּנֵי יִשְׂרָאֵל וַיַּחֲנוּ בַּמִּצְפָּה:

18 The troops – the officers of *Gilad* – said to one another, "Let the man who is the first to fight the Ammonites be chieftain over all the inhabitants of *Gilad*."

יח וַיֹּאמְרוּ הָעָם שָׂרֵי גִלְעָד אִישׁ אֶל־רֵעֵהוּ מִי הָאִישׁ אֲשֶׁר יָחֵל לְהִלָּחֵם בִּבְנֵי עַמּוֹן יִהְיֶה לְרֹאשׁ לְכֹל יֹשְׁבֵי גִלְעָד:

11 1 *Yiftach* the Giladite was an able warrior, who was the son of a prostitute. *Yiftach*'s father was *Gilad*;

יא א וְיִפְתָּח הַגִּלְעָדִי הָיָה גִּבּוֹר חַיִל וְהוּא בֶּן־אִשָּׁה זוֹנָה וַיּוֹלֶד גִּלְעָד אֶת־יִפְתָּח:

2 but *Gilad* also had sons by his wife, and when the wife's sons grew up, they drove *Yiftach* out. They said to him, "You shall have no share in our father's property, for you are the son of an outsider."

ב וַתֵּלֶד אֵשֶׁת־גִּלְעָד לוֹ בָּנִים וַיִּגְדְּלוּ בְנֵי־הָאִשָּׁה וַיְגָרְשׁוּ אֶת־יִפְתָּח וַיֹּאמְרוּ לוֹ לֹא־תִנְחַל בְּבֵית־אָבִינוּ כִּי בֶּן־אִשָּׁה אַחֶרֶת אָתָּה:

3 So *Yiftach* fled from his brothers and settled in the Tob country. Men of low character gathered about *Yiftach* and went out raiding with him.

ג וַיִּבְרַח יִפְתָּח מִפְּנֵי אֶחָיו וַיֵּשֶׁב בְּאֶרֶץ טוֹב וַיִּתְלַקְּטוּ אֶל־יִפְתָּח אֲנָשִׁים רֵיקִים וַיֵּצְאוּ עִמּוֹ:

4 Some time later, the Ammonites went to war against *Yisrael*.

ד וַיְהִי מִיָּמִים וַיִּלָּחֲמוּ בְנֵי־עַמּוֹן עִם־יִשְׂרָאֵל:

5 And when the Ammonites attacked *Yisrael*, the elders of *Gilad* went to bring *Yiftach* back from the Tob country.

ה וַיְהִי כַּאֲשֶׁר־נִלְחֲמוּ בְנֵי־עַמּוֹן עִם־יִשְׂרָאֵל וַיֵּלְכוּ זִקְנֵי גִלְעָד לָקַחַת אֶת־יִפְתָּח מֵאֶרֶץ טוֹב:

6 They said to *Yiftach*, "Come be our chief, so that we can fight the Ammonites."

ו וַיֹּאמְרוּ לְיִפְתָּח לְכָה וְהָיִיתָה לָּנוּ לְקָצִין וְנִלָּחֲמָה בִּבְנֵי עַמּוֹן:

7 *Yiftach* replied to the elders of *Gilad*, "You are the very people who rejected me and drove me out of my father's house. How can you come to me now when you are in trouble?"

ז וַיֹּאמֶר יִפְתָּח לְזִקְנֵי גִלְעָד הֲלֹא אַתֶּם שְׂנֵאתֶם אוֹתִי וַתְּגָרְשׁוּנִי מִבֵּית אָבִי וּמַדּוּעַ בָּאתֶם אֵלַי עַתָּה כַּאֲשֶׁר צַר לָכֶם:

8 The elders of *Gilad* said to *Yiftach*, "Honestly, we have now turned back to you. If you come with us and fight the Ammonites, you shall be our commander over all the inhabitants of *Gilad*."

ח וַיֹּאמְרוּ זִקְנֵי גִלְעָד אֶל־יִפְתָּח לָכֵן עַתָּה שַׁבְנוּ אֵלֶיךָ וְהָלַכְתָּ עִמָּנוּ וְנִלְחַמְתָּ בִּבְנֵי עַמּוֹן וְהָיִיתָ לָּנוּ לְרֹאשׁ לְכֹל יֹשְׁבֵי גִלְעָד:

9 *Yiftach* said to the elders of *Gilad*, "[Very well,] if you bring me back to fight the Ammonites and *Hashem* delivers them to me, I am to be your commander."

ט וַיֹּאמֶר יִפְתָּח אֶל־זִקְנֵי גִלְעָד אִם־מְשִׁיבִים אַתֶּם אוֹתִי לְהִלָּחֵם בִּבְנֵי עַמּוֹן וְנָתַן יְהֹוָה אוֹתָם לְפָנָי אָנֹכִי אֶהְיֶה לָכֶם לְרֹאשׁ:

10 And the elders of *Gilad* answered Jepthah, "*Hashem* Himself shall be witness between us: we will do just as you have said."

י וַיֹּאמְרוּ זִקְנֵי־גִלְעָד אֶל־יִפְתָּח יְהֹוָה יִהְיֶה שֹׁמֵעַ בֵּינוֹתֵינוּ אִם־לֹא כִדְבָרְךָ כֵּן נַעֲשֶׂה:

11 *Yiftach* went with the elders of *Gilad*, and the people made him their commander and chief. And *Yiftach* repeated all these terms before *Hashem* at Mitzpa.

יא וַיֵּלֶךְ יִפְתָּח עִם־זִקְנֵי גִלְעָד וַיָּשִׂימוּ הָעָם אוֹתוֹ עֲלֵיהֶם לְרֹאשׁ וּלְקָצִין וַיְדַבֵּר יִפְתָּח אֶת־כָּל־דְּבָרָיו לִפְנֵי יְהֹוָה בַּמִּצְפָּה:

12 *Yiftach* then sent messengers to the king of the Ammonites, saying, "What have you against me that you have come to make war on my country?"

יב וַיִּשְׁלַח יִפְתָּח מַלְאָכִים אֶל־מֶלֶךְ בְּנֵי־עַמּוֹן לֵאמֹר מַה־לִּי וָלָךְ כִּי־בָאתָ אֵלַי לְהִלָּחֵם בְּאַרְצִי:

va-yish-LAKH yif-TAKH mal-a-KHEEM el ME-lekh b'-nay a-MON lay-MOR mah LEE va-LAKH kee VA-ta ay-LAI l'-hi-la-KHAYM b'-ar-TZEE

13 The king of the Ammonites replied to *Yiftach's* messengers, "When *Yisrael* came from Egypt, they seized the land which is mine, from the Arnon to the Jabbok as far as the *Yarden*. Now, then, restore it peaceably."

יג וַיֹּאמֶר מֶלֶךְ בְּנֵי־עַמּוֹן אֶל־מַלְאֲכֵי יִפְתָּח כִּי־לָקַח יִשְׂרָאֵל אֶת־אַרְצִי בַּעֲלוֹתוֹ מִמִּצְרַיִם מֵאַרְנוֹן וְעַד־הַיַּבֹּק וְעַד־הַיַּרְדֵּן וְעַתָּה הָשִׁיבָה אֶתְהֶן בְּשָׁלוֹם:

14 *Yiftach* again sent messengers to the king of the Ammonites.

יד וַיּוֹסֶף עוֹד יִפְתָּח וַיִּשְׁלַח מַלְאָכִים אֶל־מֶלֶךְ בְּנֵי עַמּוֹן:

15 He said to him, "Thus said *Yiftach*: *Yisrael* did not seize the land of Moab or the land of the Ammonites.

טו וַיֹּאמֶר לוֹ כֹּה אָמַר יִפְתָּח לֹא־לָקַח יִשְׂרָאֵל אֶת־אֶרֶץ מוֹאָב וְאֶת־אֶרֶץ בְּנֵי עַמּוֹן:

16 When they left Egypt, *Yisrael* traveled through the wilderness to the Sea of Reeds and went on to Kadesh.

טז כִּי בַּעֲלוֹתָם מִמִּצְרָיִם וַיֵּלֶךְ יִשְׂרָאֵל בַּמִּדְבָּר עַד־יַם־סוּף וַיָּבֹא קָדֵשָׁה:

17 *Yisrael* then sent messengers to the king of Edom, saying, 'Allow us to cross your country.' But the king of Edom would not consent. They also sent a mission to the king of Moab, and he refused. So *Yisrael*, after staying at Kadesh,

יז וַיִּשְׁלַח יִשְׂרָאֵל מַלְאָכִים אֶל־מֶלֶךְ אֱדוֹם לֵאמֹר אֶעְבְּרָה־נָּא בְאַרְצֶךָ וְלֹא שָׁמַע מֶלֶךְ אֱדוֹם וְגַם אֶל־מֶלֶךְ מוֹאָב שָׁלַח וְלֹא אָבָה וַיֵּשֶׁב יִשְׂרָאֵל בְּקָדֵשׁ:

 11:12 *Yiftach* then sent messengers to the king of the Ammonites As *Moshe* and *Yehoshua* did before him, *Yiftach* tries to avoid war by sending a message to the enemy. The Children of Israel always offer their adversaries a choice between three options: make peace, flee the land, or fight. Although war is the least desirable choice, peace is not to be obtained at any price. In his message to the Ammonites, *Yiftach* emphasized that they were seeking to make war *b'artzee* (בארצי), meaning 'on my country' or, more literally, 'in my land.' *Hashem* has given the Land of Israel to the Children of Israel, and therefore their struggle to possess it is by divine right.

An Israeli flag flying near the Western Wall

18 traveled on through the wilderness, skirting the land of Edom and the land of Moab. They kept to the east of the land of Moab until they encamped on the other side of the Arnon; and, since Moab ends at the Arnon, they never entered Moabite territory.

יח וַיֵּלֶךְ בַּמִּדְבָּר וַיָּסָב אֶת־אֶרֶץ אֱדוֹם וְאֶת־אֶרֶץ מוֹאָב וַיָּבֹא מִמִּזְרַח־שֶׁמֶשׁ לְאֶרֶץ מוֹאָב וַיַּחֲנוּן בְּעֵבֶר אַרְנוֹן וְלֹא־בָאוּ בִּגְבוּל מוֹאָב כִּי אַרְנוֹן גְּבוּל מוֹאָב:

19 "Then *Yisrael* sent messengers to Sihon king of the Amorites, the king of Heshbon. *Yisrael* said to him, 'Allow us to cross through your country to our homeland.'

יט וַיִּשְׁלַח יִשְׂרָאֵל מַלְאָכִים אֶל־סִיחוֹן מֶלֶךְ־הָאֱמֹרִי מֶלֶךְ חֶשְׁבּוֹן וַיֹּאמֶר לוֹ יִשְׂרָאֵל נַעְבְּרָה־נָּא בְאַרְצְךָ עַד־מְקוֹמִי:

20 But Sihon would not trust *Yisrael* to pass through his territory. Sihon mustered all his troops, and they encamped at Jahaz; he engaged *Yisrael* in battle.

כ וְלֹא־הֶאֱמִין סִיחוֹן אֶת־יִשְׂרָאֵל עֲבֹר בִּגְבֻלוֹ וַיֶּאֱסֹף סִיחוֹן אֶת־כָּל־עַמּוֹ וַיַּחֲנוּ בְּיָהְצָה וַיִּלָּחֶם עִם־יִשְׂרָאֵל:

21 But *Hashem*, the God of *Yisrael*, delivered Sihon and all his troops into *Yisrael*'s hands, and they defeated them; and *Yisrael* took possession of all the land of the Amorites, the inhabitants of that land.

כא וַיִּתֵּן יְהֹוָה אֱלֹהֵי־יִשְׂרָאֵל אֶת־סִיחוֹן וְאֶת־כָּל־עַמּוֹ בְּיַד יִשְׂרָאֵל וַיַּכּוּם וַיִּירַשׁ יִשְׂרָאֵל אֵת כָּל־אֶרֶץ הָאֱמֹרִי יוֹשֵׁב הָאָרֶץ הַהִיא:

22 Thus they possessed all the territory of the Amorites from the Arnon to the Jabbok and from the wilderness to the *Yarden*.

כב וַיִּירְשׁוּ אֵת כָּל־גְּבוּל הָאֱמֹרִי מֵאַרְנוֹן וְעַד־הַיַּבֹּק וּמִן־הַמִּדְבָּר וְעַד־הַיַּרְדֵּן:

23 "Now, then, *Hashem*, the God of *Yisrael*, dispossessed the Amorites before His people *Yisrael*; and should you possess their land?

כג וְעַתָּה יְהֹוָה אֱלֹהֵי יִשְׂרָאֵל הוֹרִישׁ אֶת־הָאֱמֹרִי מִפְּנֵי עַמּוֹ יִשְׂרָאֵל וְאַתָּה תִּירָשֶׁנּוּ:

24 Do you not hold what Chemosh your god gives you to possess? So we will hold on to everything that *Hashem* our God has given us to possess.

כד הֲלֹא אֵת אֲשֶׁר יוֹרִישְׁךָ כְּמוֹשׁ אֱלֹהֶיךָ אוֹתוֹ תִירָשׁ וְאֵת כָּל־אֲשֶׁר הוֹרִישׁ יְהֹוָה אֱלֹהֵינוּ מִפָּנֵינוּ אוֹתוֹ נִירָשׁ:

25 "Besides, are you any better than Balak son of Zippor, king of Moab? Did he start a quarrel with *Yisrael* or go to war with them?

כה וְעַתָּה הֲטוֹב טוֹב אַתָּה מִבָּלָק בֶּן־צִפּוֹר מֶלֶךְ מוֹאָב הֲרוֹב רָב עִם־יִשְׂרָאֵל אִם־נִלְחֹם נִלְחַם בָּם:

26 "While *Yisrael* has been inhabiting Heshbon and its dependencies, and Aroer and its dependencies, and all the towns along the Arnon for three hundred years, why have you not tried to recover them all this time?

כו בְּשֶׁבֶת יִשְׂרָאֵל בְּחֶשְׁבּוֹן וּבִבְנוֹתֶיהָ וּבְעַרְעוֹר וּבִבְנוֹתֶיהָ וּבְכָל־הֶעָרִים אֲשֶׁר עַל־יְדֵי אַרְנוֹן שְׁלֹשׁ מֵאוֹת שָׁנָה וּמַדּוּעַ לֹא־הִצַּלְתֶּם בָּעֵת הַהִיא:

27 I have done you no wrong; yet you are doing me harm and making war on me. May *Hashem*, who judges, decide today between the Israelites and the Ammonites!"

כז וְאָנֹכִי לֹא־חָטָאתִי לָךְ וְאַתָּה עֹשֶׂה אִתִּי רָעָה לְהִלָּחֶם בִּי יִשְׁפֹּט יְהֹוָה הַשֹּׁפֵט הַיּוֹם בֵּין בְּנֵי יִשְׂרָאֵל וּבֵין בְּנֵי עַמּוֹן:

28 But the king of the Ammonites paid no heed to the message that *Yiftach* sent him.

כח וְלֹא שָׁמַע מֶלֶךְ בְּנֵי עַמּוֹן אֶל־דִּבְרֵי יִפְתָּח אֲשֶׁר שָׁלַח אֵלָיו:

Judges

²⁹ Then the spirit of *Hashem* came upon *Yiftach*. He marched through *Gilad* and *Menashe*, passing Mizpeh of *Gilad*; and from Mizpeh of *Gilad* he crossed over [to] the Ammonites.

כט וַתְּהִי עַל־יִפְתָּח רוּחַ יְהֹוָה וַיַּעֲבֹר אֶת־הַגִּלְעָד וְאֶת־מְנַשֶּׁה וַיַּעֲבֹר אֶת־מִצְפֵּה גִלְעָד וּמִמִּצְפֵּה גִלְעָד עָבַר בְּנֵי עַמּוֹן:

³⁰ And *Yiftach* made the following vow to *Hashem*: "If you deliver the Ammonites into my hands,

ל וַיִּדַּר יִפְתָּח נֶדֶר לַיהֹוָה וַיֹּאמַר אִם־נָתוֹן תִּתֵּן אֶת־בְּנֵי עַמּוֹן בְּיָדִי:

³¹ then whatever comes out of the door of my house to meet me on my safe return from the Ammonites shall be *Hashem*'s and shall be offered by me as a burnt offering."

לא וְהָיָה הַיּוֹצֵא אֲשֶׁר יֵצֵא מִדַּלְתֵי בֵיתִי לִקְרָאתִי בְּשׁוּבִי בְשָׁלוֹם מִבְּנֵי עַמּוֹן וְהָיָה לַיהֹוָה וְהַעֲלִיתִהוּ עוֹלָה:

³² *Yiftach* crossed over to the Ammonites and attacked them, and *Hashem* delivered them into his hands.

לב וַיַּעֲבֹר יִפְתָּח אֶל־בְּנֵי עַמּוֹן לְהִלָּחֶם בָּם וַיִּתְּנֵם יְהֹוָה בְּיָדוֹ:

³³ He utterly routed them – from Aroer as far as Minnith, twenty towns – all the way to Abel-cheramim. So the Ammonites submitted to the Israelites.

לג וַיַּכֵּם מֵעֲרוֹעֵר וְעַד־בּוֹאֲךָ מִנִּית עֶשְׂרִים עִיר וְעַד אָבֵל כְּרָמִים מַכָּה גְּדוֹלָה מְאֹד וַיִּכָּנְעוּ בְּנֵי עַמּוֹן מִפְּנֵי בְּנֵי יִשְׂרָאֵל:

³⁴ When *Yiftach* arrived at his home in *Mitzpa*, there was his daughter coming out to meet him, with timbrel and dance! She was an only child; he had no other son or daughter.

לד וַיָּבֹא יִפְתָּח הַמִּצְפָּה אֶל־בֵּיתוֹ וְהִנֵּה בִתּוֹ יֹצֵאת לִקְרָאתוֹ בְּתֻפִּים וּבִמְחֹלוֹת וְרַק הִיא יְחִידָה אֵין־לוֹ מִמֶּנּוּ בֵּן אוֹ־בַת:

³⁵ On seeing her, he rent his clothes and said, "Alas, daughter! You have brought me low; you have become my troubler! For I have uttered a vow to *Hashem* and I cannot retract."

לה וַיְהִי כִרְאוֹתוֹ אוֹתָהּ וַיִּקְרַע אֶת־בְּגָדָיו וַיֹּאמֶר אֲהָהּ בִּתִּי הַכְרֵעַ הִכְרַעְתִּנִי וְאַתְּ הָיִית בְּעֹכְרָי וְאָנֹכִי פָּצִיתִי־פִי אֶל־יְהֹוָה וְלֹא אוּכַל לָשׁוּב:

³⁶ "Father," she said, "you have uttered a vow to *Hashem*; do to me as you have vowed, seeing that *Hashem* has vindicated you against your enemies, the Ammonites."

לו וַתֹּאמֶר אֵלָיו אָבִי פָּצִיתָה אֶת־פִּיךָ אֶל־יְהֹוָה עֲשֵׂה לִי כַּאֲשֶׁר יָצָא מִפִּיךָ אַחֲרֵי אֲשֶׁר עָשָׂה לְךָ יְהֹוָה נְקָמוֹת מֵאֹיְבֶיךָ מִבְּנֵי עַמּוֹן:

³⁷ She further said to her father, "Let this be done for me: let me be for two months, and I will go with my companions and lament upon the hills and there bewail my maidenhood."

לז וַתֹּאמֶר אֶל־אָבִיהָ יֵעָשֶׂה לִּי הַדָּבָר הַזֶּה הַרְפֵּה מִמֶּנִּי שְׁנַיִם חֳדָשִׁים וְאֵלְכָה וְיָרַדְתִּי עַל־הֶהָרִים וְאֶבְכֶּה עַל־בְּתוּלַי אָנֹכִי וְרֵעוֹתָי [וְרֵעוֹתָי]:

³⁸ "Go," he replied. He let her go for two months, and she and her companions went and bewailed her maidenhood upon the hills.

לח וַיֹּאמֶר לֵכִי וַיִּשְׁלַח אוֹתָהּ שְׁנֵי חֳדָשִׁים וַתֵּלֶךְ הִיא וְרֵעוֹתֶיהָ וַתֵּבְךְּ עַל־בְּתוּלֶיהָ עַל־הֶהָרִים:

³⁹ After two months' time, she returned to her father, and he did to her as he had vowed. She had never known a man. So it became a custom in *Yisrael*

לט וַיְהִי מִקֵּץ שְׁנַיִם חֳדָשִׁים וַתָּשָׁב אֶל־אָבִיהָ וַיַּעַשׂ לָהּ אֶת־נִדְרוֹ אֲשֶׁר נָדָר וְהִיא לֹא־יָדְעָה אִישׁ וַתְּהִי־חֹק בְּיִשְׂרָאֵל:

⁴⁰ for the maidens of *Yisrael* to go every year, for four days in the year, and chant dirges for the daughter of *Yiftach* the Giladite.

מ מִיָּמִים יָמִימָה תֵּלַכְנָה בְּנוֹת יִשְׂרָאֵל לְתַנּוֹת לְבַת־יִפְתָּח הַגִּלְעָדִי אַרְבַּעַת יָמִים בַּשָּׁנָה:

12 1 The men of *Efraim* mustered and crossed [the *Yarden*] to Zaphon. They said to *Yiftach*, "Why did you march to fight the Ammonites without calling us to go with you? We'll burn your house down over you!"

2 *Yiftach* answered them, "I and my people were in a bitter conflict with the Ammonites; and I summoned you, but you did not save me from them.

3 When I saw that you were no saviors, I risked my life and advanced against the Ammonites; and *Hashem* delivered them into my hands. Why have you come here now to fight against me?"

4 And *Yiftach* gathered all the men of *Gilad* and fought the Ephraimites. The men of *Gilad* defeated the Ephraimites; for they had said, "You Giladites are nothing but fugitives from *Efraim* – being in *Menashe* is like being in *Efraim*."

5 The Giladites held the fords of the *Yarden* against the Ephraimites. And when any fugitive from *Efraim* said, "Let me cross," the men of *Gilad* would ask him, "Are you an Ephraimites?"; if he said "No,"

6 they would say to him, "Then say shibboleth"; but he would say "sibboleth," not being able to pronounce it correctly. Thereupon they would seize him and slay him by the fords of the *Yarden*. Forty-two thousand Ephraimites fell at that time.

7 *Yiftach* led *Yisrael* six years. Then *Yiftach* the Giladite died and he was buried in one of the towns of *Gilad*.

8 After him, *Ivtzan* of *Beit Lechem* led *Yisrael*.

va-yish-POT a-kha-RAV et yis-ra-AYL iv-TZAN mi-BAYT LA-khem

9 He had thirty sons, and he married off thirty daughters outside the clan and brought in thirty girls from outside the clan for his sons. He led *Yisrael* seven years.

יב א וַיִּצָּעֵק אִישׁ אֶפְרַיִם וַיַּעֲבֹר צָפוֹנָה וַיֹּאמְרוּ לְיִפְתָּח מַדּוּעַ עָבַרְתָּ לְהִלָּחֵם בִּבְנֵי־עַמּוֹן וְלָנוּ לֹא קָרָאתָ לָלֶכֶת עִמָּךְ בֵּיתְךָ נִשְׂרֹף עָלֶיךָ בָּאֵשׁ:

ב וַיֹּאמֶר יִפְתָּח אֲלֵיהֶם אִישׁ רִיב הָיִיתִי אֲנִי וְעַמִּי וּבְנֵי־עַמּוֹן מְאֹד וָאֶזְעַק אֶתְכֶם וְלֹא־הוֹשַׁעְתֶּם אוֹתִי מִיָּדָם:

ג וָאֶרְאֶה כִּי־אֵינְךָ מוֹשִׁיעַ וָאָשִׂימָה נַפְשִׁי בְכַפִּי וָאֶעְבְּרָה אֶל־בְּנֵי עַמּוֹן וַיִּתְּנֵם יְהוָה בְּיָדִי וְלָמָה עֲלִיתֶם אֵלַי הַיּוֹם הַזֶּה לְהִלָּחֶם בִּי:

ד וַיִּקְבֹּץ יִפְתָּח אֶת־כָּל־אַנְשֵׁי גִלְעָד וַיִּלָּחֶם אֶת־אֶפְרָיִם וַיַּכּוּ אַנְשֵׁי גִלְעָד אֶת־אֶפְרַיִם כִּי אָמְרוּ פְּלִיטֵי אֶפְרַיִם אַתֶּם גִּלְעָד בְּתוֹךְ אֶפְרַיִם בְּתוֹךְ מְנַשֶּׁה:

ה וַיִּלְכֹּד גִּלְעָד אֶת־מַעְבְּרוֹת הַיַּרְדֵּן לְאֶפְרָיִם וְהָיָה כִּי יֹאמְרוּ פְּלִיטֵי אֶפְרַיִם אֶעֱבֹרָה וַיֹּאמְרוּ לוֹ אַנְשֵׁי־גִלְעָד הַאֶפְרָתִי אַתָּה וַיֹּאמֶר לֹא:

ו וַיֹּאמְרוּ לוֹ אֱמָר־נָא שִׁבֹּלֶת וַיֹּאמֶר סִבֹּלֶת וְלֹא יָכִין לְדַבֵּר כֵּן וַיֹּאחֲזוּ אוֹתוֹ וַיִּשְׁחָטוּהוּ אֶל־מַעְבְּרוֹת הַיַּרְדֵּן וַיִּפֹּל בָּעֵת הַהִיא מֵאֶפְרַיִם אַרְבָּעִים וּשְׁנַיִם אָלֶף:

ז וַיִּשְׁפֹּט יִפְתָּח אֶת־יִשְׂרָאֵל שֵׁשׁ שָׁנִים וַיָּמָת יִפְתָּח הַגִּלְעָדִי וַיִּקָּבֵר בְּעָרֵי גִלְעָד:

ח וַיִּשְׁפֹּט אַחֲרָיו אֶת־יִשְׂרָאֵל אִבְצָן מִבֵּית לָחֶם:

ט וַיְהִי־לוֹ שְׁלֹשִׁים בָּנִים וּשְׁלֹשִׁים בָּנוֹת שִׁלַּח הַחוּצָה וּשְׁלֹשִׁים בָּנוֹת הֵבִיא לְבָנָיו מִן־הַחוּץ וַיִּשְׁפֹּט אֶת־יִשְׂרָאֵל שֶׁבַע שָׁנִים:

12:8 *Ivtzan* of *Beit Lechem* led *Yisrael* According to the Talmud (*Bava Batra* 91a), the judge called *Ivtzan* mentioned in this verse is none other than *Boaz*, one of the heroes of *Megillat Rut*. At the climax of that dramatic narrative, *Boaz* marries the poor Moabite convert *Rut*. Their descendants include King *David*, and will ultimately

Statue of King *David* in *Yerushalayim*

also include the righteous *Mashiach*. *Ivtzan* has sixty children. But it is a unique child, born as a result of his kindness to a poor convert, who is the ancestor of the redeemer of Israel. *Hashem* indeed finds many ways to take care of the People of Israel, and to reward acts of kindness.

Judges

¹⁰ Then *Ivtzan* died and was buried in *Beit Lechem*.

י וַיָּמׇת אִבְצָן וַיִּקָּבֵר בְּבֵית לָחֶם׃

¹¹ After him, *Eilon* the Zebulunite led *Yisrael*; he led *Yisrael* for ten years.

יא וַיִּשְׁפֹּט אַחֲרָיו אֶת־יִשְׂרָאֵל אֵילוֹן הַזְּבֽוּלֹנִי וַיִּשְׁפֹּט אֶת־יִשְׂרָאֵל עֶשֶׂר שָׁנִֽים׃

¹² Then *Eilon* the Zebulunite died and was buried in Aijalon, in the territory of *Zevulun*.

יב וַיָּמׇת אֵלוֹן הַזְּבֽוּלֹנִי וַיִּקָּבֵר בְּאַיָּלוֹן בְּאֶרֶץ זְבוּלֻֽן׃

¹³ After him, *Avdon* son of Hillel the Pirathonite led *Yisrael*.

יג וַיִּשְׁפֹּט אַחֲרָיו אֶת־יִשְׂרָאֵל עַבְדּוֹן בֶּן־הִלֵּל הַפִּרְעָתֽוֹנִי׃

¹⁴ He had forty sons and thirty grandsons, who rode on seventy jackasses. He led *Yisrael* for eight years.

יד וַֽיְהִי־לוֹ אַרְבָּעִים בָּנִים וּשְׁלֹשִׁים בְּנֵי בָנִים רֹֽכְבִים עַל־שִׁבְעִים עֲיָרִם וַיִּשְׁפֹּט אֶת־יִשְׂרָאֵל שְׁמֹנֶה שָׁנִֽים׃

¹⁵ Then *Avdon* son of Hillel the Pirathonite died. He was buried in Pirathon, in the territory of *Efraim*, on the hill of the Amalekites.

טו וַיָּמׇת עַבְדּוֹן בֶּן־הִלֵּל הַפִּרְעָתוֹנִי וַיִּקָּבֵר בְּפִרְעָתוֹן בְּאֶרֶץ אֶפְרַיִם בְּהַר הָעֲמָלֵקִֽי׃

13 ¹ *B'nei Yisrael* again did what was offensive to *Hashem*, and *Hashem* delivered them into the hands of the Philistines for forty years.

א וַיֹּסִפוּ בְּנֵי יִשְׂרָאֵל לַעֲשׂוֹת הָרַע בְּעֵינֵי יְהֹוָה וַיִּתְּנֵם יְהֹוָה בְּיַד־פְּלִשְׁתִּים אַרְבָּעִים שָׁנָֽה׃

² There was a certain man from *Tzora*, of the stock of *Dan*, whose name was *Manoach*. His wife was barren and had borne no children.

ב וַיְהִי אִישׁ אֶחָד מִצׇּרְעָה מִמִּשְׁפַּחַת הַדָּנִי וּשְׁמוֹ מָנוֹחַ וְאִשְׁתּוֹ עֲקָרָה וְלֹא יָלָֽדָה׃

³ An angel of *Hashem* appeared to the woman and said to her, "You are barren and have borne no children; but you shall conceive and bear a son.

ג וַיֵּרָא מַלְאַךְ־יְהֹוָה אֶל־הָאִשָּׁה וַיֹּאמֶר אֵלֶיהָ הִנֵּה־נָא אַתְּ־עֲקָרָה וְלֹא יָלַדְתְּ וְהָרִית וְיָלַדְתְּ בֵּֽן׃

⁴ Now be careful not to drink wine or other intoxicant, or to eat anything unclean.

ד וְעַתָּה הִשָּׁמְרִי נָא וְאַל־תִּשְׁתִּי יַיִן וְשֵׁכָר וְאַל־תֹּאכְלִי כׇּל־טָמֵֽא׃

⁵ For you are going to conceive and bear a son; let no razor touch his head, for the boy is to be a nazirite to *Hashem* from the womb on. He shall be the first to deliver *Yisrael* from the Philistines."

ה כִּי הִנָּךְ הָרָה וְיֹלַדְתְּ בֵּן וּמוֹרָה לֹא־יַעֲלֶה עַל־רֹאשׁוֹ כִּי־נְזִיר אֱלֹהִים יִהְיֶה הַנַּעַר מִן־הַבָּטֶן וְהוּא יָחֵל לְהוֹשִׁיעַ אֶת־יִשְׂרָאֵל מִיַּד פְּלִשְׁתִּֽים׃

KEE hi-NAKH ha-RAH v'-yo-LAD-t' BAYN u-mo-RAH lo ya-a-LEH al ro-SHO kee n'-ZEER e-lo-HEEM yih-YEH ha-NA-ar min ha-BA-ten v'-HU ya-KHAYL l'-ho-SHEE-a et yis-ra-AYL mi-YAD p'-lish-TEEM

Rabbi David Cohen, Nazir of Jerusalem (1887–1972)

13:5 For the boy is to be a nazirite to *Hashem* from the womb on The promised child, who will be the strong and fearless judge *Shimshon*, is to be a nazirite from birth. This is an unusual situation; most nazirites choose this status temporarily, for a limited period. Though typically people do not take such vows nowadays, a famous exception was Rabbi David Cohen (1887–1972). Known as "The *Nazir*," 'nazirite,' he was a close student of Rabbi Abraham Isaac Kook, and was a nazirite for most of his life. Following his move to *Eretz Yisrael*,

Rabbi Cohen also refused to leave Jerusalem. Along with Rabbi Tzvi Yehuda Kook, he was brought by his students serving in the Israeli Army to the Western Wall shortly after its liberation during the Six Day War. When secular Israeli soldiers saw Rabbis Cohen and Kook at the *Kotel* in the midst of the war, they gasped and pointed, assuming the two saintly rabbis were none other than the *Mashiach* and the Prophet *Eliyahu*. The *Nazir of Yerushalayim* was a reminder of the holiness that special people can achieve, even today.

6 The woman went and told her husband, "A man of *Hashem* came to me; he looked like an angel of *Hashem*, very frightening. I did not ask him where he was from, nor did he tell me his name.

7 He said to me, 'You are going to conceive and bear a son. Drink no wine or other intoxicant, and eat nothing unclean, for the boy is to be a nazirite to *Hashem* from the womb to the day of his death!'"

8 *Manoach* pleaded with *Hashem*. "Oh, my Lord!" he said, "please let the man of *Hashem* that You sent come to us again, and let him instruct us how to act with the child that is to be born."

9 *Hashem* heeded *Manoach*'s plea, and the angel of *Hashem* came to the woman again. She was sitting in the field and her husband *Manoach* was not with her.

10 The woman ran in haste to tell her husband. She said to him, "The man who came to me before has just appeared to me."

11 *Manoach* promptly followed his wife. He came to the man and asked him: "Are you the man who spoke to my wife?" "Yes," he answered.

12 Then *Manoach* said, "May your words soon come true! What rules shall be observed for the boy?"

13 The angel of *Hashem* said to *Manoach*, "The woman must abstain from all the things against which I warned her.

14 She must not eat anything that comes from the grapevine, or drink wine or other intoxicant, or eat anything unclean. She must observe all that I commanded her."

15 *Manoach* said to the angel of *Hashem*, "Let us detain you and prepare a kid for you."

16 But the angel of *Hashem* said to *Manoach*, "If you detain me, I shall not eat your food; and if you present a burnt offering, offer it to *Hashem*." – For *Manoach* did not know that he was an angel of *Hashem*.

17 So *Manoach* said to the angel of *Hashem*, "What is your name? We should like to honor you when your words come true."

ו וַתָּבֹא הָאִשָּׁה וַתֹּאמֶר לְאִישָׁהּ לֵאמֹר אִישׁ הָאֱלֹהִים בָּא אֵלַי וּמַרְאֵהוּ כְּמַרְאֵה מַלְאַךְ הָאֱלֹהִים נוֹרָא מְאֹד וְלֹא שְׁאִלְתִּיהוּ אֵי־מִזֶּה הוּא וְאֶת־שְׁמוֹ לֹא־הִגִּיד לִי:

ז וַיֹּאמֶר לִי הִנָּךְ הָרָה וְיֹלַדְתְּ בֵּן וְעַתָּה אַל־תִּשְׁתִּי יַיִן וְשֵׁכָר וְאַל־תֹּאכְלִי כָּל־טֻמְאָה כִּי־נְזִיר אֱלֹהִים יִהְיֶה הַנַּעַר מִן־הַבֶּטֶן עַד־יוֹם מוֹתוֹ:

ח וַיֶּעְתַּר מָנוֹחַ אֶל־יְהֹוָה וַיֹּאמַר בִּי אֲדוֹנָי אִישׁ הָאֱלֹהִים אֲשֶׁר שָׁלַחְתָּ יָבוֹא־נָא עוֹד אֵלֵינוּ וְיוֹרֵנוּ מַה־נַּעֲשֶׂה לַנַּעַר הַיּוּלָּד:

ט וַיִּשְׁמַע הָאֱלֹהִים בְּקוֹל מָנוֹחַ וַיָּבֹא מַלְאַךְ הָאֱלֹהִים עוֹד אֶל־הָאִשָּׁה וְהִיא יוֹשֶׁבֶת בַּשָּׂדֶה וּמָנוֹחַ אִישָׁהּ אֵין עִמָּהּ:

י וַתְּמַהֵר הָאִשָּׁה וַתָּרָץ וַתַּגֵּד לְאִישָׁהּ וַתֹּאמֶר אֵלָיו הִנֵּה נִרְאָה אֵלַי הָאִישׁ אֲשֶׁר־בָּא בַיּוֹם אֵלָי:

יא וַיָּקָם וַיֵּלֶךְ מָנוֹחַ אַחֲרֵי אִשְׁתּוֹ וַיָּבֹא אֶל־הָאִישׁ וַיֹּאמֶר לוֹ הַאַתָּה הָאִישׁ אֲשֶׁר־דִּבַּרְתָּ אֶל־הָאִשָּׁה וַיֹּאמֶר אָנִי:

יב וַיֹּאמֶר מָנוֹחַ עַתָּה יָבֹא דְבָרֶיךָ מַה־יִּהְיֶה מִשְׁפַּט־הַנַּעַר וּמַעֲשֵׂהוּ:

יג וַיֹּאמֶר מַלְאַךְ יְהֹוָה אֶל־מָנוֹחַ מִכֹּל אֲשֶׁר־אָמַרְתִּי אֶל־הָאִשָּׁה תִּשָּׁמֵר:

יד מִכֹּל אֲשֶׁר־יֵצֵא מִגֶּפֶן הַיַּיִן לֹא תֹאכַל וְיַיִן וְשֵׁכָר אַל־תֵּשְׁתְּ וְכָל־טֻמְאָה אַל־תֹּאכַל כֹּל אֲשֶׁר־צִוִּיתִיהָ תִּשְׁמֹר:

טו וַיֹּאמֶר מָנוֹחַ אֶל־מַלְאַךְ יְהֹוָה נַעְצְרָה־נָּא אוֹתָךְ וְנַעֲשֶׂה לְפָנֶיךָ גְּדִי עִזִּים:

טז וַיֹּאמֶר מַלְאַךְ יְהֹוָה אֶל־מָנוֹחַ אִם־תַּעְצְרֵנִי לֹא־אֹכַל בְּלַחְמֶךָ וְאִם־תַּעֲשֶׂה עֹלָה לַיהֹוָה תַּעֲלֶנָּה כִּי לֹא־יָדַע מָנוֹחַ כִּי־מַלְאַךְ יְהֹוָה הוּא:

יז וַיֹּאמֶר מָנוֹחַ אֶל־מַלְאַךְ יְהֹוָה מִי שְׁמֶךָ כִּי־יָבֹא דבריך [דְבָרְךָ] וְכִבַּדְנוּךָ:

18 The angel said to him, "You must not ask for my name; it is unknowable!"

יח וַיֹּאמֶר לוֹ מַלְאַךְ יְהוָה לָמָּה זֶּה תִּשְׁאַל לִשְׁמִי וְהוּא־פֶלִאי:

19 *Manoach* took the kid and the meal offering and offered them up on the rock to *Hashem*; and a marvelous thing happened while *Manoach* and his wife looked on.

יט וַיִּקַּח מָנוֹחַ אֶת־גְּדִי הָעִזִּים וְאֶת־הַמִּנְחָה וַיַּעַל עַל־הַצּוּר לַיהוָה וּמַפְלִא לַעֲשׂוֹת וּמָנוֹחַ וְאִשְׁתּוֹ רֹאִים:

20 As the flames leaped up from the *Mizbayach* toward the sky, the angel of *Hashem* ascended in the flames of the *Mizbayach*, while *Manoach* and his wife looked on; and they flung themselves on their faces to the ground.

כ וַיְהִי בַעֲלוֹת הַלַּהַב מֵעַל הַמִּזְבֵּחַ הַשָּׁמַיְמָה וַיַּעַל מַלְאַךְ־יְהוָה בְּלַהַב הַמִּזְבֵּחַ וּמָנוֹחַ וְאִשְׁתּוֹ רֹאִים וַיִּפְּלוּ עַל־פְּנֵיהֶם אָרְצָה:

21 The angel of *Hashem* never appeared again to *Manoach* and his wife. – *Manoach* then realized that it had been an angel of *Hashem*.

כא וְלֹא־יָסַף עוֹד מַלְאַךְ יְהוָה לְהֵרָאֹה אֶל־מָנוֹחַ וְאֶל־אִשְׁתּוֹ אָז יָדַע מָנוֹחַ כִּי־מַלְאַךְ יְהוָה הוּא:

22 And *Manoach* said to his wife, "We shall surely die, for we have seen a divine being."

כב וַיֹּאמֶר מָנוֹחַ אֶל־אִשְׁתּוֹ מוֹת נָמוּת כִּי אֱלֹהִים רָאִינוּ:

23 But his wife said to him, "Had *Hashem* meant to take our lives, He would not have accepted a burnt offering and meal offering from us, nor let us see all these things; and He would not have made such an announcement to us."

כג וַתֹּאמֶר לוֹ אִשְׁתּוֹ לוּ חָפֵץ יְהוָה לַהֲמִיתֵנוּ לֹא־לָקַח מִיָּדֵנוּ עֹלָה וּמִנְחָה וְלֹא הֶרְאָנוּ אֶת־כָּל־אֵלֶּה וְכָעֵת לֹא הִשְׁמִיעָנוּ כָּזֹאת:

24 The woman bore a son, and she named him *Shimshon*. The boy grew up, and *Hashem* blessed him.

כד וַתֵּלֶד הָאִשָּׁה בֵּן וַתִּקְרָא אֶת־שְׁמוֹ שִׁמְשׁוֹן וַיִּגְדַּל הַנַּעַר וַיְבָרְכֵהוּ יְהוָה:

25 The spirit of *Hashem* first moved him in the encampment of *Dan*, between *Tzora* and *Eshtaol*.

כה וַתָּחֶל רוּחַ יְהוָה לְפַעֲמוֹ בְּמַחֲנֵה־דָן בֵּין צָרְעָה וּבֵין אֶשְׁתָּאֹל:

14 1 Once *Shimshon* went down to Timnah; and while in Timnah, he noticed a girl among the Philistine women.

יד א וַיֵּרֶד שִׁמְשׁוֹן תִּמְנָתָה וַיַּרְא אִשָּׁה בְּתִמְנָתָה מִבְּנוֹת פְּלִשְׁתִּים:

2 On his return, he told his father and mother, "I noticed one of the Philistine women in Timnah; please get her for me as a wife."

ב וַיַּעַל וַיַּגֵּד לְאָבִיו וּלְאִמּוֹ וַיֹּאמֶר אִשָּׁה רָאִיתִי בְתִמְנָתָה מִבְּנוֹת פְּלִשְׁתִּים וְעַתָּה קְחוּ־אוֹתָהּ לִּי לְאִשָּׁה:

3 His father and mother said to him, "Is there no one among the daughters of your own kinsmen and among all our people, that you must go and take a wife from the uncircumcised Philistines?" But *Shimshon* answered his father, "Get me that one, for she is the one that pleases me."

ג וַיֹּאמֶר לוֹ אָבִיו וְאִמּוֹ הַאֵין בִּבְנוֹת אַחֶיךָ וּבְכָל־עַמִּי אִשָּׁה כִּי־אַתָּה הוֹלֵךְ לָקַחַת אִשָּׁה מִפְּלִשְׁתִּים הָעֲרֵלִים וַיֹּאמֶר שִׁמְשׁוֹן אֶל־אָבִיו אוֹתָהּ קַח־לִי כִּי־הִיא יָשְׁרָה בְעֵינָי:

4 His father and mother did not realize that this was *Hashem*'s doing: He was seeking a pretext against the Philistines, for the Philistines were ruling over *Yisrael* at that time.

ד וְאָבִיו וְאִמּוֹ לֹא יָדְעוּ כִּי מֵיְהוָה הִיא כִּי־תֹאֲנָה הוּא־מְבַקֵּשׁ מִפְּלִשְׁתִּים וּבָעֵת הַהִיא פְּלִשְׁתִּים מֹשְׁלִים בְּיִשְׂרָאֵל:

5 So *Shimshon* and his father and mother went down to Timnah. When he came to the vineyards of Timnah [for the first time], a full-grown lion came roaring at him.

ה וַיֵּ֧רֶד שִׁמְשׁ֛וֹן וְאָבִ֥יו וְאִמּ֖וֹ תִּמְנָ֑תָה וַיָּבֹ֙אוּ֙ עַד־כַּרְמֵ֣י תִמְנָ֔תָה וְהִנֵּה֙ כְּפִ֣יר אֲרָי֔וֹת שֹׁאֵ֖ג לִקְרָאתֽוֹ:

6 The spirit of *Hashem* gripped him, and he tore him asunder with his bare hands as one might tear a kid asunder; but he did not tell his father and mother what he had done.

ו וַתִּצְלַ֨ח עָלָ֜יו ר֣וּחַ יְהֹוָ֗ה וַֽיְשַׁסְּעֵ֙הוּ֙ כְּשַׁסַּ֣ע הַגְּדִ֔י וּמְא֖וּמָה אֵ֣ין בְּיָד֑וֹ וְלֹ֤א הִגִּיד֙ לְאָבִ֣יו וּלְאִמּ֔וֹ אֵ֖ת אֲשֶׁ֥ר עָשָֽׂה:

7 Then he went down and spoke to the woman, and she pleased *Shimshon*.

ז וַיֵּ֖רֶד וַיְדַבֵּ֣ר לָֽאִשָּׁ֑ה וַתִּישַׁ֖ר בְּעֵינֵ֥י שִׁמְשֽׁוֹן:

8 Returning the following year to marry her, he turned aside to look at the remains of the lion; and in the lion's skeleton he found a swarm of bees, and honey.

ח וַיָּ֤שׇׁב מִיָּמִים֙ לְקַחְתָּ֔הּ וַיָּ֣סַר לִרְא֔וֹת אֵ֖ת מַפֶּ֣לֶת הָאַרְיֵ֑ה וְהִנֵּ֨ה עֲדַ֧ת דְּבוֹרִ֛ים בִּגְוִיַּ֥ת הָאַרְיֵ֖ה וּדְבָֽשׁ:

9 He scooped it into his palms and ate it as he went along. When he rejoined his father and mother, he gave them some and they ate it; but he did not tell them that he had scooped the honey out of a lion's skeleton.

ט וַיִּרְדֵּ֣הוּ אֶל־כַּפָּ֗יו וַיֵּ֤לֶךְ הָלוֹךְ֙ וְאָכֹ֔ל וַיֵּ֙לֶךְ֙ אֶל־אָבִ֣יו וְאֶל־אִמּ֔וֹ וַיִּתֵּ֥ן לָהֶ֖ם וַיֹּאכֵ֑לוּ וְלֹֽא־הִגִּ֣יד לָהֶ֔ם כִּ֛י מִגְּוִיַּ֥ת הָאַרְיֵ֖ה רָדָ֥ה הַדְּבָֽשׁ:

10 So his father came down to the woman, and *Shimshon* made a feast there, as young men used to do.

י וַיֵּ֥רֶד אָבִ֖יהוּ אֶל־הָאִשָּׁ֑ה וַיַּ֨עַשׂ שָׁ֤ם שִׁמְשׁוֹן֙ מִשְׁתֶּ֔ה כִּ֛י כֵּ֥ן יַעֲשׂ֖וּ הַבַּחוּרִֽים:

11 When they saw him, they designated thirty companions to be with him.

יא וַיְהִ֖י כִּרְאוֹתָ֣ם אוֹת֑וֹ וַיִּקְח֙וּ שְׁלֹשִׁ֣ים מֵֽרֵעִ֔ים וַיִּהְי֖וּ אִתּֽוֹ:

12 Then *Shimshon* said to them, "Let me propound a riddle to you. If you can give me the right answer during the seven days of the feast, I shall give you thirty linen tunics and thirty sets of clothing;

יב וַיֹּ֤אמֶר לָהֶם֙ שִׁמְשׁ֔וֹן אָחֽוּדָה־נָּ֥א לָכֶ֖ם חִידָ֑ה אִם־הַגֵּ֣ד תַּגִּ֩ידוּ֩ אוֹתָ֨הּ לִ֜י שִׁבְעַ֨ת יְמֵ֤י הַמִּשְׁתֶּה֙ וּמְצָאתֶ֔ם וְנָתַתִּ֣י לָכֶ֗ם שְׁלֹשִׁים֙ סְדִינִ֔ים וּשְׁלֹשִׁ֖ים חֲלִפֹ֥ת בְּגָדִֽים:

13 but if you are not able to tell it to me, you must give me thirty linen tunics and thirty sets of clothing." And they said to him, "Ask your riddle and we will listen."

יג וְאִם־לֹ֤א תֽוּכְלוּ֙ לְהַגִּ֣יד לִ֔י וּנְתַתֶּ֥ם אַתֶּ֛ם לִ֗י שְׁלֹשִׁ֤ים סְדִינִים֙ וּשְׁלֹשִׁ֖ים חֲלִיפ֣וֹת בְּגָדִ֑ים וַיֹּ֣אמְרוּ ל֔וֹ ח֥וּדָה חִידָתְךָ֖ וְנִשְׁמָעֶֽנָּה:

14 So he said to them: "Out of the eater came something to eat, Out of the strong came something sweet." For three days they could not answer the riddle.

יד וַיֹּ֣אמֶר לָהֶ֗ם מֵֽהָֽאֹכֵל֙ יָצָ֣א מַֽאֲכָ֔ל וּמֵעַ֖ז יָצָ֣א מָת֑וֹק וְלֹ֥א יָֽכְל֛וּ לְהַגִּ֥יד הַֽחִידָ֖ה שְׁלֹ֥שֶׁת יָמִֽים:

15 On the seventh day, they said to *Shimshon*'s wife, "Coax your husband to provide us with the answer to the riddle; else we shall put you and your father's household to the fire; have you invited us here in order to impoverish us?"

טו וַיְהִ֣י ׀ בַּיּ֣וֹם הַשְּׁבִיעִ֗י וַיֹּאמְר֤וּ לְאֵֽשֶׁת־שִׁמְשׁוֹן֙ פַּתִּ֣י אֶת־אִישֵׁ֗ךְ וְיַגֶּד־לָ֙נוּ֙ אֶת־הַ֣חִידָ֔ה פֶּן־נִשְׂרֹ֥ף אוֹתָ֛ךְ וְאֶת־בֵּ֥ית אָבִ֖יךְ בָּאֵ֑שׁ הַלְיׇרְשֵׁ֕נוּ קְרָאתֶ֥ם לָ֖נוּ הֲלֹֽא:

Judges

16 Then *Shimshon*'s wife harassed him with tears, and she said, "You really hate me, you don't love me. You asked my countrymen a riddle, and you didn't tell me the answer." He replied, "I haven't even told my father and mother; shall I tell you?"

טז וַתֵּבְךְּ אֵשֶׁת שִׁמְשׁוֹן עָלָיו וַתֹּאמֶר רַק־שְׂנֵאתַנִי וְלֹא אֲהַבְתָּנִי הַחִידָה חַדְתָּ לִבְנֵי עַמִּי וְלִי לֹא הִגַּדְתָּה וַיֹּאמֶר לָהּ הִנֵּה לְאָבִי וּלְאִמִּי לֹא הִגַּדְתִּי וְלָךְ אַגִּיד:

17 During the rest of the seven days of the feast she continued to harass him with her tears, and on the seventh day he told her, because she nagged him so. And she explained the riddle to her countrymen.

יז וַתֵּבְךְּ עָלָיו שִׁבְעַת הַיָּמִים אֲשֶׁר־הָיָה לָהֶם הַמִּשְׁתֶּה וַיְהִי בַּיּוֹם הַשְּׁבִיעִי וַיַּגֶּד־לָהּ כִּי הֱצִיקַתְהוּ וַתַּגֵּד הַחִידָה לִבְנֵי עַמָּהּ:

18 On the seventh day, before the sunset, the townsmen said to him: "What is sweeter than honey, And what is stronger than a lion?" He responded: "Had you not plowed with my heifer, You would not have guessed my riddle!"

יח וַיֹּאמְרוּ לוֹ אַנְשֵׁי הָעִיר בַּיּוֹם הַשְּׁבִיעִי בְּטֶרֶם יָבֹא הַחַרְסָה מַה־מָּתוֹק מִדְּבַשׁ וּמֶה עַז מֵאֲרִי וַיֹּאמֶר לָהֶם לוּלֵא חֲרַשְׁתֶּם בְּעֶגְלָתִי לֹא מְצָאתֶם חִידָתִי:

19 The spirit of *Hashem* gripped him. He went down to *Ashkelon* and killed thirty of its men. He stripped them and gave the sets of clothing to those who had answered the riddle. And he left in a rage for his father's house.

יט וַתִּצְלַח עָלָיו רוּחַ יְהֹוָה וַיֵּרֶד אַשְׁקְלוֹן וַיַּךְ מֵהֶם שְׁלֹשִׁים אִישׁ וַיִּקַּח אֶת־חֲלִיצוֹתָם וַיִּתֵּן הַחֲלִיפוֹת לְמַגִּידֵי הַחִידָה וַיִּחַר אַפּוֹ וַיַּעַל בֵּית אָבִיהוּ:

va-titz-LAKH a-LAV RU-akh a-do-NAI va-YAY-red ash-k'-LON
va-YAKH may-HEM sh'-lo-SHEEM eesh va-yi-KAKH et
kha-lee-tzo-TAM va-yi-TAYN ha-kha-lee-FOT l'-ma-gee-DAY
ha-khee-DAH va-yi-KHAR a-PO va-YA-al BAYT a-VEE-hu

20 *Shimshon*'s wife then married one of those who had been his wedding companions.

כ וַתְּהִי אֵשֶׁת שִׁמְשׁוֹן לְמֵרֵעֵהוּ אֲשֶׁר רֵעָה לוֹ:

15 1 Some time later, in the season of the wheat harvest, *Shimshon* came to visit his wife, bringing a kid as a gift. He said, "Let me go into the chamber to my wife." But her father would not let him go in.

א וַיְהִי מִיָּמִים בִּימֵי קְצִיר־חִטִּים וַיִּפְקֹד שִׁמְשׁוֹן אֶת־אִשְׁתּוֹ בִּגְדִי עִזִּים וַיֹּאמֶר אָבֹאָה אֶל־אִשְׁתִּי הֶחָדְרָה וְלֹא־נְתָנוֹ אָבִיהָ לָבוֹא:

2 "I was sure," said her father, "that you had taken a dislike to her, so I gave her to your wedding companion. But her younger sister is more beautiful than she; let her become your wife instead."

ב וַיֹּאמֶר אָבִיהָ אָמֹר אָמַרְתִּי כִּי־שָׂנֹא שְׂנֵאתָהּ וָאֶתְּנֶנָּה לְמֵרֵעֶךָ הֲלֹא אֲחֹתָהּ הַקְּטַנָּה טוֹבָה מִמֶּנָּה תְּהִי־נָא לְךָ תַּחְתֶּיהָ:

3 Thereupon *Shimshon* declared, "Now the Philistines can have no claim against me for the harm I shall do them."

ג וַיֹּאמֶר לָהֶם שִׁמְשׁוֹן נִקֵּיתִי הַפַּעַם מִפְּלִשְׁתִּים כִּי־עֹשֶׂה אֲנִי עִמָּם רָעָה:

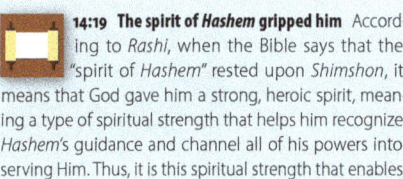

14:19 The spirit of *Hashem* gripped him According to *Rashi*, when the Bible says that the "spirit of *Hashem*" rested upon *Shimshon*, it means that God gave him a strong, heroic spirit, meaning a type of spiritual strength that helps him recognize *Hashem*'s guidance and channel all of his powers into serving Him. Thus, it is this spiritual strength that enables *Shimshon* to use his great physical strength against the Philistines. There is a difference between the physical strength within our bodies and spiritual strength, which helps us meet all challenges to do God's will. *Shimshon* has both.

Israeli soldiers waving
the Israeli flag

4 *Shimshon* went and caught three hundred foxes. He took torches and, turning [the foxes] tail to tail, he placed a torch between each pair of tails.

ד וַיֵּ֣לֶךְ שִׁמְשׁ֔וֹן וַיִּלְכֹּ֖ד שְׁלֹשׁ־מֵא֣וֹת שׁוּעָלִ֑ים וַיִּקַּ֣ח לַפִּדִ֗ים וַיֶּ֤פֶן זָנָ֣ב אֶל־זָנָ֔ב וַיָּ֣שֶׂם לַפִּ֞יד אֶחָ֛ד בֵּין־שְׁנֵ֥י הַזְּנָב֖וֹת בַּתָּֽוֶךְ׃

5 He lit the torches and turned [the foxes] loose among the standing grain of the Philistines, setting fire to stacked grain, standing grain, vineyards, [and] olive trees.

ה וַיַּבְעֶר־אֵשׁ֙ בַּלַּפִּידִ֔ים וַיְשַׁלַּ֖ח בְּקָמ֣וֹת פְּלִשְׁתִּ֑ים וַיַּבְעֵ֛ר מִגָּדִ֥ישׁ וְעַד־קָמָ֖ה וְעַד־כֶּ֥רֶם זָֽיִת׃

6 The Philistines asked, "Who did this?" And they were told, "It was *Shimshon*, the son-in-law of the Timnite, who took *Shimshon*'s wife and gave her to his wedding companion." Thereupon the Philistines came up and put her and her father to the fire.

ו וַיֹּאמְר֣וּ פְלִשְׁתִּים֮ מִ֣י עָ֣שָׂה זֹאת֒ וַיֹּאמְר֗וּ שִׁמְשׁוֹן֙ חֲתַ֣ן הַתִּמְנִ֔י כִּ֤י לָקַח֙ אֶת־אִשְׁתּ֔וֹ וַֽיִּתְּנָ֖הּ לְמֵרֵעֵ֑הוּ וַיַּעֲל֣וּ פְלִשְׁתִּ֗ים וַיִּשְׂרְפ֥וּ אוֹתָ֛הּ וְאֶת־אָבִ֖יהָ בָּאֵֽשׁ׃

7 *Shimshon* said to them, "If that is how you act, I will not rest until I have taken revenge on you."

ז וַיֹּ֤אמֶר לָהֶם֙ שִׁמְשׁ֔וֹן אִֽם־תַּעֲשׂ֖וּן כָּזֹ֑את כִּ֛י אִם־נִקַּ֥מְתִּי בָכֶ֖ם וְאַחַ֥ר אֶחְדָּֽל׃

8 He gave them a sound and thorough thrashing. Then he went down and stayed in the cave of the rock of Etam.

ח וַיַּ֨ךְ אוֹתָ֥ם שׁ֛וֹק עַל־יָרֵ֖ךְ מַכָּ֣ה גְדוֹלָ֑ה וַיֵּ֣רֶד וַיֵּ֔שֶׁב בִּסְעִ֖יף סֶ֥לַע עֵיטָֽם׃

9 The Philistines came up, pitched camp in *Yehuda* and spread out over Lehi.

ט וַיַּעֲל֣וּ פְלִשְׁתִּ֔ים וַֽיַּחֲנ֖וּ בִּיהוּדָ֑ה וַיִּנָּטְשׁ֖וּ בַּלֶּֽחִי׃

va-ya-a-LU f'-lish-TEEM va-ya-kha-NU bee-hu-DAH va-yi-na-t'-SHU ba-LE-khee

10 The men of *Yehuda* asked, "Why have you come up against us?" They answered, "We have come to take *Shimshon* prisoner, and to do to him as he did to us."

י וַיֹּֽאמְרוּ֙ אִ֣ישׁ יְהוּדָ֔ה לָמָ֖ה עֲלִיתֶ֣ם עָלֵ֑ינוּ וַיֹּאמְר֗וּ לֶאֱס֤וֹר אֶת־שִׁמְשׁוֹן֙ עָלִ֔ינוּ לַעֲשׂ֣וֹת ל֔וֹ כַּאֲשֶׁ֖ר עָ֥שָׂה לָֽנוּ׃

11 Thereupon three thousand men of *Yehuda* went down to the cave of the rock of Etam, and they said to *Shimshon*, "You knew that the Philistines rule over us; why have you done this to us?" He replied, "As they did to me, so I did to them."

יא וַיֵּרְד֡וּ שְׁלֹ֣שֶׁת אֲלָפִים֩ אִ֨ישׁ מִֽיהוּדָ֜ה אֶל־סְעִיף֮ סֶ֣לַע עֵיטָם֒ וַיֹּאמְר֣וּ לְשִׁמְשׁ֗וֹן הֲלֹ֤א יָדַ֨עְתָּ֙ כִּֽי־מֹשְׁלִ֤ים בָּ֨נוּ֙ פְּלִשְׁתִּ֔ים וּמַה־זֹּ֖את עָשִׂ֣יתָ לָּ֑נוּ וַיֹּ֣אמֶר לָהֶ֔ם כַּאֲשֶׁר֙ עָ֣שׂוּ לִ֔י כֵּ֖ן עָשִׂ֥יתִי לָהֶֽם׃

12 "We have come down," they told him, "to take you prisoner and to hand you over to the Philistines." "But swear to me," said *Shimshon* to them, "that you yourselves will not attack me."

יב וַיֹּ֤אמְרוּ לוֹ֙ לֶאֱסָרְךָ֣ יָרַ֔דְנוּ לְתִתְּךָ֖ בְּיַד־פְּלִשְׁתִּ֑ים וַיֹּ֤אמֶר לָהֶם֙ שִׁמְשׁ֔וֹן הִשָּׁבְע֣וּ לִ֔י פֶּֽן־תִּפְגְּע֥וּן בִּ֖י אַתֶּֽם׃

15:9 The Philistines came up, pitched camp in *Yehuda* The land of *Yehuda* encompasses much of the biblical heartland of *Eretz Yisrael*. *Chevron* and *Beit Lechem* are in the heart of the territory of *Yehuda*, while *Yerushalayim* is on its border. Though it borders both *Yehuda* and *Binyamin*, the Talmud (*Yoma* 12a) states that *Yerushalayim* was not given to a specific tribe; rather, it belongs to all of Israel. The holiness of the city chosen by God (Deuteronomy 12:5) is a unifying force that joins everyone together in the service of the Almighty.

Yerushalayim

13 "We won't," they replied. "We will only take you prisoner and hand you over to them; we will not slay you." So they bound him with two new ropes and brought him up from the rock.

יג וַיֹּאמְרוּ לוֹ לֵאמֹר לֹא כִּי־אָסֹר נֶאֱסָרְךָ וּנְתַנּוּךָ בְיָדָם וְהָמֵת לֹא נְמִיתֶךָ וַיַּאַסְרֻהוּ בִּשְׁנַיִם עֲבֹתִים חֲדָשִׁים וַיַּעֲלוּהוּ מִן־הַסָּלַע:

14 When he reached Lehi, the Philistines came shouting to meet him. Thereupon the spirit of *Hashem* gripped him, and the ropes on his arms became like flax that catches fire; the bonds melted off his hands.

יד הוּא־בָא עַד־לֶחִי וּפְלִשְׁתִּים הֵרִיעוּ לִקְרָאתוֹ וַתִּצְלַח עָלָיו רוּחַ יְהֹוָה וַתִּהְיֶינָה הָעֲבֹתִים אֲשֶׁר עַל־זְרוֹעוֹתָיו כַּפִּשְׁתִּים אֲשֶׁר בָּעֲרוּ בָאֵשׁ וַיִּמַּסּוּ אֱסוּרָיו מֵעַל יָדָיו:

15 He came upon a fresh jawbone of an ass and he picked it up; and with it he killed a thousand men.

טו וַיִּמְצָא לְחִי־חֲמוֹר טְרִיָּה וַיִּשְׁלַח יָדוֹ וַיִּקָּחֶהָ וַיַּךְ־בָּהּ אֶלֶף אִישׁ:

16 Then *Shimshon* said: "With the jaw of an ass, Mass upon mass! With the jaw of an ass I have slain a thousand men."

טז וַיֹּאמֶר שִׁמְשׁוֹן בִּלְחִי הַחֲמוֹר חֲמוֹר חֲמֹרָתָיִם בִּלְחִי הַחֲמוֹר הִכֵּיתִי אֶלֶף אִישׁ:

17 As he finished speaking, he threw the jawbone away; hence that place was called Ramath-lehi.

יז וַיְהִי כְּכַלֹּתוֹ לְדַבֵּר וַיַּשְׁלֵךְ הַלְּחִי מִיָּדוֹ וַיִּקְרָא לַמָּקוֹם הַהוּא רָמַת לֶחִי:

18 He was very thirsty and he called to *Hashem*, "You Yourself have granted this great victory through Your servant; and must I now die of thirst and fall into the hands of the uncircumcised?"

יח וַיִּצְמָא מְאֹד וַיִּקְרָא אֶל־יְהֹוָה וַיֹּאמַר אַתָּה נָתַתָּ בְיַד־עַבְדְּךָ אֶת־הַתְּשׁוּעָה הַגְּדֹלָה הַזֹּאת וְעַתָּה אָמוּת בַּצָּמָא וְנָפַלְתִּי בְּיַד הָעֲרֵלִים:

19 So *Hashem* split open the hollow which is at Lehi, and the water gushed out of it; he drank, regained his strength, and revived. That is why it is called to this day "En-hakkore of Lehi."

יט וַיִּבְקַע אֱלֹהִים אֶת־הַמַּכְתֵּשׁ אֲשֶׁר־בַּלֶּחִי וַיֵּצְאוּ מִמֶּנּוּ מַיִם וַיֵּשְׁתְּ וַתָּשָׁב רוּחוֹ וַיֶּחִי עַל־כֵּן קָרָא שְׁמָהּ עֵין הַקּוֹרֵא אֲשֶׁר בַּלֶּחִי עַד הַיּוֹם הַזֶּה:

20 He led *Yisrael* in the days of the Philistines for twenty years.

כ וַיִּשְׁפֹּט אֶת־יִשְׂרָאֵל בִּימֵי פְלִשְׁתִּים עֶשְׂרִים שָׁנָה:

16 1 Once *Shimshon* went to *Azza*; there he met a whore and slept with her.

טז א וַיֵּלֶךְ שִׁמְשׁוֹן עַזָּתָה וַיַּרְא־שָׁם אִשָּׁה זוֹנָה וַיָּבֹא אֵלֶיהָ:

2 The Gazites [learned] that *Shimshon* had come there, so they gathered and lay in ambush for him in the town gate the whole night; and all night long they kept whispering to each other, "When daylight comes, we'll kill him."

ב לַעַזָּתִים לֵאמֹר בָּא שִׁמְשׁוֹן הֵנָּה וַיָּסֹבּוּ וַיֶּאֶרְבוּ־לוֹ כָל־הַלַּיְלָה בְּשַׁעַר הָעִיר וַיִּתְחָרְשׁוּ כָל־הַלַּיְלָה לֵאמֹר עַד־אוֹר הַבֹּקֶר וַהֲרַגְנֻהוּ:

3 But *Shimshon* lay in bed only till midnight. At midnight he got up, grasped the doors of the town gate together with the two gateposts, and pulled them out along with the bar. He placed them on his shoulders and carried them off to the top of the hill that is near *Chevron*.

ג וַיִּשְׁכַּב שִׁמְשׁוֹן עַד־חֲצִי הַלַּיְלָה וַיָּקָם בַּחֲצִי הַלַּיְלָה וַיֶּאֱחֹז בְּדַלְתוֹת שַׁעַר־הָעִיר וּבִשְׁתֵּי הַמְּזוּזוֹת וַיִּסָּעֵם עִם־הַבְּרִיחַ וַיָּשֶׂם עַל־כְּתֵפָיו וַיַּעֲלֵם אֶל־רֹאשׁ הָהָר אֲשֶׁר עַל־פְּנֵי חֶבְרוֹן:

4 After that, he fell in love with a woman in the Wadi Sorek, named Delilah.

ד וַיְהִי אַחֲרֵי־כֵן וַיֶּאֱהַב אִשָּׁה בְּנַחַל שֹׂרֵק וּשְׁמָהּ דְּלִילָה:

5 The lords of the Philistines went up to her and said, "Coax him and find out what makes him so strong, and how we can overpower him, tie him up, and make him helpless; and we'll each give you eleven hundred *shekalim* of silver."

ה וַיַּעֲלוּ אֵלֶיהָ סַרְנֵי פְלִשְׁתִּים וַיֹּאמְרוּ לָהּ פַּתִּי אוֹתוֹ וּרְאִי בַּמֶּה כֹּחוֹ גָדוֹל וּבַמֶּה נוּכַל לוֹ וַאֲסַרְנֻהוּ לְעַנֹּתוֹ וַאֲנַחְנוּ נִתַּן־לָךְ אִישׁ אֶלֶף וּמֵאָה כָּסֶף:

6 So Delilah said to *Shimshon*, "Tell me, what makes you so strong? And how could you be tied up and made helpless?"

ו וַתֹּאמֶר דְּלִילָה אֶל־שִׁמְשׁוֹן הַגִּידָה־נָּא לִי בַּמֶּה כֹּחֲךָ גָדוֹל וּבַמֶּה תֵאָסֵר לְעַנּוֹתֶךָ:

7 *Shimshon* replied, "If I were to be tied with seven fresh tendons that had not been dried, I should become as weak as an ordinary man."

ז וַיֹּאמֶר אֵלֶיהָ שִׁמְשׁוֹן אִם־יַאַסְרֻנִי בְּשִׁבְעָה יְתָרִים לַחִים אֲשֶׁר לֹא־חֹרָבוּ וְחָלִיתִי וְהָיִיתִי כְּאַחַד הָאָדָם:

8 So the lords of the Philistines brought up to her seven fresh tendons that had not been dried. She bound him with them,

ח וַיַּעֲלוּ־לָהּ סַרְנֵי פְלִשְׁתִּים שִׁבְעָה יְתָרִים לַחִים אֲשֶׁר לֹא־חֹרָבוּ וַתַּאַסְרֵהוּ בָּהֶם:

9 while an ambush was waiting in her room. Then she called out to him, "*Shimshon*, the Philistines are upon you!" Whereat he pulled the tendons apart, as a strand of tow comes apart at the touch of fire. So the secret of his strength remained unknown.

ט וְהָאֹרֵב יֹשֵׁב לָהּ בַּחֶדֶר וַתֹּאמֶר אֵלָיו פְּלִשְׁתִּים עָלֶיךָ שִׁמְשׁוֹן וַיְנַתֵּק אֶת־הַיְתָרִים כַּאֲשֶׁר יִנָּתֵק פְּתִיל־הַנְּעֹרֶת בַּהֲרִיחוֹ אֵשׁ וְלֹא נוֹדַע כֹּחוֹ:

10 Then Delilah said to *Shimshon*, "Oh, you deceived me; you lied to me! Do tell me now how you could be tied up."

י וַתֹּאמֶר דְּלִילָה אֶל־שִׁמְשׁוֹן הִנֵּה הֵתַלְתָּ בִּי וַתְּדַבֵּר אֵלַי כְּזָבִים עַתָּה הַגִּידָה־נָּא לִי בַּמֶּה תֵּאָסֵר:

11 He said, "If I were to be bound with new ropes that had never been used, I would become as weak as an ordinary man."

יא וַיֹּאמֶר אֵלֶיהָ אִם־אָסוֹר יַאַסְרוּנִי בַּעֲבֹתִים חֲדָשִׁים אֲשֶׁר לֹא־נַעֲשָׂה בָהֶם מְלָאכָה וְחָלִיתִי וְהָיִיתִי כְּאַחַד הָאָדָם:

12 So Delilah took new ropes and bound him with them, while an ambush was waiting in a room. And she cried, "*Shimshon*, the Philistines are upon you!" But he tore them off his arms like a thread.

יב וַתִּקַּח דְּלִילָה עֲבֹתִים חֲדָשִׁים וַתַּאַסְרֵהוּ בָהֶם וַתֹּאמֶר אֵלָיו פְּלִשְׁתִּים עָלֶיךָ שִׁמְשׁוֹן וְהָאֹרֵב יֹשֵׁב בֶּחָדֶר וַיְנַתְּקֵם מֵעַל זְרֹעֹתָיו כַּחוּט:

13 Then Delilah said to *Shimshon*, "You have been deceiving me all along; you have been lying to me! Tell me, how could you be tied up?" He answered her, "If you weave seven locks of my head into the web."

יג וַתֹּאמֶר דְּלִילָה אֶל־שִׁמְשׁוֹן עַד־הֵנָּה הֵתַלְתָּ בִּי וַתְּדַבֵּר אֵלַי כְּזָבִים הַגִּידָה לִּי בַּמֶּה תֵּאָסֵר וַיֹּאמֶר אֵלֶיהָ אִם־תַּאַרְגִי אֶת־שֶׁבַע מַחְלְפוֹת רֹאשִׁי עִם־הַמַּסָּכֶת:

14 And she pinned it with a peg and cried to him, "*Shimshon*, the Philistines are upon you!" Awaking from his sleep, he pulled out the peg, the loom, and the web.

יד וַתִּתְקַע בַּיָּתֵד וַתֹּאמֶר אֵלָיו פְּלִשְׁתִּים עָלֶיךָ שִׁמְשׁוֹן וַיִּיקַץ מִשְּׁנָתוֹ וַיִּסַּע אֶת־הַיְתַד הָאֶרֶג וְאֶת־הַמַּסָּכֶת:

15 Then she said to him, "How can you say you love me, when you don't confide in me? This makes three times that you've deceived me and haven't told me what makes you so strong."

טו וַתֹּאמֶר אֵלָיו אֵיךְ תֹּאמַר אֲהַבְתִּיךְ וְלִבְּךָ אֵין אִתִּי זֶה שָׁלֹשׁ פְּעָמִים הֵתַלְתָּ בִּי וְלֹא־הִגַּדְתָּ לִּי בַּמֶּה כֹּחֲךָ גָדוֹל:

16 Finally, after she had nagged him and pressed him constantly, he was wearied to death

טז וַיְהִי כִּי־הֵצִיקָה לּוֹ בִדְבָרֶיהָ כָּל־הַיָּמִים וַתְּאַלְצֵהוּ וַתִּקְצַר נַפְשׁוֹ לָמוּת:

17 and he confided everything to her. He said to her, "No razor has ever touched my head, for I have been a nazirite to *Hashem* since I was in my mother's womb. If my hair were cut, my strength would leave me and I should become as weak as an ordinary man."

יז וַיַּגֶּד־לָהּ אֶת־כָּל־לִבּוֹ וַיֹּאמֶר לָהּ מוֹרָה לֹא־עָלָה עַל־רֹאשִׁי כִּי־נְזִיר אֱלֹהִים אֲנִי מִבֶּטֶן אִמִּי אִם־גֻּלַּחְתִּי וְסָר מִמֶּנִּי כֹחִי וְחָלִיתִי וְהָיִיתִי כְּכָל־הָאָדָם:

18 Sensing that he had confided everything to her, Delilah sent for the lords of the Philistines, with this message: "Come up once more, for he has confided everything to me." And the lords of the Philistines came up and brought the money with them.

יח וַתֵּרֶא דְּלִילָה כִּי־הִגִּיד לָהּ אֶת־כָּל־לִבּוֹ וַתִּשְׁלַח וַתִּקְרָא לְסַרְנֵי פְלִשְׁתִּים לֵאמֹר עֲלוּ הַפַּעַם כִּי־הִגִּיד לה [לִי] אֶת־כָּל־לִבּוֹ וְעָלוּ אֵלֶיהָ סַרְנֵי פְלִשְׁתִּים וַיַּעֲלוּ הַכֶּסֶף בְּיָדָם:

19 She lulled him to sleep on her lap. Then she called in a man, and she had him cut off the seven locks of his head; thus she weakened him and made him helpless: his strength slipped away from him.

יט וַתְּיַשְּׁנֵהוּ עַל־בִּרְכֶּיהָ וַתִּקְרָא לָאִישׁ וַתְּגַלַּח אֶת־שֶׁבַע מַחְלְפוֹת רֹאשׁוֹ וַתָּחֶל לְעַנּוֹתוֹ וַיָּסַר כֹּחוֹ מֵעָלָיו:

20 She cried, "*Shimshon*, the Philistines are upon you!" And he awoke from his sleep, thinking he would break loose and shake himself free as he had the other times. For he did not know that *Hashem* had departed from him.

כ וַתֹּאמֶר פְּלִשְׁתִּים עָלֶיךָ שִׁמְשׁוֹן וַיִּקַץ מִשְּׁנָתוֹ וַיֹּאמֶר אֵצֵא כְּפַעַם בְּפַעַם וְאִנָּעֵר וְהוּא לֹא יָדַע כִּי יְהֹוָה סָר מֵעָלָיו:

21 The Philistines seized him and gouged out his eyes. They brought him down to *Azza* and shackled him in bronze fetters, and he became a mill slave in the prison.

כא וַיֹּאחֲזוּהוּ פְלִשְׁתִּים וַיְנַקְּרוּ אֶת־עֵינָיו וַיּוֹרִידוּ אוֹתוֹ עַזָּתָה וַיַּאַסְרוּהוּ בַּנְחֻשְׁתַּיִם וַיְהִי טוֹחֵן בְּבֵית הָאֲסִירִים [הָאֲסוּרִים]:

22 After his hair was cut off, it began to grow back.

כב וַיָּחֶל שְׂעַר־רֹאשׁוֹ לְצַמֵּחַ כַּאֲשֶׁר גֻּלָּח:

23 Now the lords of the Philistines gathered to offer a great sacrifice to their god Dagon and to make merry. They chanted, "Our god has delivered into our hands Our enemy *Shimshon*."

כג וְסַרְנֵי פְלִשְׁתִּים נֶאֶסְפוּ לִזְבֹּחַ זֶבַח־גָּדוֹל לְדָגוֹן אֱלֹהֵיהֶם וּלְשִׂמְחָה וַיֹּאמְרוּ נָתַן אֱלֹהֵינוּ בְּיָדֵנוּ אֵת שִׁמְשׁוֹן אוֹיְבֵינוּ:

24 When the people saw him, they sang praises to their god, chanting, "Our god has delivered into our hands The enemy who devastated our land, And who slew so many of us."

כד וַיִּרְאוּ אֹתוֹ הָעָם וַיְהַלְלוּ אֶת־אֱלֹהֵיהֶם כִּי אָמְרוּ נָתַן אֱלֹהֵינוּ בְּיָדֵנוּ אֶת־אוֹיְבֵנוּ וְאֵת מַחֲרִיב אַרְצֵנוּ וַאֲשֶׁר הִרְבָּה אֶת־חֲלָלֵינוּ:

25 As their spirits rose, they said, "Call *Shimshon* here and let him dance for us." *Shimshon* was fetched from the prison, and he danced for them. Then they put him between the pillars.

כה וַיְהִי כִּי טוֹב [כְּטוֹב] לִבָּם וַיֹּאמְרוּ קִרְאוּ לְשִׁמְשׁוֹן וִישַׂחֶק־לָנוּ וַיִּקְרְאוּ לְשִׁמְשׁוֹן מִבֵּית הָאֲסִירִים [הָאֲסוּרִים] וַיְצַחֵק לִפְנֵיהֶם וַיַּעֲמִידוּ אוֹתוֹ בֵּין הָעַמּוּדִים:

26 And *Shimshon* said to the boy who was leading him by the hand, "Let go of me and let me feel the pillars that the temple rests upon, that I may lean on them."

כו וַיֹּאמֶר שִׁמְשׁוֹן אֶל־הַנַּעַר הַמַּחֲזִיק בְּיָדוֹ הַנִּיחָה אוֹתִי והימשני [וַהֲמִשֵׁנִי] אֶת־הָעַמֻּדִים אֲשֶׁר הַבַּיִת נָכוֹן עֲלֵיהֶם וְאֶשָּׁעֵן עֲלֵיהֶם:

27 Now the temple was full of men and women; all the lords of the Philistines were there, and there were some three thousand men and women on the roof watching *Shimshon* dance.

28 Then *Shimshon* called to *Hashem*, "O *Hashem*! Please remember me, and give me strength just this once, O *Hashem*, to take revenge of the Philistines, if only for one of my two eyes."

29 He embraced the two middle pillars that the temple rested upon, one with his right arm and one with his left, and leaned against them;

30 *Shimshon* cried, "Let me die with the Philistines!" and he pulled with all his might. The temple came crashing down on the lords and on all the people in it. Those who were slain by him as he died outnumbered those who had been slain by him when he lived.

כז וְהַבַּ֤יִת מָלֵא֙ הָאֲנָשִׁ֣ים וְהַנָּשִׁ֔ים וְשָׁ֕מָּה כֹּ֖ל סַרְנֵ֣י פְלִשְׁתִּ֑ים וְעַל־הַגָּ֗ג כִּשְׁלֹ֤שֶׁת אֲלָפִים֙ אִ֣ישׁ וְאִשָּׁ֔ה הָרֹאִ֖ים בִּשְׂח֥וֹק שִׁמְשֽׁוֹן׃

כח וַיִּקְרָ֨א שִׁמְשׁ֥וֹן אֶל־יְהֹוָ֖ה וַיֹּאמַ֑ר אֲדֹנָ֣י יֱהֹוִ֡ה זׇכְרֵ֣נִי נָא֩ וְחַזְּקֵ֨נִי נָ֜א אַ֣ךְ הַפַּ֤עַם הַזֶּה֙ הָאֱלֹהִ֔ים וְאִנָּקְמָ֛ה נְקַם־אַחַ֥ת מִשְּׁתֵ֥י עֵינַ֖י מִפְּלִשְׁתִּֽים׃

כט וַיִּלְפֹּ֨ת שִׁמְשׁ֜וֹן אֶת־שְׁנֵ֣י ׀ עַמּוּדֵ֣י הַתָּ֗וֶךְ אֲשֶׁ֤ר הַבַּ֙יִת֙ נָכ֣וֹן עֲלֵיהֶ֔ם וַיִּסָּמֵ֖ךְ עֲלֵיהֶ֑ם אֶחָ֥ד בִּימִינ֖וֹ וְאֶחָ֥ד בִּשְׂמֹאלֽוֹ׃

ל וַיֹּ֣אמֶר שִׁמְשׁ֗וֹן תָּמ֣וֹת נַפְשִׁי֮ עִם־פְּלִשְׁתִּים֒ וַיֵּ֣ט בְּכֹ֔חַ וַיִּפֹּ֤ל הַבַּ֙יִת֙ עַל־הַסְּרָנִ֔ים וְעַל־כׇּל־הָעָ֖ם אֲשֶׁר־בּ֑וֹ וַיִּהְי֤וּ הַמֵּתִים֙ אֲשֶׁ֣ר הֵמִ֣ית בְּמוֹת֔וֹ רַבִּ֕ים מֵאֲשֶׁ֥ר הֵמִ֖ית בְּחַיָּֽיו׃

va-YO-mer shim-SHON ta-MOT naf-SHEE im p'-lish-TEEM va-YAYT b'-KHO-akh va-yi-POL ha-BA-yit al ha-s'-ra-NEEM v'-al kol ha-AM a-sher BO va-yih-YU ha-may-TEEM a-SHER hay-MEET b'-mo-TO ra-BEEM may-a-SHER hay-MEET b'-kha-YAV

31 His brothers and all his father's household came down and carried him up and buried him in the tomb of his father *Manoach*, between *Tzora* and *Eshtaol*. He had led *Yisrael* for twenty years.

לא וַיֵּרְד֨וּ אֶחָ֜יו וְכׇל־בֵּ֣ית אָבִ֘יהוּ֮ וַיִּשְׂא֣וּ אֹתוֹ֒ וַֽיַּעֲל֣וּ ׀ וַיִּקְבְּר֣וּ אוֹת֗וֹ בֵּ֤ין צׇרְעָה֙ וּבֵ֣ין אֶשְׁתָּאֹ֔ל בְּקֶ֖בֶר מָנ֣וֹחַ אָבִ֑יו וְה֛וּא שָׁפַ֥ט אֶת־יִשְׂרָאֵ֖ל עֶשְׂרִ֥ים שָׁנָֽה׃

17 ¹ There was a man in the hill country of *Efraim* whose name was *Micha*.

יז א וַֽיְהִי־אִ֥ישׁ מֵהַר־אֶפְרָ֖יִם וּשְׁמ֥וֹ מִיכָֽיְהוּ׃

² He said to his mother, "The eleven hundred *shekalim* of silver that were taken from you, so that you uttered an imprecation which you repeated in my hearing – I have that silver; I took it." "Blessed of *Hashem* be my son," said his mother.

ב וַיֹּ֣אמֶר לְאִמּ֗וֹ אֶ֣לֶף וּמֵאָ֤ה הַכֶּ֙סֶף֙ אֲשֶׁ֣ר לֻקַּֽח־לָ֗ךְ וְאַ֤תְּ [וְאַתְּ] אָלִית֙ וְגַם֙ אָמַ֣רְתְּ בְּאׇזְנַ֔י הִנֵּֽה־הַכֶּ֥סֶף אִתִּ֖י אֲנִ֣י לְקַחְתִּ֑יו וַתֹּ֣אמֶר אִמּ֔וֹ בָּר֥וּךְ בְּנִ֖י לַֽיהֹוָֽה׃

³ He returned the eleven hundred *shekalim* of silver to his mother; but his mother said, "I herewith consecrate the silver to *Hashem*, transferring it to my son to make a sculptured image and a molten image. I now return it to you."

ג וַיָּ֛שֶׁב אֶת־אֶֽלֶף־וּמֵאָ֥ה הַכֶּ֖סֶף לְאִמּ֑וֹ וַתֹּ֣אמֶר אִמּ֡וֹ הַקְדֵּ֣שׁ הִקְדַּ֣שְׁתִּי אֶת־הַכֶּ֩סֶף֩ לַיהֹוָ֨ה מִיָּדִ֜י לִבְנִ֗י לַעֲשׂוֹת֙ פֶּ֣סֶל וּמַסֵּכָ֔ה וְעַתָּ֖ה אֲשִׁיבֶ֥נּוּ לָֽךְ׃

16:30 ***Shimshon* cried, "Let me die with the Philistines!"*** *Shimshon's* prayer to die among his Philistine oppressors, taking his own life for the sake of his people, is one of the most stirring scenes in the Bible. *Shimshon* has served as a model for soldiers of Israel who have been willing to give up their lives to save the Jewish people. A moving modern example is the story of Major Ro'i Klein, who, during the Second Lebanon War in 2006, jumped on a grenade, shielding his comrades from the explosion with his own body. Dying with the holy words of *Shema Yisrael* (שמע ישראל), "Hear O Israel, *Hashem* is Our God, *Hashem* is One" on his lips, Ro'i Klein sacrificed his life to save other soldiers who were fighting for *Eretz Yisrael*.

Major Roi Klein
(1975–2006)

4 So when he gave the silver back to his mother, his mother took two hundred *shekalim* of silver and gave it to a smith. He made of it a sculptured image and a molten image, which were kept in the house of *Micha*.

ד וַיָּשֶׁב אֶת־הַכֶּסֶף לְאִמּוֹ וַתִּקַּח אִמּוֹ מָאתַיִם כֶּסֶף וַתִּתְּנֵהוּ לַצּוֹרֵף וַיַּעֲשֵׂהוּ פֶּסֶל וּמַסֵּכָה וַיְהִי בְּבֵית מִיכָיְהוּ:

5 Now the man *Micha* had a house of *Hashem*; he had made an ephod and teraphim and he had inducted one of his sons to be his *Kohen*.

ה וְהָאִישׁ מִיכָה לוֹ בֵּית אֱלֹהִים וַיַּעַשׂ אֵפוֹד וּתְרָפִים וַיְמַלֵּא אֶת־יַד אַחַד מִבָּנָיו וַיְהִי־לוֹ לְכֹהֵן:

6 In those days there was no king in *Yisrael*; every man did as he pleased.

ו בַּיָּמִים הָהֵם אֵין מֶלֶךְ בְּיִשְׂרָאֵל אִישׁ הַיָּשָׁר בְּעֵינָיו יַעֲשֶׂה:

ba-ya-MEEM ha-HAYM AYN ME-lekh b'-yis-ra-AYL
EESH ha-ya-SHAR b'-ay-NAV ya-a-SEH

7 There was a young man from *Beit Lechem* of *Yehuda*, from the clan seat of *Yehuda*; he was a Levite and had resided there as a sojourner.

ז וַיְהִי־נַעַר מִבֵּית לֶחֶם יְהוּדָה מִמִּשְׁפַּחַת יְהוּדָה וְהוּא לֵוִי וְהוּא גָר־שָׁם:

8 This man had left the town of *Beit Lechem* of *Yehuda* to take up residence wherever he could find a place. On his way, he came to the house of *Micha* in the hill country of *Efraim*.

ח וַיֵּלֶךְ הָאִישׁ מֵהָעִיר מִבֵּית לֶחֶם יְהוּדָה לָגוּר בַּאֲשֶׁר יִמְצָא וַיָּבֹא הַר־אֶפְרַיִם עַד־בֵּית מִיכָה לַעֲשׂוֹת דַּרְכּוֹ:

9 "Where do you come from?" *Micha* asked him. He replied, "I am a Levite from *Beit Lechem* of *Yehuda*, and I am traveling to take up residence wherever I can find a place."

ט וַיֹּאמֶר־לוֹ מִיכָה מֵאַיִן תָּבוֹא וַיֹּאמֶר אֵלָיו לֵוִי אָנֹכִי מִבֵּית לֶחֶם יְהוּדָה וְאָנֹכִי הֹלֵךְ לָגוּר בַּאֲשֶׁר אֶמְצָא:

10 "Stay with me," *Micha* said to him, "and be a father and a *Kohen* to me, and I will pay you ten *shekalim* of silver a year, an allowance of clothing, and your food." The Levite went.

י וַיֹּאמֶר לוֹ מִיכָה שְׁבָה עִמָּדִי וֶהְיֵה־לִי לְאָב וּלְכֹהֵן וְאָנֹכִי אֶתֶּן־לְךָ עֲשֶׂרֶת כֶּסֶף לַיָּמִים וְעֵרֶךְ בְּגָדִים וּמִחְיָתֶךָ וַיֵּלֶךְ הַלֵּוִי:

11 The Levite agreed to stay with the man, and the youth became like one of his own sons.

יא וַיּוֹאֶל הַלֵּוִי לָשֶׁבֶת אֶת־הָאִישׁ וַיְהִי הַנַּעַר לוֹ כְּאַחַד מִבָּנָיו:

12 *Micha* inducted the Levite, and the young man became his *Kohen* and remained in *Micha*'s shrine.

יב וַיְמַלֵּא מִיכָה אֶת־יַד הַלֵּוִי וַיְהִי־לוֹ הַנַּעַר לְכֹהֵן וַיְהִי בְּבֵית מִיכָה:

King *David*'s tomb in *Yerushalayim*

17:6 In those days there was no king in *Yisrael*; every man did as he pleased. *Sefer Shoftim* repeatedly teaches that the lack of a king, enabling everyone to do whatever was right in their eyes, is the preeminent problem of this era. According to the Bible, the king should not be responsible only for the legal, military and economic affairs of the nation. He should also be responsible for ensuring that the society is moral and follows *Hashem*'s *Torah*. Having a righteous king in *Yerushalayim* will be part of the complete redemption.

13 "Now I know," *Micha* told himself, "that *Hashem* will prosper me, since the Levite has become my *Kohen*."

יג וַיֹּאמֶר מִיכָה עַתָּה יָדַעְתִּי כִּי־יֵיטִיב יְהוָה לִי כִּי הָיָה־לִי הַלֵּוִי לְכֹהֵן:

18 1 In those days there was no king in *Yisrael*, and in those days the tribe of *Dan* was seeking a territory in which to settle; for to that day no territory had fallen to their lot among the tribes of *Yisrael*.

יח א בַּיָּמִים הָהֵם אֵין מֶלֶךְ בְּיִשְׂרָאֵל וּבַיָּמִים הָהֵם שֵׁבֶט הַדָּנִי מְבַקֶּשׁ־לוֹ נַחֲלָה לָשֶׁבֶת כִּי לֹא־נָפְלָה לּוֹ עַד־הַיּוֹם הַהוּא בְּתוֹךְ־שִׁבְטֵי יִשְׂרָאֵל בְּנַחֲלָה:

2 The Danites sent out five of their number, from their clan seat at *Tzora* and *Eshtaol* – valiant men – to spy out the land and explore it. "Go," they told them, "and explore the land." When they had advanced into the hill country of *Efraim* as far as the house of *Micha*, they stopped there for the night.

ב וַיִּשְׁלְחוּ בְנֵי־דָן מִמִּשְׁפַּחְתָּם חֲמִשָּׁה אֲנָשִׁים מִקְצוֹתָם אֲנָשִׁים בְּנֵי־חַיִל מִצָּרְעָה וּמֵאֶשְׁתָּאֹל לְרַגֵּל אֶת־הָאָרֶץ וּלְחָקְרָהּ וַיֹּאמְרוּ אֲלֵהֶם לְכוּ חִקְרוּ אֶת־הָאָרֶץ וַיָּבֹאוּ הַר־אֶפְרַיִם עַד־בֵּית מִיכָה וַיָּלִינוּ שָׁם:

3 While in the vicinity of *Micha*'s house, they recognized the speech of the young Levite, so they went over and asked him, "Who brought you to these parts? What are you doing in this place? What is your business here?"

ג הֵמָּה עִם־בֵּית מִיכָה וְהֵמָּה הִכִּירוּ אֶת־קוֹל הַנַּעַר הַלֵּוִי וַיָּסוּרוּ שָׁם וַיֹּאמְרוּ לוֹ מִי־הֱבִיאֲךָ הֲלֹם וּמָה־אַתָּה עֹשֶׂה בָּזֶה וּמַה־לְּךָ פֹּה:

4 He replied, "Thus and thus *Micha* did for me – he hired me and I became his *Kohen*."

ד וַיֹּאמֶר אֲלֵהֶם כָּזֹה וְכָזֶה עָשָׂה לִי מִיכָה וַיִּשְׂכְּרֵנִי וָאֱהִי־לוֹ לְכֹהֵן:

5 They said to him, "Please, inquire of *Hashem*; we would like to know if the mission on which we are going will be successful."

ה וַיֹּאמְרוּ לוֹ שְׁאַל־נָא בֵאלֹהִים וְנֵדְעָה הֲתַצְלִיחַ דַּרְכֵּנוּ אֲשֶׁר אֲנַחְנוּ הֹלְכִים עָלֶיהָ:

6 "Go in peace," the *Kohen* said to them, "*Hashem* views with favor the mission you are going on."

ו וַיֹּאמֶר לָהֶם הַכֹּהֵן לְכוּ לְשָׁלוֹם נֹכַח יְהוָה דַּרְכְּכֶם אֲשֶׁר תֵּלְכוּ־בָהּ:

7 The five men went on and came to Laish. They observed the people in it dwelling carefree, after the manner of the Sidonians, a tranquil and unsuspecting people, with no one in the land to molest them and with no hereditary ruler. Moreover, they were distant from the Sidonians and had no dealings with anybody.

ז וַיֵּלְכוּ חֲמֵשֶׁת הָאֲנָשִׁים וַיָּבֹאוּ לָיְשָׁה וַיִּרְאוּ אֶת־הָעָם אֲשֶׁר־בְּקִרְבָּהּ יוֹשֶׁבֶת־לָבֶטַח כְּמִשְׁפַּט צִדֹנִים שֹׁקֵט וּבֹטֵחַ וְאֵין־מַכְלִים דָּבָר בָּאָרֶץ יוֹרֵשׁ עֶצֶר וּרְחֹקִים הֵמָּה מִצִּדֹנִים וְדָבָר אֵין־לָהֶם עִם־אָדָם:

8 When [the men] came back to their kinsmen at *Tzora* and *Eshtaol*, their kinsmen asked them, "How did you fare?"

ח וַיָּבֹאוּ אֶל־אֲחֵיהֶם צָרְעָה וְאֶשְׁתָּאֹל וַיֹּאמְרוּ לָהֶם אֲחֵיהֶם מָה אַתֶּם:

9 They replied, "Let us go at once and attack them! For we found that the land was very good, and you are sitting idle! Don't delay; go and invade the land and take possession of it,

ט וַיֹּאמְרוּ קוּמָה וְנַעֲלֶה עֲלֵיהֶם כִּי רָאִינוּ אֶת־הָאָרֶץ וְהִנֵּה טוֹבָה מְאֹד וְאַתֶּם מַחְשִׁים אַל־תֵּעָצְלוּ לָלֶכֶת לָבֹא לָרֶשֶׁת אֶת־הָאָרֶץ:

10 for *Hashem* has delivered it into your hand. When you come, you will come to an unsuspecting people; and the land is spacious and nothing on earth is lacking there."

י כְּבֹאֲכֶם תָּבֹאוּ אֶל־עַם בֹּטֵחַ וְהָאָרֶץ רַחֲבַת יָדַיִם כִּי־נְתָנָהּ אֱלֹהִים בְּיֶדְכֶם מָקוֹם אֲשֶׁר אֵין־שָׁם מַחְסוֹר כָּל־דָּבָר אֲשֶׁר בָּאָרֶץ:

11 They departed from there, from the clan seat of the Danites, from *Tzora* and *Eshtaol*, six hundred strong, girt with weapons of war.

יא וַיִּסְעוּ מִשָּׁם מִמִּשְׁפַּחַת הַדָּנִי מִצָּרְעָה וּמֵאֶשְׁתָּאֹל שֵׁשׁ־מֵאוֹת אִישׁ חָגוּר כְּלֵי מִלְחָמָה:

12 They went up and encamped at *Kiryat Ye'arim* in *Yehuda*. That is why that place is called "the Camp of *Dan*" to this day; it lies west of *Kiryat Ye'arim*.

יב וַיַּעֲלוּ וַיַּחֲנוּ בְּקִרְיַת יְעָרִים בִּיהוּדָה עַל־כֵּן קָרְאוּ לַמָּקוֹם הַהוּא מַחֲנֵה־דָן עַד הַיּוֹם הַזֶּה הִנֵּה אַחֲרֵי קִרְיַת יְעָרִים:

13 From there they passed on to the hill country of *Efraim* and arrived at the house of *Micha*.

יג וַיַּעֲבֹר מִשָּׁם הַר־אֶפְרָיִם וַיָּבֹאוּ עַד־בֵּית מִיכָה:

14 Here the five men who had gone to spy out the Laish region remarked to their kinsmen, "Do you know, there is an ephod in these houses, and teraphim, and a sculptured image and a molten image? Now you know what you have to do."

יד וַיַּעֲנוּ חֲמֵשֶׁת הָאֲנָשִׁים הַהֹלְכִים לְרַגֵּל אֶת־הָאָרֶץ לַיִשׁ וַיֹּאמְרוּ אֶל־אֲחֵיהֶם הַיְדַעְתֶּם כִּי יֵשׁ בַּבָּתִּים הָאֵלֶּה אֵפוֹד וּתְרָפִים וּפֶסֶל וּמַסֵּכָה וְעַתָּה דְּעוּ מַה־תַּעֲשׂוּ:

15 So they turned off there and entered the home of the young Levite at *Micha*'s house and greeted him.

טו וַיָּסוּרוּ שָׁמָּה וַיָּבֹאוּ אֶל־בֵּית־הַנַּעַר הַלֵּוִי בֵּית מִיכָה וַיִּשְׁאֲלוּ־לוֹ לְשָׁלוֹם:

16 The six hundred Danite men, girt with their weapons of war, stood at the entrance of the gate,

טז וְשֵׁשׁ־מֵאוֹת אִישׁ חֲגוּרִים כְּלֵי מִלְחַמְתָּם נִצָּבִים פֶּתַח הַשָּׁעַר אֲשֶׁר מִבְּנֵי־דָן:

17 while the five men who had gone to spy out the land went inside and took the sculptured image, the ephod, the teraphim, and the molten image. The *Kohen* was standing at the entrance of the gate, and the six hundred men girt with their weapons of war,

יז וַיַּעֲלוּ חֲמֵשֶׁת הָאֲנָשִׁים הַהֹלְכִים לְרַגֵּל אֶת־הָאָרֶץ בָּאוּ שָׁמָּה לָקְחוּ אֶת־הַפֶּסֶל וְאֶת־הָאֵפוֹד וְאֶת־הַתְּרָפִים וְאֶת־הַמַּסֵּכָה וְהַכֹּהֵן נִצָּב פֶּתַח הַשַּׁעַר וְשֵׁשׁ־מֵאוֹת הָאִישׁ הֶחָגוּר כְּלֵי הַמִּלְחָמָה:

18 while those men entered *Micha*'s house and took the sculptured image, the molten image, the ephod, and the household gods. The *Kohen* said to them, "What are you doing?"

יח וְאֵלֶּה בָּאוּ בֵּית מִיכָה וַיִּקְחוּ אֶת־פֶּסֶל הָאֵפוֹד וְאֶת־הַתְּרָפִים וְאֶת־הַמַּסֵּכָה וַיֹּאמֶר אֲלֵיהֶם הַכֹּהֵן מָה אַתֶּם עֹשִׂים:

19 But they said to him, "Be quiet; put your hand on your mouth! Come with us and be our father and *Kohen*. Would you rather be *Kohen* to one man's household or be *Kohen* to a tribe and clan in *Yisrael*?"

יט וַיֹּאמְרוּ לוֹ הַחֲרֵשׁ שִׂים־יָדְךָ עַל־פִּיךָ וְלֵךְ עִמָּנוּ וֶהְיֵה־לָנוּ לְאָב וּלְכֹהֵן הֲטוֹב הֱיוֹתְךָ כֹהֵן לְבֵית אִישׁ אֶחָד אוֹ הֱיוֹתְךָ כֹהֵן לְשֵׁבֶט וּלְמִשְׁפָּחָה בְּיִשְׂרָאֵל:

20 The *Kohen* was delighted. He took the ephod, the household gods, and the sculptured image, and he joined the people.

כ וַיִּיטַב לֵב הַכֹּהֵן וַיִּקַּח אֶת־הָאֵפוֹד וְאֶת־הַתְּרָפִים וְאֶת־הַפָּסֶל וַיָּבֹא בְּקֶרֶב הָעָם:

21 They set out again, placing the children, the cattle, and their household goods in front.

כא וַיִּפְנוּ וַיֵּלֵכוּ וַיָּשִׂימוּ אֶת־הַטַּף וְאֶת־הַמִּקְנֶה וְאֶת־הַכְּבוּדָּה לִפְנֵיהֶם:

22 They had already gone some distance from *Micha*'s house, when the men in the houses near *Micha*'s mustered and caught up with the Danites.

כב הֵמָּה הִרְחִיקוּ מִבֵּית מִיכָה וְהָאֲנָשִׁים אֲשֶׁר בַּבָּתִּים אֲשֶׁר עִם־בֵּית מִיכָה נִזְעֲקוּ וַיַּדְבִּיקוּ אֶת־בְּנֵי־דָן:

23 They called out to the Danites, who turned around and said to *Micha*, "What's the matter? Why have you mustered?"

כג וַיִּקְרְאוּ אֶל־בְּנֵי־דָן וַיַּסֵּבּוּ פְּנֵיהֶם וַיֹּאמְרוּ לְמִיכָה מַה־לְּךָ כִּי נִזְעָקְתָּ:

24 He said, "You have taken my *Kohen* and the gods that I made, and walked off! What do I have left? How can you ask, 'What's the matter'?"

כד וַיֹּאמֶר אֶת־אֱלֹהַי אֲשֶׁר־עָשִׂיתִי לְקַחְתֶּם וְאֶת־הַכֹּהֵן וַתֵּלְכוּ וּמַה־לִּי עוֹד וּמַה־זֶּה תֹּאמְרוּ אֵלַי מַה־לָּךְ:

25 But the Danites replied, "Don't do any shouting at us, or some desperate men might attack you, and you and your family would lose your lives."

כה וַיֹּאמְרוּ אֵלָיו בְּנֵי־דָן אַל־תַּשְׁמַע קוֹלְךָ עִמָּנוּ פֶּן־יִפְגְּעוּ בָכֶם אֲנָשִׁים מָרֵי נֶפֶשׁ וְאָסַפְתָּה נַפְשְׁךָ וְנֶפֶשׁ בֵּיתֶךָ:

26 So *Micha*, realizing that they were stronger than he, turned back and went home; and the Danites went on their way,

כו וַיֵּלְכוּ בְּנֵי־דָן לְדַרְכָּם וַיַּרְא מִיכָה כִּי־חֲזָקִים הֵמָּה מִמֶּנּוּ וַיִּפֶן וַיָּשָׁב אֶל־בֵּיתוֹ:

27 taking the things *Micha* had made and the *Kohen* he had acquired. They proceeded to Laish, a people tranquil and unsuspecting, and they put them to the sword and burned down the town.

כז וְהֵמָּה לָקְחוּ אֵת אֲשֶׁר־עָשָׂה מִיכָה וְאֶת־הַכֹּהֵן אֲשֶׁר הָיָה־לוֹ וַיָּבֹאוּ עַל־לַיִשׁ עַל־עַם שֹׁקֵט וּבֹטֵחַ וַיַּכּוּ אוֹתָם לְפִי־חָרֶב וְאֶת־הָעִיר שָׂרְפוּ בָאֵשׁ:

28 There was none to come to the rescue, for it was distant from Sidon and they had no dealings with anyone; it lay in the valley of Beth-rehob. They rebuilt the town and settled there,

כח וְאֵין מַצִּיל כִּי רְחוֹקָה־הִיא מִצִּידוֹן וְדָבָר אֵין־לָהֶם עִם־אָדָם וְהִיא בָּעֵמֶק אֲשֶׁר לְבֵית־רְחוֹב וַיִּבְנוּ אֶת־הָעִיר וַיֵּשְׁבוּ בָהּ:

29 and they named the town *Dan*, after their ancestor *Dan* who was *Yisrael*'s son. Originally, however, the name of the town was Laish.

כט וַיִּקְרְאוּ שֵׁם־הָעִיר דָּן בְּשֵׁם דָּן אֲבִיהֶם אֲשֶׁר יוּלַּד לְיִשְׂרָאֵל וְאוּלָם לַיִשׁ שֵׁם־הָעִיר לָרִאשֹׁנָה:

30 The Danites set up the sculptured image for themselves; and *Yonatan* son of *Gershom* son of *Menashe*, and his descendants, served as *Kohanim* to the Danite tribe until the land went into exile.

ל וַיָּקִימוּ לָהֶם בְּנֵי־דָן אֶת־הַפָּסֶל וִיהוֹנָתָן בֶּן־גֵּרְשֹׁם בֶּן־מְנַשֶּׁה הוּא וּבָנָיו הָיוּ כֹהֲנִים לְשֵׁבֶט הַדָּנִי עַד־יוֹם גְּלוֹת הָאָרֶץ:

*va-ya-KEE-mu la-HEM b'-nay DAN et ha-PA-sel vee-ho-na-TAN
ben gay-r'-SHOM ben m'-na-SHEH HU u-va-NAV ha-YU
kho-ha-NEEM l'-SHAY-vet ha-da-NEE ad yom g'-LOT ha-A-retz*

Sunset prayer

18:30 *Yonatan* son of *Gershom* son of *Menashe*
The idolatrous priest *Yonatan* is identified as being the son of *Gershom*, the son of *Menashe* (מנשה). However, *Rashi* writes that *Yonatan*'s actual grandfather was *Moshe* (משה). Out of respect for the greatest prophet in history, the prophet *Shmuel* (who authored this book) disguised *Moshe*'s name, inserting the letter *nun* (נ) between the first two letters, *mem* (מ) and *shin* (ש). The sad fact is that the grandson of *Moshe* left the ways of the *Torah*. This tragic betrayal was the result of living in a society that was spiritually adrift. Clearly, if this can happen to a grandchild of the greatest prophet in history, it can happen to any person, in any family. *Moshe*'s grandson *Yonatan* is a sobering reminder of the importance of making sure that our children are surrounded by positive role models, have a strong religious education and grow up in a just society that seeks to do *Hashem*'s will.

31 They maintained the sculptured image that *Micha* had made throughout the time that the House of *Hashem* stood at *Shilo*.

לא וַיָּשִׂימוּ לָהֶם אֶת־פֶּסֶל מִיכָה אֲשֶׁר עָשָׂה כָּל־יְמֵי הֱיוֹת בֵּית־הָאֱלֹהִים בְּשִׁלֹה:

19 1 In those days, when there was no king in *Yisrael*, a Levite residing at the other end of the hill country of *Efraim* took to himself a concubine from *Beit Lechem* in *Yehuda*.

יט א וַיְהִי בַּיָּמִים הָהֵם וּמֶלֶךְ אֵין בְּיִשְׂרָאֵל וַיְהִי אִישׁ לֵוִי גָּר בְּיַרְכְּתֵי הַר־אֶפְרַיִם וַיִּקַּח־לוֹ אִשָּׁה פִילֶגֶשׁ מִבֵּית לֶחֶם יְהוּדָה:

2 Once his concubine deserted him, leaving him for her father's house in *Beit Lechem* in *Yehuda*; and she stayed there a full four months.

ב וַתִּזְנֶה עָלָיו פִּילַגְשׁוֹ וַתֵּלֶךְ מֵאִתּוֹ אֶל־בֵּית אָבִיהָ אֶל־בֵּית לֶחֶם יְהוּדָה וַתְּהִי־שָׁם יָמִים אַרְבָּעָה חֳדָשִׁים:

3 Then her husband set out, with an attendant and a pair of donkeys, and went after her to woo her and to win her back. She admitted him into her father's house; and when the girl's father saw him, he received him warmly.

ג וַיָּקָם אִישָׁהּ וַיֵּלֶךְ אַחֲרֶיהָ לְדַבֵּר עַל־לִבָּהּ להשיבו [לַהֲשִׁיבָהּ] וְנַעֲרוֹ עִמּוֹ וְצֶמֶד חֲמֹרִים וַתְּבִיאֵהוּ בֵּית אָבִיהָ וַיִּרְאֵהוּ אֲבִי הַנַּעֲרָה וַיִּשְׂמַח לִקְרָאתוֹ:

4 His father-in-law, the girl's father, pressed him, and he stayed with him three days; they ate and drank and lodged there.

ד וַיֶּחֱזַק־בּוֹ חֹתְנוֹ אֲבִי הַנַּעֲרָה וַיֵּשֶׁב אִתּוֹ שְׁלֹשֶׁת יָמִים וַיֹּאכְלוּ וַיִּשְׁתּוּ וַיָּלִינוּ שָׁם:

5 Early in the morning of the fourth day, he started to leave; but the girl's father said to his son-in-law, "Eat something to give you strength, then you can leave."

ה וַיְהִי בַּיּוֹם הָרְבִיעִי וַיַּשְׁכִּימוּ בַבֹּקֶר וַיָּקָם לָלֶכֶת וַיֹּאמֶר אֲבִי הַנַּעֲרָה אֶל־חֲתָנוֹ סְעָד לִבְּךָ פַּת־לֶחֶם וְאַחַר תֵּלֵכוּ:

6 So the two of them sat down and they feasted together. Then the girl's father said to the man, "Won't you stay overnight and enjoy yourself?"

ו וַיֵּשְׁבוּ וַיֹּאכְלוּ שְׁנֵיהֶם יַחְדָּו וַיִּשְׁתּוּ וַיֹּאמֶר אֲבִי הַנַּעֲרָה אֶל־הָאִישׁ הוֹאֶל־נָא וְלִין וְיִטַב לִבֶּךָ:

7 The man started to leave, but his father-in-law kept urging him until he turned back and spent the night there.

ז וַיָּקָם הָאִישׁ לָלֶכֶת וַיִּפְצַר־בּוֹ חֹתְנוֹ וַיָּשָׁב וַיָּלֶן שָׁם:

8 Early in the morning of the fifth day, he was about to leave, when the girl's father said, "Come, have a bite." The two of them ate, dawdling until past noon.

ח וַיַּשְׁכֵּם בַּבֹּקֶר בַּיּוֹם הַחֲמִישִׁי לָלֶכֶת וַיֹּאמֶר אֲבִי הַנַּעֲרָה סְעָד־נָא לְבָבְךָ וְהִתְמַהְמְהוּ עַד־נְטוֹת הַיּוֹם וַיֹּאכְלוּ שְׁנֵיהֶם:

9 Then the man, his concubine, and his attendant started to leave. His father-in-law, the girl's father, said to him, "Look, the day is waning toward evening; do stop for the night. See, the day is declining; spend the night here and enjoy yourself. You can start early tomorrow on your journey and head for home."

ט וַיָּקָם הָאִישׁ לָלֶכֶת הוּא וּפִילַגְשׁוֹ וְנַעֲרוֹ וַיֹּאמֶר לוֹ חֹתְנוֹ אֲבִי הַנַּעֲרָה הִנֵּה נָא רָפָה הַיּוֹם לַעֲרֹב לִינוּ־נָא הִנֵּה חֲנוֹת הַיּוֹם לִין פֹּה וְיִיטַב לְבָבֶךָ וְהִשְׁכַּמְתֶּם מָחָר לְדַרְכְּכֶם וְהָלַכְתָּ לְאֹהָלֶךָ:

10 But the man refused to stay for the night. He set out and traveled as far as the vicinity of Jebus – that is, *Yerushalayim*; he had with him a pair of laden donkeys, and his concubine was with him.

י וְלֹא־אָבָה הָאִישׁ לָלוּן וַיָּקָם וַיֵּלֶךְ וַיָּבֹא עַד־נֹכַח יְבוּס הִיא יְרוּשָׁלָ͏ִם וְעִמּוֹ צֶמֶד חֲמוֹרִים חֲבוּשִׁים וּפִילַגְשׁוֹ עִמּוֹ:

11 Since they were close to Jebus, and the day was very far spent, the attendant said to his master, "Let us turn aside to this town of the Jebusites and spend the night in it."

יא הֵם עִם־יְבוּס וְהַיּוֹם רַד מְאֹד וַיֹּאמֶר הַנַּעַר אֶל־אֲדֹנָיו לְכָה־נָּא וְנָסוּרָה אֶל־עִיר־הַיְבוּסִי הַזֹּאת וְנָלִין בָּהּ:

12 But his master said to him, "We will not turn aside to a town of aliens who are not of *Yisrael*, but will continue to *Giva*.

יב וַיֹּאמֶר אֵלָיו אֲדֹנָיו לֹא נָסוּר אֶל־עִיר נָכְרִי אֲשֶׁר לֹא־מִבְּנֵי יִשְׂרָאֵל הֵנָּה וְעָבַרְנוּ עַד־גִּבְעָה:

13 Come," he said to his attendant, "let us approach one of those places and spend the night either in *Giva* or in *Rama*."

יג וַיֹּאמֶר לְנַעֲרוֹ לֵךְ וְנִקְרְבָה בְּאַחַד הַמְּקֹמוֹת וְלַנּוּ בַגִּבְעָה אוֹ בָרָמָה:

14 So they traveled on, and the sun set when they were near *Giva* of *Binyamin*.

יד וַיַּעַבְרוּ וַיֵּלֵכוּ וַתָּבֹא לָהֶם הַשֶּׁמֶשׁ אֵצֶל הַגִּבְעָה אֲשֶׁר לְבִנְיָמִן:

15 They turned off there and went in to spend the night in *Giva*. He went and sat down in the town square, but nobody took them indoors to spend the night.

טו וַיָּסֻרוּ שָׁם לָבוֹא לָלוּן בַּגִּבְעָה וַיָּבֹא וַיֵּשֶׁב בִּרְחוֹב הָעִיר וְאֵין אִישׁ מְאַסֵּף־אוֹתָם הַבַּיְתָה לָלוּן:

16 In the evening, an old man came along from his property outside the town. (This man hailed from the hill country of *Efraim* and resided at *Giva*, where the townspeople were Benjaminites.)

טז וְהִנֵּה אִישׁ זָקֵן בָּא מִן־מַעֲשֵׂהוּ מִן־הַשָּׂדֶה בָּעֶרֶב וְהָאִישׁ מֵהַר אֶפְרַיִם וְהוּא־גָר בַּגִּבְעָה וְאַנְשֵׁי הַמָּקוֹם בְּנֵי יְמִינִי:

17 He happened to see the wayfarer in the town square. "Where," the old man inquired, "are you going to, and where do you come from?"

יז וַיִּשָּׂא עֵינָיו וַיַּרְא אֶת־הָאִישׁ הָאֹרֵחַ בִּרְחֹב הָעִיר וַיֹּאמֶר הָאִישׁ הַזָּקֵן אָנָה תֵלֵךְ וּמֵאַיִן תָּבוֹא:

18 He replied, "We are traveling from *Beit Lechem* in *Yehuda* to the other end of the hill country of *Efraim*. That is where I live. I made a journey to *Beit Lechem* of *Yehuda*, and now I am on my way to the House of *Hashem*, and nobody has taken me indoors.

יח וַיֹּאמֶר אֵלָיו עֹבְרִים אֲנַחְנוּ מִבֵּית־לֶחֶם יְהוּדָה עַד־יַרְכְּתֵי הַר־אֶפְרַיִם מִשָּׁם אָנֹכִי וָאֵלֵךְ עַד־בֵּית לֶחֶם יְהוּדָה וְאֶת־בֵּית יְהֹוָה אֲנִי הֹלֵךְ וְאֵין אִישׁ מְאַסֵּף אוֹתִי הַבָּיְתָה:

19 We have both bruised straw and feed for our donkeys, and bread and wine for me and your handmaid, and for the attendant with your servants. We lack nothing."

יט וְגַם־תֶּבֶן גַּם־מִסְפּוֹא יֵשׁ לַחֲמוֹרֵינוּ וְגַם לֶחֶם וָיַיִן יֶשׁ־לִי וְלַאֲמָתֶךָ וְלַנַּעַר עִם־עֲבָדֶיךָ אֵין מַחְסוֹר כָּל־דָּבָר:

20 "Rest easy," said the old man. "Let me take care of all your needs. Do not on any account spend the night in the square."

כ וַיֹּאמֶר הָאִישׁ הַזָּקֵן שָׁלוֹם לָךְ רַק כָּל־מַחְסוֹרְךָ עָלָי רַק בָּרְחוֹב אַל־תָּלַן:

21 And he took him into his house. He mixed fodder for the donkeys; then they bathed their feet and ate and drank.

כא וַיְבִיאֵהוּ לְבֵיתוֹ וַיָּבָל לַחֲמוֹרִים וַיִּרְחֲצוּ רַגְלֵיהֶם וַיֹּאכְלוּ וַיִּשְׁתּוּ:

22 While they were enjoying themselves, the men of the town, a depraved lot, had gathered about the house and were pounding on the door. They calledto the aged owner of the house, "Bring out the man who has come into your house, so that we can be intimate with him."

כב הֵמָּה מֵיטִיבִים אֶת־לִבָּם וְהִנֵּה אַנְשֵׁי הָעִיר אַנְשֵׁי בְנֵי־בְלִיַּעַל נָסַבּוּ אֶת־הַבַּיִת מִתְדַּפְּקִים עַל־הַדָּלֶת וַיֹּאמְרוּ אֶל־הָאִישׁ בַּעַל הַבַּיִת הַזָּקֵן לֵאמֹר הוֹצֵא אֶת־הָאִישׁ אֲשֶׁר־בָּא אֶל־בֵּיתְךָ וְנֵדָעֶנּוּ:

Judges

23 The owner of the house went out and said to them, "Please, my friends, do not commit such a wrong. Since this man has entered my house, do not perpetrate this outrage.

כג וַיֵּצֵא אֲלֵיהֶם הָאִישׁ בַּעַל הַבַּיִת וַיֹּאמֶר אֲלֵהֶם אַל־אַחַי אַל־תָּרֵעוּ נָא אַחֲרֵי אֲשֶׁר־בָּא הָאִישׁ הַזֶּה אֶל־בֵּיתִי אַל־תַּעֲשׂוּ אֶת־הַנְּבָלָה הַזֹּאת:

24 Look, here is my virgin daughter, and his concubine. Let me bring them out to you. Have your pleasure of them, do what you like with them; but don't do that outrageous thing to this man."

כד הִנֵּה בִתִּי הַבְּתוּלָה וּפִילַגְשֵׁהוּ אוֹצִיאָה־נָּא אוֹתָם וְעַנּוּ אוֹתָם וַעֲשׂוּ לָהֶם הַטּוֹב בְּעֵינֵיכֶם וְלָאִישׁ הַזֶּה לֹא תַעֲשׂוּ דְּבַר הַנְּבָלָה הַזֹּאת:

25 But the men would not listen to him, so the man seized his concubine and pushed her out to them. They raped her and abused her all night long until morning; and they let her go when dawn broke.

כה וְלֹא־אָבוּ הָאֲנָשִׁים לִשְׁמֹעַ לוֹ וַיַּחֲזֵק הָאִישׁ בְּפִילַגְשׁוֹ וַיֹּצֵא אֲלֵיהֶם הַחוּץ וַיֵּדְעוּ אוֹתָהּ וַיִּתְעַלְּלוּ־בָהּ כָּל־הַלַּיְלָה עַד־הַבֹּקֶר וַיְשַׁלְּחוּהָ בעלות [כַּעֲלוֹת] הַשָּׁחַר:

26 Toward morning the woman came back; and as it was growing light, she collapsed at the entrance of the man's house where her husband was.

כו וַתָּבֹא הָאִשָּׁה לִפְנוֹת הַבֹּקֶר וַתִּפֹּל פֶּתַח בֵּית־הָאִישׁ אֲשֶׁר־אֲדוֹנֶיהָ שָּׁם עַד־הָאוֹר:

27 When her husband arose in the morning, he opened the doors of the house and went out to continue his journey; and there was the woman, his concubine, lying at the entrance of the house, with her hands on the threshold.

כז וַיָּקָם אֲדֹנֶיהָ בַּבֹּקֶר וַיִּפְתַּח דַּלְתוֹת הַבַּיִת וַיֵּצֵא לָלֶכֶת לְדַרְכּוֹ וְהִנֵּה הָאִשָּׁה פִילַגְשׁוֹ נֹפֶלֶת פֶּתַח הַבַּיִת וְיָדֶיהָ עַל־הַסַּף:

28 "Get up," he said to her, "let us go." But there was no reply. So the man placed her on the donkey and set out for home.

כח וַיֹּאמֶר אֵלֶיהָ קוּמִי וְנֵלֵכָה וְאֵין עֹנֶה וַיִּקָּחֶהָ עַל־הַחֲמוֹר וַיָּקָם הָאִישׁ וַיֵּלֶךְ לִמְקֹמוֹ:

29 When he came home, he picked up a knife, and took hold of his concubine and cut her up limb by limb into twelve parts. He sent them throughout the territory of *Yisrael*.

כט וַיָּבֹא אֶל־בֵּיתוֹ וַיִּקַּח אֶת־הַמַּאֲכֶלֶת וַיַּחֲזֵק בְּפִילַגְשׁוֹ וַיְנַתְּחֶהָ לַעֲצָמֶיהָ לִשְׁנֵים עָשָׂר נְתָחִים וַיְשַׁלְּחֶהָ בְּכֹל גְּבוּל יִשְׂרָאֵל:

30 And everyone who saw it cried out, "Never has such a thing happened or been seen from the day the Israelites came out of the land of Egypt to this day! Put your mind to this; take counsel and decide."

ל וְהָיָה כָל־הָרֹאֶה וְאָמַר לֹא־נִהְיְתָה וְלֹא־נִרְאֲתָה כָּזֹאת לְמִיּוֹם עֲלוֹת בְּנֵי־יִשְׂרָאֵל מֵאֶרֶץ מִצְרַיִם עַד הַיּוֹם הַזֶּה שִׂימוּ־לָכֶם עָלֶיהָ עֻצוּ וְדַבֵּרוּ:

v'-ha-YAH khol ha-ro-EH v'-a-MAR lo nih-y'-TAH v'-lo nir-a-TAH
ka-ZOT l'-mi-YOM a-LOT b'-nay yis-ra-AYL may-E-retz mitz-RA-yim
AD ha-YOM ha-ZEH see-mu la-KHEM a-LE-ha U-tzu v'-da-BAY-ru

19:30 Never has such a thing happened or been seen Jewish tradition understands that the passages of the *Tanakh* are not always presented in chronological order. According to *Rashi*, this story, along with the narrative of *Micha*'s idol, occurred at the beginning of the era of the Judges. Rabbi Shlomo Aviner suggests that these narratives were placed here, at the end of the book, as another reminder of the sad results of having no king: disunity, disorder and violence.

Inside the Knesset

20 **1** *Thereupon all the Israelites – from Dan to Be'er Sheva and [from] the land of Gilad – marched forth, and the community assembled to a man before Hashem at Mitzpa.*

כ א וַיֵּצְאוּ כָּל־בְּנֵי יִשְׂרָאֵל וַתִּקָּהֵל הָעֵדָה כְּאִישׁ אֶחָד לְמִדָּן וְעַד־בְּאֵר שֶׁבַע וְאֶרֶץ הַגִּלְעָד אֶל־יְהוָה הַמִּצְפָּה:

va-yay-tz'-U kol b'-NAY yis-ra-AYL va-ti-ka-HAYL ha-ay-DAH k'-EESH e-KHAD l'-mi-DAN v'-ad b'-AYR SHE-va v'-E-retz ha-gil-AD el a-do-NAI ha-mitz-PAH

2 All the leaders of the people [and] all the tribes of *Yisrael* presented themselves in the assembly of *Hashem*'s people, 400,000 fighting men on foot.

ב וַיִּתְיַצְּבוּ פִּנּוֹת כָּל־הָעָם כֹּל שִׁבְטֵי יִשְׂרָאֵל בִּקְהַל עַם הָאֱלֹהִים אַרְבַּע מֵאוֹת אֶלֶף אִישׁ רַגְלִי שֹׁלֵף חָרֶב:

3 The Benjaminites heard that the Israelites had come up to *Mitzpa*. – The Israelites said, "Tell us, how did this evil thing happen?"

ג וַיִּשְׁמְעוּ בְּנֵי בִנְיָמִן כִּי־עָלוּ בְנֵי־יִשְׂרָאֵל הַמִּצְפָּה וַיֹּאמְרוּ בְּנֵי יִשְׂרָאֵל דַּבְּרוּ אֵיכָה נִהְיְתָה הָרָעָה הַזֹּאת:

4 And the Levite, the husband of the murdered woman, replied, "My concubine and I came to *Giva* of *Binyamin* to spend the night.

ד וַיַּעַן הָאִישׁ הַלֵּוִי אִישׁ הָאִשָּׁה הַנִּרְצָחָה וַיֹּאמַר הַגִּבְעָתָה אֲשֶׁר לְבִנְיָמִן בָּאתִי אֲנִי וּפִילַגְשִׁי לָלוּן:

5 The citizens of *Giva* set out to harm me. They gathered against me around the house in the night; they meant to kill me, and they ravished my concubine until she died.

ה וַיָּקֻמוּ עָלַי בַּעֲלֵי הַגִּבְעָה וַיָּסֹבּוּ עָלַי אֶת־הַבַּיִת לָיְלָה אוֹתִי דִּמּוּ לַהֲרֹג וְאֶת־פִּילַגְשִׁי עִנּוּ וַתָּמֹת:

6 So I took hold of my concubine and I cut her in pieces and sent them through every part of *Yisrael*'s territory. For an outrageous act of depravity had been committed in *Yisrael*.

ו וָאֹחֵז בְּפִילַגְשִׁי וָאֲנַתְּחֶהָ וָאֲשַׁלְּחֶהָ בְּכָל־שְׂדֵה נַחֲלַת יִשְׂרָאֵל כִּי עָשׂוּ זִמָּה וּנְבָלָה בְּיִשְׂרָאֵל:

7 Now you are all Israelites; produce a plan of action here and now!"

ז הִנֵּה כֻלְּכֶם בְּנֵי יִשְׂרָאֵל הָבוּ לָכֶם דָּבָר וְעֵצָה הֲלֹם:

8 Then all the people rose, as one man, and declared, "We will not go back to our homes, we will not enter our houses!

ח וַיָּקָם כָּל־הָעָם כְּאִישׁ אֶחָד לֵאמֹר לֹא נֵלֵךְ אִישׁ לְאָהֳלוֹ וְלֹא נָסוּר אִישׁ לְבֵיתוֹ:

Seeing these repeated tragedies at the end of the book of *Shoftim* highlights the importance of the rise of the monarchy, described in the next book, *Shmuel*. Though the contemporary State of Israel has no king, Rabbi Abraham Isaac Kook says that a democratically elected Jewish government has a status similar to that of a monarchy. The Jewish people are fortunate that the State of Israel has a set and ordered government to protect society and to care for the nation.

20:1 From *Dan* to *Be'er Sheva* *Be'er Sheva*, mentioned in this verse as the southern boundary of Jewish settlement in *Eretz Yisrael*, was a vital city in biblical times. *Be'er Sheva* is one of the primary places where *Avraham* lives and digs a well, *be'er* (באר) in Hebrew. *Yitzchak* builds an altar there, and *Yaakov* passes through on the way to *Beit El* and later stops to bring sacrifices there on his way down to Egypt. In contemporary Israel, *Be'er Sheva* is known as "the capital of the *Negev* Desert." It is a thriving, multicultural city with a population including many Jews from Ethiopia and the former Soviet Union, a major hospital and a large university. The city is one of the many ancient cities in the Land of Israel that the Children of Israel have revived and developed.

Modern Court House in *Beer Sheva*

9 But this is what we will do to *Giva*: [we will wage war] against it according to lot.

ט וְעַתָּה זֶה הַדָּבָר אֲשֶׁר נַעֲשֶׂה לַגִּבְעָה עָלֶיהָ בְּגוֹרָל:

10 We will take from all the tribes of *Yisrael* ten men to the hundred, a hundred to the thousand, and a thousand to the ten thousand to supply provisions for the troops – to prepare for their going to Geba in *Binyamin* for all the outrage it has committed in *Yisrael*."

י וְלָקַחְנוּ עֲשָׂרָה אֲנָשִׁים לַמֵּאָה לְכֹל שִׁבְטֵי יִשְׂרָאֵל וּמֵאָה לָאֶלֶף וְאֶלֶף לָרְבָבָה לָקַחַת צֵדָה לָעָם לַעֲשׂוֹת לְבוֹאָם לְגֶבַע בִּנְיָמִן כְּכָל־הַנְּבָלָה אֲשֶׁר עָשָׂה בְּיִשְׂרָאֵל:

11 So all the men of *Yisrael*, united as one man, massed against the town.

יא וַיֵּאָסֵף כָּל־אִישׁ יִשְׂרָאֵל אֶל־הָעִיר כְּאִישׁ אֶחָד חֲבֵרִים:

12 And the tribes of *Yisrael* sent men through the whole tribe of *Binyamin*, saying, "What is this evil thing that has happened among you?

יב וַיִּשְׁלְחוּ שִׁבְטֵי יִשְׂרָאֵל אֲנָשִׁים בְּכָל־ שִׁבְטֵי בִנְיָמִן לֵאמֹר מָה הָרָעָה הַזֹּאת אֲשֶׁר נִהְיְתָה בָּכֶם:

13 Come, hand over those scoundrels in *Giva* so that we may put them to death and stamp out the evil from *Yisrael*." But the Benjaminites would not yield to the demand of their fellow Israelites.

יג וְעַתָּה תְּנוּ אֶת־הָאֲנָשִׁים בְּנֵי־בְלִיַּעַל אֲשֶׁר בַּגִּבְעָה וּנְמִיתֵם וּנְבַעֲרָה רָעָה מִיִּשְׂרָאֵל וְלֹא אָבוּ [בְּנֵי] בִּנְיָמִן לִשְׁמֹעַ בְּקוֹל אֲחֵיהֶם בְּנֵי־יִשְׂרָאֵל:

14 So the Benjaminites gathered from their towns to *Giva* in order to take the field against the Israelites.

יד וַיֵּאָסְפוּ בְנֵי־בִנְיָמִן מִן־הֶעָרִים הַגִּבְעָתָה לָצֵאת לַמִּלְחָמָה עִם־בְּנֵי יִשְׂרָאֵל:

15 On that day the Benjaminites mustered from the towns 26,000 fighting men, mustered apart from the inhabitants of *Giva*; 700 picked men

טו וַיִּתְפָּקְדוּ בְנֵי בִנְיָמִן בַּיּוֹם הַהוּא מֵהֶעָרִים עֶשְׂרִים וְשִׁשָּׁה אֶלֶף אִישׁ שֹׁלֵף חָרֶב לְבַד מִיֹּשְׁבֵי הַגִּבְעָה הִתְפָּקְדוּ שְׁבַע מֵאוֹת אִישׁ בָּחוּר:

16 of all this force – 700 picked men – were left-handed. Every one of them could sling a stone at a hair and not miss.

טז מִכֹּל הָעָם הַזֶּה שְׁבַע מֵאוֹת אִישׁ בָּחוּר אִטֵּר יַד־יְמִינוֹ כָּל־זֶה קֹלֵעַ בָּאֶבֶן אֶל־ הַשַּׂעֲרָה וְלֹא יַחֲטִא:

17 The men of *Yisrael* other than *Binyamin* mustered 400,000 fighting men, warriors to a man.

יז וְאִישׁ יִשְׂרָאֵל הִתְפָּקְדוּ לְבַד מִבִּנְיָמִן אַרְבַּע מֵאוֹת אֶלֶף אִישׁ שֹׁלֵף חָרֶב כָּל־ זֶה אִישׁ מִלְחָמָה:

18 They proceeded to *Beit El* and inquired of *Hashem*; the Israelites asked, "Who of us shall advance first to fight the Benjaminites?" And *Hashem* replied, "*Yehuda* first."

יח וַיָּקֻמוּ וַיַּעֲלוּ בֵית־אֵל וַיִּשְׁאֲלוּ בֵאלֹהִים וַיֹּאמְרוּ בְּנֵי יִשְׂרָאֵל מִי יַעֲלֶה־לָּנוּ בַתְּחִלָּה לַמִּלְחָמָה עִם־בְּנֵי בִנְיָמִן וַיֹּאמֶר יְהוָה יְהוּדָה בַתְּחִלָּה:

19 So the Israelites arose in the morning and encamped against *Giva*.

יט וַיָּקוּמוּ בְנֵי־יִשְׂרָאֵל בַּבֹּקֶר וַיַּחֲנוּ עַל־ הַגִּבְעָה:

20 The men of *Yisrael* took the field against the Benjaminites; the men of *Yisrael* drew up in battle order against them at *Giva*.

כ וַיֵּצֵא אִישׁ יִשְׂרָאֵל לַמִּלְחָמָה עִם־בִּנְיָמִן וַיַּעַרְכוּ אִתָּם אִישׁ־יִשְׂרָאֵל מִלְחָמָה אֶל־הַגִּבְעָה:

21 But the Benjaminites issued from *Giva*, and that day they struck down 22,000 men of *Yisrael*.

כא וַיֵּצְאוּ בְנֵי־בִנְיָמִן מִן־הַגִּבְעָה וַיַּשְׁחִיתוּ בְיִשְׂרָאֵל בַּיּוֹם הַהוּא שְׁנַיִם וְעֶשְׂרִים אֶלֶף אִישׁ אָרְצָה:

22 Now the army – the men of *Yisrael* – rallied and again drew up in battle order at the same place as they had on the first day.

כב וַיִּתְחַזֵּק הָעָם אִישׁ יִשְׂרָאֵל וַיֹּסִפוּ לַעֲרֹךְ מִלְחָמָה בַּמָּקוֹם אֲשֶׁר־עָרְכוּ שָׁם בַּיּוֹם הָרִאשׁוֹן:

23 For the Israelites had gone up and wept before *Hashem* until evening. They had inquired of *Hashem*, "Shall we again join battle with our kinsmen the Benjaminites?" And *Hashem* had replied, "March against them."

כג וַיַּעֲלוּ בְנֵי־יִשְׂרָאֵל וַיִּבְכּוּ לִפְנֵי־יְהוָה עַד־הָעֶרֶב וַיִּשְׁאֲלוּ בַיהוָה לֵאמֹר הַאוֹסִיף לָגֶשֶׁת לַמִּלְחָמָה עִם־בְּנֵי בִנְיָמִן אָחִי וַיֹּאמֶר יְהוָה עֲלוּ אֵלָיו:

24 The Israelites advanced against the *Binyaminites* on the second day.

כד וַיִּקְרְבוּ בְנֵי־יִשְׂרָאֵל אֶל־בְּנֵי בִנְיָמִן בַּיּוֹם הַשֵּׁנִי:

25 But the Benjaminites came out from *Giva* against them on the second day and struck down 18,000 more of the Israelites, all of them fighting men.

כה וַיֵּצֵא בִנְיָמִן לִקְרָאתָם מִן־הַגִּבְעָה בַּיּוֹם הַשֵּׁנִי וַיַּשְׁחִיתוּ בִבְנֵי יִשְׂרָאֵל עוֹד שְׁמֹנַת עָשָׂר אֶלֶף אִישׁ אָרְצָה כָּל־אֵלֶּה שֹׁלְפֵי חָרֶב:

26 Then all the Israelites, all the army, went up and came to *Beit El* and they sat there, weeping before *Hashem*. They fasted that day until evening, and presented burnt offerings and offerings of well-being to *Hashem*.

כו וַיַּעֲלוּ כָל־בְּנֵי יִשְׂרָאֵל וְכָל־הָעָם וַיָּבֹאוּ בֵית־אֵל וַיִּבְכּוּ וַיֵּשְׁבוּ שָׁם לִפְנֵי יְהוָה וַיָּצוּמוּ בַיּוֹם־הַהוּא עַד־הָעָרֶב וַיַּעֲלוּ עֹלוֹת וּשְׁלָמִים לִפְנֵי יְהוָה:

27 The Israelites inquired of *Hashem* (for the *Aron Brit Hashem* was there in those days,

כז וַיִּשְׁאֲלוּ בְנֵי־יִשְׂרָאֵל בַּיהוָה וְשָׁם אֲרוֹן בְּרִית הָאֱלֹהִים בַּיָּמִים הָהֵם:

28 and *Pinchas* son of *Elazar* son of *Aharon* the *Kohen* ministered before Him in those days), "Shall we again take the field against our kinsmen the Benjaminites, or shall we not?" *Hashem* answered, "Go up, for tomorrow I will deliver them into your hands."

כח וּפִינְחָס בֶּן־אֶלְעָזָר בֶּן־אַהֲרֹן עֹמֵד לְפָנָיו בַּיָּמִים הָהֵם לֵאמֹר הַאוֹסִף עוֹד לָצֵאת לַמִּלְחָמָה עִם־בְּנֵי־בִנְיָמִן אָחִי אִם־אֶחְדָּל וַיֹּאמֶר יְהוָה עֲלוּ כִּי מָחָר אֶתְּנֶנּוּ בְיָדֶךָ:

29 *Yisrael* put men in ambush against *Giva* on all sides.

כט וַיָּשֶׂם יִשְׂרָאֵל אֹרְבִים אֶל־הַגִּבְעָה סָבִיב:

30 And on the third day, the Israelites went up against the Benjaminites, as before, and engaged them in battle at *Giva*.

ל וַיַּעֲלוּ בְנֵי־יִשְׂרָאֵל אֶל־בְּנֵי בִנְיָמִן בַּיּוֹם הַשְּׁלִישִׁי וַיַּעַרְכוּ אֶל־הַגִּבְעָה כְּפַעַם בְּפָעַם:

31 The Benjaminites dashed out to meet the army and were drawn away from the town onto the roads, of which one runs to *Beit El* and the other to *Giva*. As before, they started out by striking some of the men dead in the open field, about 30 men of *Yisrael*.

לא וַיֵּצְאוּ בְנֵי־בִנְיָמִן לִקְרַאת הָעָם הָנְתְּקוּ מִן־הָעִיר וַיָּחֵלּוּ לְהַכּוֹת מֵהָעָם חֲלָלִים כְּפַעַם בְּפַעַם בַּמְסִלּוֹת אֲשֶׁר אַחַת עֹלָה בֵית־אֵל וְאַחַת גִּבְעָתָה בַּשָּׂדֶה כִּשְׁלֹשִׁים אִישׁ בְּיִשְׂרָאֵל:

32 The Benjaminites thought, "They are being routed before us as previously." But the Israelites had planned: "We will take to flight and draw them away from the town to the roads."

לב וַיֹּאמְרוּ בְּנֵי בִנְיָמִן נִגָּפִים הֵם לְפָנֵינוּ כְּבָרִאשֹׁנָה וּבְנֵי יִשְׂרָאֵל אָמְרוּ נָנוּסָה וּנְתַקְנֻהוּ מִן־הָעִיר אֶל־הַמְסִלּוֹת:

33 And while the main body of the Israelites had moved away from their positions and had drawn up in battle order at Baal-tamar, the Israelite ambush was rushing out from its position at Maareh-geba.

לג וְכֹל אִישׁ יִשְׂרָאֵל קָמוּ מִמְּקוֹמוֹ וַיַּעַרְכוּ בְּבַעַל תָּמָר וְאֹרֵב יִשְׂרָאֵל מֵגִיחַ מִמְּקֹמוֹ מִמַּעֲרֵה־גָבַע:

34 Thus 10,000 picked men of all *Yisrael* came to a point south of *Giva*, and the battle was furious. Before they realized that disaster was approaching,

לד וַיָּבֹאוּ מִנֶּגֶד לַגִּבְעָה עֲשֶׂרֶת אֲלָפִים אִישׁ בָּחוּר מִכָּל־יִשְׂרָאֵל וְהַמִּלְחָמָה כָּבֵדָה וְהֵם לֹא יָדְעוּ כִּי־נֹגַעַת עֲלֵיהֶם הָרָעָה:

35 *Hashem* routed the Benjaminites before *Yisrael*. That day the Israelites slew 25,100 men of *Binyamin*, all of them fighting men.

לה וַיִּגֹּף יְהֹוָה אֶת־בִּנְיָמִן לִפְנֵי יִשְׂרָאֵל וַיַּשְׁחִיתוּ בְנֵי יִשְׂרָאֵל בְּבִנְיָמִן בַּיּוֹם הַהוּא עֶשְׂרִים וַחֲמִשָּׁה אֶלֶף וּמֵאָה אִישׁ כָּל־אֵלֶּה שֹׁלֵף חָרֶב:

36 Then the Benjaminites realized that they were routed. Now the Israelites had yielded ground to the Benjaminites, for they relied on the ambush which they had laid against *Giva*.

לו וַיִּרְאוּ בְנֵי־בִנְיָמִן כִּי נִגָּפוּ וַיִּתְּנוּ אִישׁ־יִשְׂרָאֵל מָקוֹם לְבִנְיָמִן כִּי בָטְחוּ אֶל־הָאֹרֵב אֲשֶׁר שָׂמוּ אֶל־הַגִּבְעָה:

37 One ambush quickly deployed against *Giva*, and the other ambush advanced and put the whole town to the sword.

לז וְהָאֹרֵב הֵחִישׁוּ וַיִּפְשְׁטוּ אֶל־הַגִּבְעָה וַיִּמְשֹׁךְ הָאֹרֵב וַיַּךְ אֶת־כָּל־הָעִיר לְפִי־חָרֶב:

38 A time had been agreed upon by the Israelite men with those in ambush: When a huge column of smoke was sent up from the town,

לח וְהַמּוֹעֵד הָיָה לְאִישׁ יִשְׂרָאֵל עִם־הָאֹרֵב הֶרֶב לְהַעֲלוֹתָם מַשְׂאַת הֶעָשָׁן מִן־הָעִיר:

39 the Israelite men were to turn about in battle. *Binyamin* had begun by striking dead about 30 Israelite men, and they thought, "They are being routed before us as in the previous fighting."

לט וַיַּהֲפֹךְ אִישׁ־יִשְׂרָאֵל בַּמִּלְחָמָה וּבִנְיָמִן הֵחֵל לְהַכּוֹת חֲלָלִים בְּאִישׁ־יִשְׂרָאֵל כִּשְׁלֹשִׁים אִישׁ כִּי אָמְרוּ אַךְ נִגּוֹף נִגָּף הוּא לְפָנֵינוּ כַּמִּלְחָמָה הָרִאשֹׁנָה:

40 But when the column, the pillar of smoke, began to rise from the city, the Benjaminites looked behind them, and there was the whole town going up in smoke to the sky!

מ וְהַמַּשְׂאֵת הֵחֵלָּה לַעֲלוֹת מִן־הָעִיר עַמּוּד עָשָׁן וַיִּפֶן בִּנְיָמִן אַחֲרָיו וְהִנֵּה עָלָה כְלִיל־הָעִיר הַשָּׁמָיְמָה:

41 And now the Israelites turned about, and the men of *Binyamin* were thrown into panic, for they realized that disaster had overtaken them.

מא וְאִישׁ יִשְׂרָאֵל הָפַךְ וַיִּבָּהֵל אִישׁ בִּנְיָמִן כִּי רָאָה כִּי־נָגְעָה עָלָיו הָרָעָה:

42 They retreated before the men of *Yisrael* along the road to the wilderness, where the fighting caught up with them; meanwhile those from the towns were massacring them in it.

מב וַיִּפְנוּ לִפְנֵי אִישׁ יִשְׂרָאֵל אֶל־דֶּרֶךְ הַמִּדְבָּר וְהַמִּלְחָמָה הִדְבִּיקָתְהוּ וַאֲשֶׁר מֵהֶעָרִים מַשְׁחִיתִים אוֹתוֹ בְּתוֹכוֹ:

43 They encircled the Benjaminites, pursued them, and trod them down [from] Menuhah to a point opposite *Giva* on the east.

מג כִּתְּרוּ אֶת־בִּנְיָמִן הִרְדִיפֻהוּ מְנוּחָה הִדְרִיכֻהוּ עַד נֹכַח הַגִּבְעָה מִמִּזְרַח־שָׁמֶשׁ:

44 That day 18,000 men of *Binyamin* fell, all of them brave men.

מד וַיִּפְּלוּ מִבִּנְיָמִן שְׁמֹנָה־עָשָׂר אֶלֶף אִישׁ אֶת־כָּל־אֵלֶּה אַנְשֵׁי־חָיִל:

45 They turned and fled to the wilderness, to the Rock of Rimmon; but [the Israelites] picked off another 5,000 on the roads and, continuing in hot pursuit of them up to Gidom, they slew 2,000 more.

מה וַיִּפְנוּ וַיָּנֻסוּ הַמִּדְבָּרָה אֶל־סֶלַע הָרִמּוֹן וַיְעֹלְלֻהוּ בַּמְסִלּוֹת חֲמֵשֶׁת אֲלָפִים אִישׁ וַיַּדְבִּיקוּ אַחֲרָיו עַד־גִּדְעֹם וַיַּכּוּ מִמֶּנּוּ אַלְפַּיִם אִישׁ:

46 Thus the total number of Benjaminites who fell that day came to 25,000 fighting men, all of them brave.

מו וַיְהִי כָל־הַנֹּפְלִים מִבִּנְיָמִן עֶשְׂרִים וַחֲמִשָּׁה אֶלֶף אִישׁ שֹׁלֵף חֶרֶב בַּיּוֹם הַהוּא אֶת־כָּל־אֵלֶּה אַנְשֵׁי־חָיִל:

47 But 600 men turned and fled to the wilderness, to the Rock of Rimmon; they remained at the Rock of Rimmon four months.

מז וַיִּפְנוּ וַיָּנֻסוּ הַמִּדְבָּרָה אֶל־סֶלַע הָרִמּוֹן שֵׁשׁ מֵאוֹת אִישׁ וַיֵּשְׁבוּ בְּסֶלַע רִמּוֹן אַרְבָּעָה חֳדָשִׁים:

48 The men of *Yisrael*, meanwhile, turned back to the rest of the Benjaminites and put them to the sword – towns, people, cattle – everything that remained. Finally, they set fire to all the towns that were left.

מח וְאִישׁ יִשְׂרָאֵל שָׁבוּ אֶל־בְּנֵי בִנְיָמִן וַיַּכּוּם לְפִי־חֶרֶב מֵעִיר מְתֹם עַד־בְּהֵמָה עַד כָּל־הַנִּמְצָא גַּם כָּל־הֶעָרִים הַנִּמְצָאוֹת שִׁלְּחוּ בָאֵשׁ:

21 1 Now the men of *Yisrael* had taken an oath at *Mitzpa*: "None of us will give his daughter in marriage to a Benjaminite."

כא א וְאִישׁ יִשְׂרָאֵל נִשְׁבַּע בַּמִּצְפָּה לֵאמֹר אִישׁ מִמֶּנּוּ לֹא־יִתֵּן בִּתּוֹ לְבִנְיָמִן לְאִשָּׁה:

2 The people came to *Beit El* and sat there before *Hashem* until evening. They wailed and wept bitterly,

ב וַיָּבֹא הָעָם בֵּית־אֵל וַיֵּשְׁבוּ שָׁם עַד־הָעֶרֶב לִפְנֵי הָאֱלֹהִים וַיִּשְׂאוּ קוֹלָם וַיִּבְכּוּ בְּכִי גָדוֹל:

3 and they said, "O God of *Yisrael*, why has this happened in *Yisrael*, that one tribe must now be missing from *Yisrael*?"

ג וַיֹּאמְרוּ לָמָה יְהֹוָה אֱלֹהֵי יִשְׂרָאֵל הָיְתָה זֹּאת בְּיִשְׂרָאֵל לְהִפָּקֵד הַיּוֹם מִיִּשְׂרָאֵל שֵׁבֶט אֶחָד:

4 Early the next day, the people built a *Mizbayach* there, and they brought burnt offerings and offerings of well-being.

ד וַיְהִי מִמָּחֳרָת וַיַּשְׁכִּימוּ הָעָם וַיִּבְנוּ־שָׁם מִזְבֵּחַ וַיַּעֲלוּ עֹלוֹת וּשְׁלָמִים:

5 The Israelites asked, "Is there anyone from all the tribes of *Yisrael* who failed to come up to the assembly before *Hashem*?" For a solemn oath had been taken concerning anyone who did not go up to *Hashem* at *Mitzpa*: "He shall be put to death."

ה וַיֹּאמְרוּ בְּנֵי יִשְׂרָאֵל מִי אֲשֶׁר לֹא־עָלָה בַקָּהָל מִכָּל־שִׁבְטֵי יִשְׂרָאֵל אֶל־יְהֹוָה כִּי הַשְּׁבוּעָה הַגְּדוֹלָה הָיְתָה לַאֲשֶׁר לֹא־עָלָה אֶל־יְהֹוָה הַמִּצְפָּה לֵאמֹר מוֹת יוּמָת:

6 The Israelites now relented toward their kinsmen the Benjaminites, and they said, "This day one tribe has been cut off from *Yisrael*!

ו וַיִּנָּחֲמוּ בְּנֵי יִשְׂרָאֵל אֶל־בִּנְיָמִן אָחִיו וַיֹּאמְרוּ נִגְדַּע הַיּוֹם שֵׁבֶט אֶחָד מִיִּשְׂרָאֵל:

7 What can we do to provide wives for those who are left, seeing that we have sworn by *Hashem* not to give any of our daughters to them in marriage?"

ז מַה־נַּעֲשֶׂה לָהֶם לַנּוֹתָרִים לְנָשִׁים וַאֲנַחְנוּ נִשְׁבַּעְנוּ בַיהֹוָה לְבִלְתִּי תֵּת־לָהֶם מִבְּנוֹתֵינוּ לְנָשִׁים:

8 They inquired, "Is there anyone from the tribes of *Yisrael* who did not go up to *Hashem* at *Mitzpa*?" Now no one from Jabesh-gilead had come to the camp, to the assembly.

ח וַיֹּאמְרוּ מִי אֶחָד מִשִּׁבְטֵי יִשְׂרָאֵל אֲשֶׁר לֹא־עָלָה אֶל־יְהֹוָה הַמִּצְפָּה וְהִנֵּה לֹא בָא־אִישׁ אֶל־הַמַּחֲנֶה מִיָּבֵישׁ גִּלְעָד אֶל־הַקָּהָל:

9 For, when the roll of the troops was taken, not one of the inhabitants of Jabesh-gilead was present.

ט וַיִּתְפָּקֵד הָעָם וְהִנֵּה אֵין־שָׁם אִישׁ מִיּוֹשְׁבֵי יָבֵשׁ גִּלְעָד:

10 So the assemblage dispatched 12,000 of the warriors, instructing them as follows: "Go and put the inhabitants of Jabesh-gilead to the sword, women and children included.

י וַיִּשְׁלְחוּ־שָׁם הָעֵדָה שְׁנֵים־עָשָׂר אֶלֶף אִישׁ מִבְּנֵי הֶחָיִל וַיְצַוּוּ אוֹתָם לֵאמֹר לְכוּ וְהִכִּיתֶם אֶת־יוֹשְׁבֵי יָבֵשׁ גִּלְעָד לְפִי־ חֶרֶב וְהַנָּשִׁים וְהַטָּף:

11 This is what you are to do: Proscribe every man, and every woman who has known a man carnally."

יא וְזֶה הַדָּבָר אֲשֶׁר תַּעֲשׂוּ כָּל־זָכָר וְכָל־ אִשָּׁה יֹדַעַת מִשְׁכַּב־זָכָר תַּחֲרִימוּ:

12 They found among the inhabitants of Jabesh-gilead 400 maidens who had not known a man carnally; and they brought them to the camp at *Shilo*, which is in the land of Canaan.

יב וַיִּמְצְאוּ מִיּוֹשְׁבֵי יָבֵישׁ גִּלְעָד אַרְבַּע מֵאוֹת נַעֲרָה בְתוּלָה אֲשֶׁר לֹא־יָדְעָה אִישׁ לְמִשְׁכַּב זָכָר וַיָּבִיאוּ אוֹתָם אֶל־ הַמַּחֲנֶה שִׁלֹה אֲשֶׁר בְּאֶרֶץ כְּנָעַן:

13 Then the whole community sent word to the Benjaminites who were at the Rock of Rimmon, and offered them terms of peace.

יג וַיִּשְׁלְחוּ כָּל־הָעֵדָה וַיְדַבְּרוּ אֶל־בְּנֵי בִנְיָמִן אֲשֶׁר בְּסֶלַע רִמּוֹן וַיִּקְרְאוּ לָהֶם שָׁלוֹם:

14 Thereupon the Benjaminites returned, and they gave them the girls who had been spared from the women of Jabesh-gilead. But there were not enough of them.

יד וַיָּשָׁב בִּנְיָמִן בָּעֵת הַהִיא וַיִּתְּנוּ לָהֶם הַנָּשִׁים אֲשֶׁר חִיּוּ מִנְּשֵׁי יָבֵשׁ גִּלְעָד וְלֹא־מָצְאוּ לָהֶם כֵּן:

15 Now the people had relented toward *Binyamin*, for *Hashem* had made a breach in the tribes of *Yisrael*.

טו וְהָעָם נִחָם לְבִנְיָמִן כִּי־עָשָׂה יְהֹוָה פֶּרֶץ בְּשִׁבְטֵי יִשְׂרָאֵל:

16 So the elders of the community asked, "What can we do about wives for those who are left, since the women of *Binyamin* have been killed off?"

טז וַיֹּאמְרוּ זִקְנֵי הָעֵדָה מַה־נַּעֲשֶׂה לַנּוֹתָרִים לְנָשִׁים כִּי־נִשְׁמְדָה מִבִּנְיָמִן אִשָּׁה:

17 For they said, "There must be a saving remnant for *Binyamin*, that a tribe may not be blotted out of *Yisrael*;

יז וַיֹּאמְרוּ יְרֻשַּׁת פְּלֵיטָה לְבִנְיָמִן וְלֹא־ יִמָּחֶה שֵׁבֶט מִיִּשְׂרָאֵל:

18 yet we cannot give them any of our daughters as wives," since the Israelites had taken an oath: "Cursed be anyone who gives a wife to *Binyamin*!"

יח וַאֲנַחְנוּ לֹא נוּכַל לָתֵת־לָהֶם נָשִׁים מִבְּנוֹתֵינוּ כִּי־נִשְׁבְּעוּ בְנֵי־יִשְׂרָאֵל לֵאמֹר אָרוּר נֹתֵן אִשָּׁה לְבִנְיָמִן:

19 They said, "The annual feast of *Hashem* is now being held at *Shilo*." (It lies north of *Beit El*, east of the highway that runs from *Beit El* to *Shechem*, and south of Lebonah.)

יט וַיֹּאמְרוּ הִנֵּה חַג־יְהֹוָה בְּשִׁלוֹ מִיָּמִים יָמִימָה אֲשֶׁר מִצְּפוֹנָה לְבֵית־אֵל מִזְרְחָה הַשֶּׁמֶשׁ לִמְסִלָּה הָעֹלָה מִבֵּית־אֵל שְׁכֶמָה וּמִנֶּגֶב לִלְבוֹנָה:

20 So they instructed the Benjaminites as follows: "Go and lie in wait in the vineyards.

כ ויצו [וַיְצַוּוּ] אֶת־בְּנֵי בִנְיָמִן לֵאמֹר לְכוּ וַאֲרַבְתֶּם בַּכְּרָמִים:

57

²¹ As soon as you see the girls of *Shilo* coming out to join in the dances, come out from the vineyards; let each of you seize a wife from among the girls of *Shilo*, and be off for the land of *Binyamin*.

כא וּרְאִיתֶם וְהִנֵּה אִם־יֵצְאוּ בְנוֹת־שִׁילוֹ לָחוּל בַּמְּחֹלוֹת וִיצָאתֶם מִן־הַכְּרָמִים וַחֲטַפְתֶּם לָכֶם אִישׁ אִשְׁתּוֹ מִבְּנוֹת שִׁילוֹ וַהֲלַכְתֶּם אֶרֶץ בִּנְיָמִן:

²² And if their fathers or brothers come to us to complain, we shall say to them, 'Be generous to them for our sake! We could not provide any of them with a wife on account of the war, and you would have incurred guilt if you yourselves had given them [wives].'"

כב וְהָיָה כִּי־יָבֹאוּ אֲבוֹתָם אוֹ אֲחֵיהֶם לָרֹב [לָרִיב] אֵלֵינוּ וְאָמַרְנוּ אֲלֵיהֶם חָנּוּנוּ אוֹתָם כִּי לֹא לָקַחְנוּ אִישׁ אִשְׁתּוֹ בַּמִּלְחָמָה כִּי לֹא אַתֶּם נְתַתֶּם לָהֶם כָּעֵת תֶּאְשָׁמוּ:

²³ The Benjaminites did so. They took to wife, from the dancers whom they carried off, as many as they themselves numbered. Then they went back to their own territory, and rebuilt their towns and settled in them.

כג וַיַּעֲשׂוּ־כֵן בְּנֵי בִנְיָמִן וַיִּשְׂאוּ נָשִׁים לְמִסְפָּרָם מִן־הַמְּחֹלְלוֹת אֲשֶׁר גָּזָלוּ וַיֵּלְכוּ וַיָּשׁוּבוּ אֶל־נַחֲלָתָם וַיִּבְנוּ אֶת־הֶעָרִים וַיֵּשְׁבוּ בָּהֶם:

va-ya-a-su KHAYN b'-NAY vin-ya-MIN va-yis-U na-SHEEM l'-mis-pa-RAM min ha-m'-kho-l'-LOT a-SHER ga-ZA-lu va-yay-l'-KHU va-ya-SHU-vu el na-kha-la-TAM va-yiv-NU et he-a-REEM va-yay-sh'-VU ba-HEM

²⁴ Thereupon the Israelites dispersed, each to his own tribe and clan; everyone departed for his own territory.

כד וַיִּתְהַלְּכוּ מִשָּׁם בְּנֵי־יִשְׂרָאֵל בָּעֵת הַהִיא אִישׁ לְשִׁבְטוֹ וּלְמִשְׁפַּחְתּוֹ וַיֵּצְאוּ מִשָּׁם אִישׁ לְנַחֲלָתוֹ:

²⁵ In those days there was no king in *Yisrael*; everyone did as he pleased.

כה בַּיָּמִים הָהֵם אֵין מֶלֶךְ בְּיִשְׂרָאֵל אִישׁ הַיָּשָׁר בְּעֵינָיו יַעֲשֶׂה:

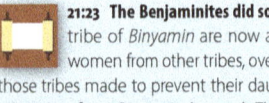

21:23 The Benjaminites did so The men of the tribe of *Binyamin* are now allowed to marry women from other tribes, overturning the oath those tribes made to prevent their daughters from marrying men from *Binyamin* (verse 1). This event brought about the reunification of the twelve tribes of Israel. The Talmud (*Taanit* 30b) records that this happened on the fifteenth day of the Hebrew month of *Av*, which helped turn that day into one of perpetual joy. The fact that the Children of Israel are once again united in the Land of Israel is indeed a cause for celebration.

Celebratory fireworks off the coast of *Tel Aviv*

List of Transliterated Words in *The Israel Bible*

The following is a list of nouns which have been transliterated into Hebrew in the English translation and commentary of *The Israel Bible*:

Hebrew Name	English Name	Pronunciation	Hebrew
Achan	Achan	a-KHAN	עָכָן
Achav	Ahab	akh-AV	אַחְאָב
Achaz	Ahaz	a-KHAZ	אָחָז
Achazyahu	Ahaziah	a-khaz-YA-hu	אֲחַזְיָהוּ
Achiezer	Ahiezer	a-khee-E-zer	אֲחִיעֶזֶר
Achihud	Ahihud	a-khee-HUD	אֲחִיהוּד
Achikam	Ahikam	a-khee-KAM	אֲחִיקָם
Achilud	Ahilud	a-khee-LUD	אֲחִילוּד
Achimelech	Ahimelech	a-khee-ME-lekh	אֲחִימֶלֶךְ
Achira	Ahira	a-khee-RA	אֲחִירַע
Achisamach	Ahisamach	a-khee-sa-MAKH	אֲחִיסָמָךְ
Achitofel	Ahithophel	a-khee-TO-fel	אֲחִיתֹפֶל
Achituv	Ahitub	a-khee-TUV	אֲחִיטוּב
Achiya	Ahijah	a-khi-YAH	אֲחִיָּה
Adam	Adam	a-DAM	אָדָם
Adar	Adar	a-DAR	אֲדָר
Adoniyahu	Adonijah	a-do-ni-YA-hu	אֲדֹנִיָּהוּ
Adulam	Adullam	a-du-LAM	עֲדֻלָּם
Agur	Agur	a-GUR	אָגוּר
Aharon	Aaron	a-ha-RON	אַהֲרֹן
Amasa	Amasa	a-ma-SA	עֲמָשָׂא
Amatzya	Amaziah	a-matz-YAH	אֲמַצְיָה
Amen	Amen	a-MAYN	אָמֵן
Amiel	Ammiel	a-mee-AYL	עַמִּיאֵל
Aminadav	Amminadab	a-mee-na-DAV	עַמִּינָדָב
Amitai	Amittai	a-mi-TAI	אֲמִתַּי
Amnon	Amnon	am-NON	אַמְנוֹן

Hebrew Name	English Name	Pronunciation	Hebrew
Amon	Amon	a-MON	אָמוֹן
Amos	Amos	a-MOS	עָמוֹס
Amotz	Amoz	a-MOTZ	אָמוֹץ
Amram	Amram	am-RAM	עַמְרָם
Anatot	Anathoth	a-na-TOT	עֲנָתוֹת
Aron	Ark	a-RON	אָרוֹן
Aron HaBrit	Ark of the Covenant	a-RON ha-b'-REET	אָרוֹן הַבְּרִית
Arpachshad	Arpachshad	ar-pakh-SHAD	אַרְפַּכְשַׁד
Asa	Asa	a-SA	אָסָא
Asael	Asahel	a-sah-AYL	עֲשָׂהאֵל
Asaf	Asaph	a-SAF	אָסָף
Ashdod	Ashdod	ash-DOD	אַשְׁדוֹד
Asher	Asher	a-SHAYR	אָשֵׁר
Ashkelon	Ashkelon	ash-k'-LON	אַשְׁקְלוֹן
Atalya	Athaliah	a-tal-YAH	עֲתַלְיָה
Avdon	Abdon	av-DON	עַבְדוֹן
Avichayil	Abihail	a-vee-KHA-yil	אֲבִיחַיִל
Avidan	Abidan	a-vee-DAN	אֲבִידָן
Avigail	Abigail	a-vee-GA-yil	אֲבִיגַיִל
Avihu	Abihu	a-vee-HU	אֲבִיהוּא
Avimelech	Abimelech	a-vee-ME-lekh	אֲבִימֶלֶךְ
Avinadav	Abinadab	a-vee-na-DAV	אֲבִינָדָב
Aviram	Abiram	a-vee-RAM	אֲבִירָם
Avishai	Abishai	a-vee-SHAI	אֲבִישַׁי
Aviya	Abijah	a-vi-YAH	אֲבִיָּה
Aviyam	Abijam	a-vi-YAM	אֲבִיָּם
Avner	Abner	av-NAYR	אַבְנֵר
Avraham	Abraham	av-ra-HAM	אַבְרָהָם
Avram	Abram	av-RAM	אַבְרָם
Avshalom	Absalom	av-sha-LOM	אַבְשָׁלוֹם
Azarya	Azariah	a-zar-YAH	עֲזַרְיָה
Azeika	Azekah	a-zay-KAH	עֲזֵקָה
Azza	Gaza	a-ZAH	עַזָּה

Hebrew Name	English Name	Pronunciation	Hebrew
B'nei Yisrael	The Children of Israel	b'-NAY yis-ra-AYL	בְּנֵי יִשְׂרָאֵל
Barak	Barak	ba-rakh-AYL	בָּרָק
Baruch	Baruch	ba-RUKH	בָּרוּךְ
Barzilai	Barzillai	bar-zi-LAI	בַּרְזִלַּי
Basha	Baasa	ba-SHA	בַּעְשָׁא
Batsheva	Bath-sheba	bat-SHE-va	בַּת־שֶׁבַע
Be'er Sheva	Beer-sheba	b'-AYR SHE-va	בְּאֵר שֶׁבַע
Be'eri	Beeri	b'-ay-REE	בְּאֵרִי
Beit Aven	Beth-aven	bayt A-ven	בֵּית אָוֶן
Beit El	Beth-el	bayt el	בֵּית אֵל
Beit Hamikdash	Temple	bayt ha-mik-DASH	בֵּית הַמִּקְדָּשׁ
Beit Lechem	Beth-lehem	bayt LE-khem	בֵּית לֶחֶם
Beit Shean	Beth-shean	bayt sh'-AN	בֵּית שְׁאָן
Beit Shemesh	Beth-shemesh	bayt SHE-mesh	בֵּית שֶׁמֶשׁ
Berechya	Berechiah	be-rekh-YAH	בֶּרֶכְיָה
Betzalel	Bezalel	b'-tzal-AYL	בְּצַלְאֵל
Bilha	Bilhah	bil-HAH	בִּלְהָה
Binyamin	Benjamin	bin-ya-MIN	בִּנְיָמִין
Boaz	Boaz	BO-az	בֹּעַז
Buki	Bukki	bu-KEE	בֻּקִּי
Buzi	Buzi	bu-ZEE	בּוּזִי
Carmel	Carmel	kar-MEL	כַּרְמֶל
Chachalya	Hacaliah	kha-khal-YAH	חֲכַלְיָה
Chagai	Haggai	kha-GAI	חַגַּי
Chana	Hannah	kha-NAH	חַנָּה
Chanamel	Hanamel	kha-nam-AYL	חֲנַמְאֵל
Chanani	Hanani	kha-NA-nee	חֲנָנִי
Chananya	Hananiah	kha-nan-YAH	חֲנַנְיָה
Chaniel	Hanniel	kha-nee-AYL	חַנִּיאֵל
Chanoch	Enoch	kha-NOKH	חֲנוֹךְ
Chava	Eve	kha-VAH	חַוָּה
Chavakuk	Habakkuk	kha-va-KUK	חֲבַקּוּק
Chermon	Hermon	kher-MON	חֶרְמוֹן

Hebrew Name	English Name	Pronunciation	Hebrew
Chetzron	Hezron	khetz-RON	חֶצְרוֹן
Chever	Heber	KHE-ver	חֶבֶר
Chevron	Hebron	khev-RON	חֶבְרוֹן
Chilkiyahu	Hilkiah	khil-ki-YA-hu	חִלְקִיָּהוּ
Chizkiyahu	Hezekiah	khiz-ki-YA-hu	חִזְקִיָּהוּ
Chofni	Hophni	khof-NEE	חָפְנִי
Chogla	Hoglah	khog-LAH	חָגְלָה
Chulda	Hulda	khul-DAH	חֻלְדָּה
Chur	Hur	Khur	חוּר
Dan	Dan	Dan	דָּן
Daniel	Daniel	da-ni-YAYL	דָּנִיֵּאל
Datan	Dathan	da-TAN	דָּתָן
David	David	da-VID	דָּוִד
Devora	Deborah	d'-vo-RAH	דְּבוֹרָה
Dina	Dinah	DEE-nah	דִּינָה
Doeg Ha'adomi	Doeg the Edomite	do-AYG ha-a-do-MEE	דּוֹאֵג הָאֲדֹמִי
Efraim	Ephraim	ef-RA-yim	אֶפְרַיִם
Efrat	Ephrat	ef-RAT	אֶפְרָתָה
Efrat	Ephrathah	ef-RA-tah	אֶפְרָתָה
Ehud	Ehud	ay-HUD	אֵהוּד
Eila	Elah	AY-lah	אֵלָה
Eilon	Elon	ay-LON	אֵילוֹן
Ein Gedi	En-gedi	ayn GE-dee	עֵין גֶּדִי
Elazar	Eleazar	el-a-ZAR	אֶלְעָזָר
Elchanan	Elhanan	el-kha-NAN	אֶלְחָנָן
Eli	Eli	ay-LEE	עֵלִי
Eliav	Eliab	e-lee-AV	אֱלִיאָב
Elidad	Elidad	e-lee-DAD	אֱלִידָד
Eliezer	Eliezer	e-lee-E-zer	אֱלִיעֶזֶר
Elimelech	Elimelech	e-lee-ME-lekh	אֱלִימָלֶךְ
Elisha	Elisha	e-lee-SHA	אֱלִישָׁע
Elishama	Elishama	e-lee-sha-MA	אֱלִישָׁמָע
Elisheva	Elisheba	e-lee-SHE-va	אֱלִישֶׁבַע

Hebrew Name	English Name	Pronunciation	Hebrew
Elitzafan	Eli-zaphan	e-lee-tza-FAN	אֱלִיצָפָן
Elitzur	Elizur	e-lee-TZUR	אֱלִיצוּר
Eliyahu	Elijah	ay-li-YA-hu	אֵלִיָּהוּ
Elkana	Elkanah	el-ka-NAH	אֶלְקָנָה
Elyasaf	Eliasaph	el-ya-SAF	אֶלְיָסָף
Elyashiv	Eliashib	el-ya-SHEEV	אֶלְיָשִׁיב
Enosh	Enosh	e-NOSH	אֱנוֹשׁ
Er	Er	ayr	עֵר
Eshtaol	Eshtaol	esh-ta-OL	אֶשְׁתָּאֹל
Esther	Esther	es-TAYR	אֶסְתֵּר
Eved Melech	Ebed-melech	E-ved ME-lekh	עֶבֶד-מֶלֶךְ
Even Ha-Ezer	Eben-Ezer	E-ven ha-E-zer	אֶבֶן הָעֵזֶר
Ever	Eber	AY-ver	עֵבֶר
Evyatar	Abiathar	ev-ya-TAR	אֶבְיָתָר
Ezra	Ezra	ez-RA	עֶזְרָא
Gad	Gad	gad	גָּד
Gadi	Gaddi	ga-DEE	גַּדִּי
Gadiel	Gaddiel	ga-dee-AYL	גַּדִּיאֵל
Gamliel	Gamaliel	gam-lee-AYL	גַּמְלִיאֵל
Gedalia	Gedaliah	g'-dal-YA (hu)	גְּדַלְיָהוּ
Gedera	Gederah	g'-day-RAH	גְּדֵרָה
Gershom	Gershom	gay-r'-SHOM	גֵּרְשׁוֹם
Gershon	Gershon	gay-r'-SHON	גֵּרְשׁוֹן
Geshem	Geshem	GE-shem	גֶּשֶׁם
Geuel	Geuel	g'-u-AYL	גְּאוּאֵל
Gidon	Gideon	gid-ON	גִּדְעוֹן
Gilad	Gilead	gil-AD	גִּלְעָד
Gilgal	Gilgal	gil-GAL	גִּלְגָּל
Giva	Gibeah	giv-AH	גִּבְעָה
Givon	Gibeon	giv-ON	גִּבְעוֹן
Hadassa	Hadassah	ha-da-SAH	הֲדַסָּה
Har Eival	Mount Ebal	ay-VAL	הַר עֵיבָל
Har Gerizim	Mount Gerizim	g'-ri-ZEEM	הַר גְּרִזִים

Hebrew Name	English Name	Pronunciation	Hebrew
Har HaBayit	Temple Mount	har ha-BA-yit	הַר הַבַּיִת
Har HaZeitim	the Mount of Olives	har ha-zay-TEEM	הַר הַזֵּיתִים
Hashem	Lord/God		
Hayman	Heman	hay-MAN	הֵימָן
Hoshea	Hosea	ho-SHAY-a	הוֹשֵׁעַ
Ido	Iddo	i-DO	עִדּוֹ
Imanu-El	Immanuel	i-MA-nu ayl	עִמָּנוּ אֵל
Ish-boshet	Ish-bosheth	eesh BO-shet	אִישׁ־בֹּשֶׁת
Itamar	Ithamar	ee-ta-MAR	אִיתָמָר
Itiel	Ithiel	ee-tee-AYL	אִיתִיאֵל
Ivtzan	Ibzan	iv-TZAN	אִבְצָן
Iyov	Job	i-YOV	אִיּוֹב
Kadmiel	Kadmiel	kad-mee-AYL	קַדְמִיאֵל
Kalev	Caleb	ka-LAYV	כָּלֵב
Keesh	Kish	keesh	קִישׁ
Kehat	Kohath	k'-HAT	קְהָת
Keinan	Kenan	kay-NAN	קֵינָן
Kemuel	Kemuel	k'-mu-AYL	קְמוּאֵל
Keruvim	Cherubim	k'-ru-VEEM	כְּרוּבִים
Kilyon	Chilion	kil-YON	כִּלְיוֹן
Kiryat Arba	Kiriath-arba	keer-YAT AR-bah	קִרְיַת אַרְבַּע
Kiryat Sefer	Kiriath-sepher	keer-YAT SAY-fer	קִרְיַת־סֵפֶר
Kiryat Ye'arim	Kiriath-jearim	keer-YAT y'-a-REEM	קִרְיַת יְעָרִים
Kislev	Chislev	kis-LAYV	כִּסְלֵו
Kohanim	Priests	ko-ha-NEEM	כֹּהֲנִים
Kohelet	Koheleth	ko-HE-let	קֹהֶלֶת
Kohen	Priest	ko-HAYN	כֹּהֵן
Kohen Gadol	High Priest	ko-HAYN ga-DOL	כֹּהֵן גָּדוֹל
Korach	Korah	KO-rakh	קֹרַח
Kushi	Cushi	ku-SHEE	כּוּשִׁי
Lachish	Lachish	la-KHEESH	לָכִישׁ
Leah	Leah	lay-AH	לֵאָה
Lemech	Lamech	LE-mekh	לֶמֶךְ

Hebrew Name	English Name	Pronunciation	Hebrew
Lemuel	Lemuel	l'-mu-AYL	לְמוֹאֵל
Levi	Levi	lay-VEE	לֵוִי
Leviim	Levites	l'-vee-IM	לְוִים
Machla	Mahlah	makh-LAH	מַחְלָה
Machlon	Mahlon	makh-LON	מַחְלוֹן
Machseya	Mahseiah	makh-say-YAH	מַחְסֵיָה
Malachi	Malachi	mal-a-KHEE	מַלְאָכִי
Manoach	Manoah	ma-NO-akh	מָנוֹחַ
Mashiach	Messiah	ma-SHEE-akh	מָשִׁיחַ
Mefiboshet	Mephibosheth	m'-fee-VO-shet	מְפִיבֹשֶׁת
Mehalalel	Mahalalel	ma-ha-lal-AYL	מַהֲלַלְאֵל
Menachem	Menahem	m'-na-KHAYM	מְנַחֵם
Menashe	Menasseh	m'-na-SHEH	מְנַשֶּׁה
Menorah	Candlestick	m'-no-RAH	מְנֹרָה
Merari	Merari	m'-ra-REE	מְרָרִי
Metushelach	Methusaleh	m'-tu-SHE-lakh	מְתוּשֶׁלַח
Micha	Micah	mee-KHAH	מִיכָה
Michael	Michael	mee-kha-AYL	מִיכָאֵל
Michaihu	Micaiah	mee-KHAI-hu	מִיכָיְהוּ
Michal	Michal	mee-KHAL	מִיכַל
Milka	Milcah	mil-KAH	מִלְכָּה
Miriam	Miriam	mir-YAM	מִרְיָם
Mishael	Mishael	mee-sha-AYL	מִישָׁאֵל
Mishkan	Tabernacle	mish-KAN	מִשְׁכַּן
Mitzpa	Mizpah	mitz-PAH	מִצְפָּה
Mizbayach	Altar	miz-BAY-akh	מִזְבֵּחַ
Mordechai	Mordecai	mor-d'-KHAI	מָרְדֳּכַי
Moriah	Moriah	mo-ri-YAH	מוֹרִיָּה
Moshe	Moses	mo-SHEH	מֹשֶׁה
Nachbi	Nahbi	nakh-BEE	נַחְבִּי
Nachor	Nahor	na-KHOR	נָחוֹר
Nachshon	Nahshon	nakh-SHON	נַחְשׁוֹן
Nachum	Nahum	na-KHUM	נַחוּם

Hebrew Name	English Name	Pronunciation	Hebrew
Nadav	Nadab	na-DAV	נָדָב
Naftali	Naphtali	naf-ta-LEE	נַפְתָּלִי
Naomi	Naomi	na-o-MEE	נָעֳמִי
Natan	Nathan	na-TAN	נָתָן
Naval	Nabal	na-VAL	נָבָל
Navi	Prophet	na-VEE	נָבִיא
Navot	Naboth	na-VAL	נָבָל
Nechemya	Nehemiah	n'-khem-YAH	נְחֶמְיָה
Negev	Negeb	NE-gev	נֶגֶב
Nerya	Neriah	nay-ri-YAH	נֵרִיָּה
Netanel	Nethanel	n'-tan-AYL	נְתַנְאֵל
Neviah	Prophetess	n'-vee-AH	נְבִיאָה
Neviim	Prophets	n'-vee-EEM	נְבִיאִים
Nisan	Nisan	nee-SAN	נִיסָן
Noa	Noah	no-AH	נֹעָה
Noach	Noah	NO-akh	נֹחַ
Nov	Nob	nov	נֹב
Nun	Nun	nun	נוּן
Oded	Oded	o-DAYD	עוֹדֵד
Ohola	Oholah	a-ho-LAH	אָהֳלָה
Oholiav	Oholiab	o-ha-lee-AV	אָהֳלִיאָב
Oholiva	Oholibah	a-ho-lee-VAH	אָהֳלִיבָה
Omri	Omri	om-REE	עָמְרִי
Onan	Onan	o-NAN	אוֹנָן
Otniel	Othniel	ot-nee-AYL	עָתְנִיאֵל
Ovadya	Obadiah	o-vad-YAH	עֹבַדְיָה
Oved	Obed	o-VAYD	עוֹבֵד
Oved Edom	Obed Edom	o-VAYD e-DOM	עוֹבֵד אֱדוֹם
Pagiel	Pagiel	pag-ee-AYL	פַּגְעִיאֵל
Palti	Palti	pal-TEE	פַּלְטִי
Paltiel	Paltiel	pal-tee-AYL	פַּלְטִיאֵל
Pekach	Pekah	PE-kakh	פֶּקַח
Pedael	Pedahel	p'-da-AYL	פְּדַהְאֵל

Hebrew Name	English Name	Pronunciation	Hebrew
Pekachya	Pekahiah	p'-kakh-YAH	פְּקַחְיָה
Peleg	Peleg	PE-leg	פֶּלֶג
Penina	Peninnah	p'-ni-NAH	פְּנִנָּה
Peretz	Perez	PE-retz	פֶּרֶץ
Petuel	Pethuel	p'-tu-AYL	פְּתוּאֵל
Pinchas	Phinehas	peen-KHAS	פִּינְחָס
Rachel	Rachel	ra-KHAYL	רָחֵל
Ram	Ram	ram	רָם
Rama	Ramah	ra-MAH	רָמָה
Re'u	Reu	r'-U	רְעוּ
Rechovam	Rehoboam	r'-khav-AM	רְחַבְעָם
Reuven	Reuben	r'-u-VAYN	רְאוּבֵן
Rivka	Rebecca	riv-KAH	רִבְקָה
Rut	Ruth	rut	רוּת
Salma	Salmon/Salmah	sal-MAH	שַׂלְמָה
Salmon	Salmon	sal-MON	שַׂלְמוֹן
Sara	Sarah	sa-RAH	שָׂרָה
Sarai	Sarai	sa-RAI	שָׂרַי
Selah	Selah	SE-lah	סֶלָה
Seraya	Seraiah	s'-ra-YAH	שְׂרָיָה
Serug	Serug	s'-RUG	שְׂרוּג
Setur	Sethur	s'-TUR	סְתוּר
Shaarayim	Shaaraim	sha-a-RA-yim	שַׁעֲרַיִם
Shabbat	Sabbath	sha-BAT	שַׁבָּת
Shabbatot	Sabbaths	sha-ba-TOT	שַׁבָּתוֹת
Shafan	Shaphan	sha-FAN	שָׁפָן
Shafat	Shaphat	sha-FAT	שָׁפָט
Shalem	Salem	sha-LAYM	שָׁלֵם
Shalum	Shallum	sha-LUM	שַׁלּוּם
Shamgar	Shamgar	sham-GAR	שַׁמְגַּר
Shamua	Shammua	sha-MU-a	שַׁמּוּעַ
Shaul	Saul	sha-UL	שָׁאוּל
Shealtiel	Shealtiel	sh'-al-tee-AYL	שְׁאַלְתִּיאֵל

Hebrew Name	English Name	Pronunciation	Hebrew
Shear Yashuv	Shear-Jashub	sh'-AR ya-SHUV	שְׁאָר יָשׁוּב
Shechanya	Shecaniah	sh'-khan-YAH	שְׁכַנְיָה
Shechem	Shechem	sh'-KHEM	שְׁכֶם
Sheila	Shelah	shay-LAH	שֵׁלָה
Shelach	Shelah	SHE-lakh	שֶׁלַח
Shelumiel	Shelumiel	sh'-lu-mee-AYL	שְׁלֻמִיאֵל
Shem	Shem	Shaym	שֵׁם
Shemaya	Shemaiah	sh'-ma-YAH	שְׁמַעְיָה
Sheshbatzar	Sheshbazzar	shaysh-ba-TZAR	שֵׁשְׁבַּצַּר
Shet	Seth	Shayt	שֵׁת
Shevat	Shebat	sh'-VAT	שְׁבָט
Shilo	Shiloh	shi-LOH	שִׁלֹה
Shim'i	Shimei	shim-EE	שִׁמְעִי
Shimon	Simeon	shim-ON	שִׁמְעוֹן
Shimshon	Samson	shim-SHON	שִׁמְשׁוֹן
Shlomo	Solomon	sh'-lo-MOH	שְׁלֹמֹה
Shmuel	Samuel	sh'-mu-AYL	שְׁמוּאֵל
Shofar	Horn	sho-FAR	שׁוֹפָר
Shofarot	Horns	sho-fa-ROT	שׁוֹפָרוֹת
Shomron	Samaria	sho-m'-RON	שֹׁמְרוֹן
Sivan	Sivan	see-VAN	סִיוָן
Tamar	Tamar	ta-MAR	תָּמָר
Tanakh	Hebrew Bible	ta-NAKH	תָּנָ"ךְ
Tapuach	Tappuah	ta-PU-akh	תַּפּוּחַ
Tavor	Tabor	ta-VOR	תָּבוֹר
Tekoa	Tekoa	t'-KO-a	תְּקוֹעַה
Terach	Terah	TE-rakh	תֶּרַח
Teveria	Tiberias	t'-ver-YAH	טְבֶרְיָה
Tevet	Tebeth	tay-VAYT	טֵבֵת
Tirtza	Tirzah	tir-TZAH	תִּרְצָה
Tola	Tola	to-LA	תּוֹלָע
Tzadok	Zadok	tza-DOK	צָדוֹק
Tzefanya	Zephaniah	tz'-fan-YAH	צְפַנְיָה

Hebrew Name	English Name	Pronunciation	Hebrew
Tzelofchad	Zelophehad	tz'-lo-f-KHAD	צְלָפְחָד
Tzeruya	Zeruiah	tz'-ru-YAH	צְרוּיָה
Tzfat	Safed	tz'-FAT	צְפַת
Tzidkiyahu	Zedekiah	tzid-ki-YA-hu	צִדְקִיָהוּ
Tziklag	Ziklag	tzi-k'-LAG	צִקְלַג
Tzion	Zion	tzi-YON	צִיּוֹן
Tzipora	Zipporah	tzi-po-RAH	צִפֹּרָה
Tzora	Zorah	tzor-AH	צָרְעָה
Tzuriel	Zuriel	tzu-ree-AYL	צוּרִיאֵל
Ukal	Ucal	u-KAL	אֻכָל
Uri	Uri	u-REE	אוּרִי
Uriya	Uriah	u-ri-YAH	אוּרִיָה
Utz	Uz	Utz	עוּץ
Uzziyahu	Uzziah	u-zi-YA-hu	עֻזִּיָהוּ
Yaakov	Jacob	ya-a-KOV	יַעֲקֹב
Yachaziel	Jahaziel	ya-kha-zee-AYL	יַחֲזִיאֵל
Yael	Jael	ya-AYL	יָעֵל
Yaffo	Joppa/Jaffa	ya-FO	יָפוֹ
Yair	Jair	ya-EER	יָאִיר
Yakeh	Jakeh	ya-KEH	יָקֶה
Yarden	Jordan	yar-DAYN	יַרְדֵּן
Yarmut	Jarmuth	yar-MUT	יַרְמוּת
Yechezkel	Ezekiel	y'-khez-KAYL	יְחֶזְקֵאל
Yechiel	Jehiel	y'-khee-AYL	יְחִיאֵל
Yechonya	Jeconiah	y'-khon-YAH	יְכָנְיָה
Yedutun	Jeduthun	y'-du-TUN	יְדוּתוּן
Yehoachaz	Jehoahaz	y'-ho-a-KHAZ	יְהוֹאָחָז
Yehoash	Jehoash	y'-ho-ASH	יְהוֹאָש
Yehochanan	Jehohanan	y'-ho-kha-NAN	יְהוֹחָנָן
Yehonatan	Jonathan	y'-ho-na-TAN	יְהוֹנָתָן
Yehoram	Jehoram	y'-ho-RAM	יְהוֹרָם
Yehoshafat	Jehoshaphat	y'-ho-sha-FAT	יְהוֹשָׁפָט
Yehoshavat	Jehoshabeath	y'-ho-shav-AT	יְהוֹשַׁבְעַת

Hebrew Name	English Name	Pronunciation	Hebrew
Yehosheva	Jehosheba	y-ho-SHE-va	יְהוֹשֶׁבַע
Yehoshua	Joshua	y'-ho-SHU-a	יְהוֹשֻׁעַ
Yehotzadak	Jehozadak	y'-ho-tza-DAK	יְהוֹצָדָק
Yehoyachin	Jehoiachin	y'-ho-ya-KHEEN	יְהוֹיָכִין
Yehoyada	Jehoiada	y'-ho-ya-DA	יְהוֹיָדָע
Yehoyakim	Jehoiakim	y'-ho-ya-KEEM	יְהוֹיָקִים
Yehu	Jehu	yay-HU	יֵהוּא
Yehuda	Judah	y'-hu-DAH	יְהוּדָה
Yehudi	Jew	y'-hu-DEE	יְהוּדִי
Yehudim	Jews	y'-hu-DEEM	יְהוּדִים
Yered	Jared	YE-red	יֶרֶד
Yericho	Jericho	y'-ree-KHO	יְרִיחוֹ
Yerovam	Jeroboam	ya-rov-AM	יָרָבְעָם
Yerubaal	Jerubbaal	y'-ru-BA-al	יְרֻבַּעַל
Yerushalayim	Jerusalem	y'-ru-sha-LA-yim	יְרוּשָׁלַיִם
Yeshayahu	Isaiah	y'-sha-YA-hu	יְשַׁעְיָהוּ
Yeshua	Jeshua	yay-SHU-a	יֵשׁוּעַ
Yiftach	Jephthah	yif-TAKH	יִפְתָּח
Yigal	Igal	yig-AL	יִגְאָל
Yirmiyahu	Jeremiah	yir-m'-YA-hu	יִרְמְיָהוּ
Yishai	Jesse	yi-SHAI	יִשַׁי
Yisrael	Israel	yis-ra-AYL	יִשְׂרָאֵל
Yissachar	Issachar	yi-sa-KHAR	יִשָּׂשכָר
Yitzchak	Issac	yitz-KHAK	יִצְחָק
Yizrael	Jezreel	yiz-r'-EL	יִזְרְעָאל
Yoash	Joash	yo-ASH	יוֹאָשׁ
Yoav	Joab	yo-AV	יוֹאָב
Yochanan	Johanan	yo-kha-NAN	יוֹחָנָן
Yocheved	Jochebed	yo-KHE-ved	יוֹכֶבֶד
Yoel	Joel	yo-AYL	יוֹאֵל
Yona	Jonah	yo-NAH	יוֹנָה
Yonadav	Jonadab	yo-na-DAV	יוֹנָדָב
Yonatan	Jonathan	yo-na-TAN	יוֹנָתָן

Hebrew Name	English Name	Pronunciation	Hebrew
Yoram	Joram	yo-RAM	יוֹרָם
Yosef	Joseph	yo-SAYF	יוֹסֵף
Yoshiyahu	Josiah	yo-shi-YA-hu	יאשִׁיָּהוּ
Yotam	Jotham	yo-TAM	יוֹתָם
Yotzaduk	Jozadak	yu-tza-DAK	יוֹצָדָק
Yozavad	Jozabad	yo-za-VAD	יוֹזָבָד
Zanoach	Zanoah	za-NO-akh	זָנוֹחַ
Zecharya	Zechariah	z'-khar-YAH	זְכַרְיָה
Zerach	Zerah	ZE-rakh	זֶרַח
Zerubavel	Zerubbabel	z'-ru-ba-VEL	זְרֻבָּבֶל
Zevulun	Zebulun	z'-vu-LUN	זְבוּלֻן
Zilpa	Zilpah	zil-PAH	זִלְפָּה
Zimri	Zimri	zim-REE	זִמְרִי

Jewish Holidays

Hebrew Name	English Name	Pronunciation	Hebrew
Chanukah	Hanukkah	kha-nu-KAH	חֲנוּכָּה
Pesach	Passover	PE-sakh	פֶּסַח
Purim	Purim	pu-REEM	פּוּרִים
Rosh Hashana	Jewish New Year	rosh ha-sha-NAH	ראֹשׁ הַשָּׁנָה
Shavuot	Feast of Weeks	sha-vu-OT	שָׁבוּעוֹת
Shemini Atzeret	Eight Day of Assembly	sh'-mee-NEE a-TZE-ret	שְׁמִינִי עֲצֶרֶת
Sukkot	Feast of Tabernacles	su-KOT	סֻכּוֹת
Yom Kippur	Day of Atonement	yom kee-PUR	יוֹם כִּיפּוּר

Biblical Measurements

Hebrew Name	English Name	Pronunciation	Hebrew
Amah	Cubit	a-MAH	אַמָּה
Amot	Cubits	a-MOT	אַמוֹת
Bat	Bath	bat	בַּת
Batim	Baths	ba-TEEM	בַּתִּים
Beka	half-shekel	BE-ka	בֶּקַע
Chomarim	Homers	kho-ma-REEM	חֳמָרִים
Chomer	Homer	KHO-mer	חֹמֶר
Efah	Ephah	ay-FAH	אֵיפָה
Geira	Gerah	gay-RAH	גֵּרָה

Hebrew Name	English Name	Pronunciation	Hebrew
Gomed	Gomed	GO- med	גֹּמֶד
Hin	Hin	heen	הִין
Kav	kab	kav	קַב
Kesita	kesitah	k'-see-TAH	קְשִׂיטָה
Kikar	talent	ki-KAR	כִּכָּר
Kikarim	talents	ki-ka-RIM	כִּכָּרִים
Kor	kor	kor	כֹּר
Letek	lethech	LE-tek	לֶתֶךְ
Log	Log	log	לֹג
Maneh	Mina	ma-NEH	מָנֶה
Manim	Minas	ma-NEEM	מָנִים
Omer	Omer	O-mer	עֹמֶר
Pim	Pim	peem	פִּים
Se'ah	Seah	say-AH	סְאָה
Se'eem	Seahs	s'-EEM	סְאִים
Shekalim	Shekels	sh'-ka-LEEM	שְׁקָלִים
Shekel	Shekel	SHE-kel	שֶׁקֶל
Tefach	Handbreadth	TE-fakh	טֶפַח
Zeret	Span	ZE-ret	זֶרֶת

Photo Credits

Map of Modern-Day Israel and its Neighbors

The following is a map of modern-day Israel and the surrounding countries

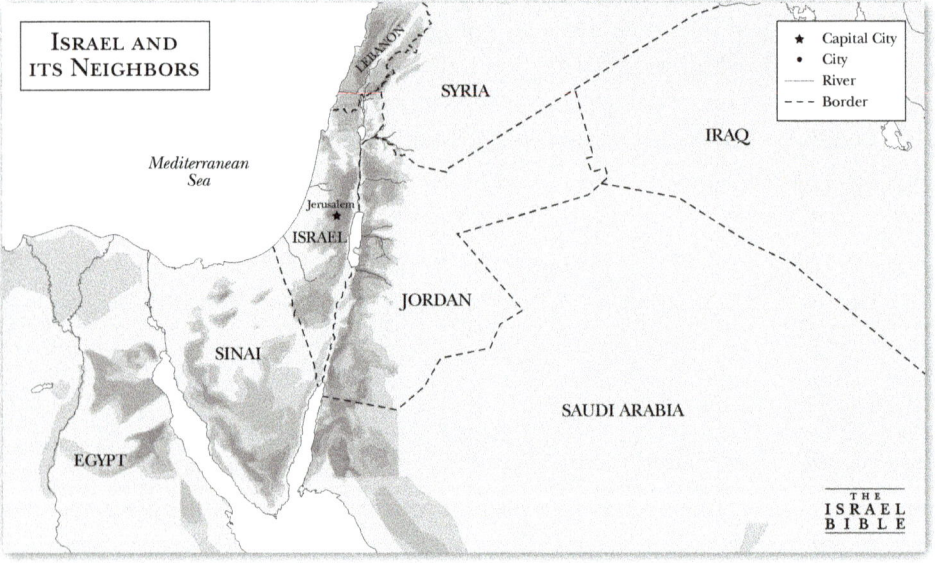

NOTES

NOTES

NOTES

NOTES

NOTES

For more inspiring commentary,
interactive maps, educational videos,
vivid photographs and more,
please visit our website

www.TheIsraelBible.com

THE
ISRAEL
BIBLE